Edwin William Streeter

Precious stones and Gems

Their history and distinguishing Characteristics

Edwin William Streeter

Precious Stones and Gems

Their history and distinguishing Characteristics

ISBN/EAN: 9783337311025

Printed in Europe, USA, Canada, Australia, Japan

Cover: Foto ©ninafisch / pixelio.de

More available books at **www.hansebooks.com**

PRECIOUS STONES

AND

GEMS,

Their History and distinguishing Characteristics.

BY

EDWIN W. STREETER

Illustrated with
COLORED PLATES, PHOTOGRAPHS, &c.

LONDON:
CHAPMAN & HALL, 193, PICCADILLY.
1877.

LIST OF ILLUSTRATIONS.

	PAGE
THE BLUE DIAMOND	*Frontispiece*
PROPER SIZES OF BRILLIANTS ...	... 31
PROPER SIZES OF ROSE DIAMONDS ...	... 32
THE "COLESBERG KOPJE" DIAMOND MINE	68—69
THE "STEWART" DIAMOND ...	72
THE "DUDLEY" DIAMOND ...	73
THE "TWIN" DIAMOND	73
TRANSPARENT STONES IN THE ROUGH ...	~~138~~
GEMS IN THE ROUGH	... 174

CONTENTS.

	PAGES
TO THE READER	v—ix

SECTION I.—PRECIOUS STONES IN GENERAL.—

CHAPTER I. ......DEFINITION OF THE TERMS "GEM" AND "PRECIOUS STONE"... ...	11—12
CHAPTER II. ......WHERE PRECIOUS STONES ARE FOUND	13—14.
CHAPTER III. ...PRECIOUS STONES AND THEIR USES IN BYGONE TIMES	15—21
CHAPTER IV. ...THE WORKING OF PRECIOUS STONES	22—40
CHAPTER V.......PRECIOUS STONES AS OBJECTS OF COMMERCE	41—44

SECTION II.—

CHAPTER I. ......THE DIAMOND	45—59
CHAPTER II.......CAPE OR SOUTH-AFRICAN DIAMONDS	60—74
CHAPTER III. ...AUSTRALIAN DIAMONDS ...	75—80
CHAPTER IV. ...BRAZILIAN DIAMONDS ...	81—90
CHAPTER V. ......INDIAN DIAMONDS	91—100
CHAPTER VI......COLORED DIAMONDS... ...	101—106
CHAPTER VII. ...BORT AND CARBONADO ...	107—110
CHAPTER VIII....CELEBRATED DIAMONDS ...	111—129
CHAPTER IX. ...ROUGH DIAMONDS	130—131

SECTION III.—

CHAPTER I. ......CORUNDUM	132—138
CHAPTER II. ......RUBY	139—144
CHAPTER III. ...SAPPHIRE	145—148
CHAPTER IV. ...EMERALD	149—155
CHAPTER V. ......SPINEL AND BALAS RUBIES...	156—160
CHAPTER VI. ...OPAL	161—165
CHAPTER VII. ...CAT'S EYE	166—168
CHAPTER VIII....TURQUOISE	169—172
CHAPTER IX. ...STAR STONES OR ASTERIA ...	173—174

SECTION IV.—STONES OF INFERIOR VALUE.—

	PAGES
CHAPTER I. ....AMBER	175—177
CHAPTER II. ......AMETHYST	178—179
CHAPTER III. ......AGATE	180—182
CHAPTER IV. ......ALEXANDRITE	183
CHAPTER V..........AQUAMARINE	184—185
CHAPTER VI. ......BLOODSTONE	186—187
CHAPTER VII. .:....CARNELIAN OR RED CHALCEDONY	188—191
CHAPTER VIII. ...CHRYSOLITE OF LAPIDARIES (CHRYSOBERYL)	192—193
CHAPTER IX. .....,.CHRYSOPRASE	194—195
CHAPTER X..........GARNET, CARBUNCLE, JACINTH, AND CINNAMON STONE	196—199
CHAPTER XI. ......JASPER	200—202
CHAPTER XII. ......LABRADOR	203—204
CHAPTER XIII.......LAPIS-LAZULI ...	205—207
CHAPTER XIV.......MALACHITE	208—209
CHAPTER XV. ......SELENITE OR MOONSTONE...	210—211
CHAPTER XVI. ......ORIENTAL ONYX ...	212—214
CHAPTER XVII. ...PERIDOT	215—216
CHAPTER XVIII....QUARTZ CAT'S EYE ...	217
CHAPTER XIX. ...ROCK CRYSTAL	218—220
CHAPTER XX. ......TOPAZ	221—223
CHAPTER XXI. ...TOURMALINE	224—225
CHAPTER XXII. ...ZIRCON, JARGOON, OR HYACINTH	226—228

SECTION V.—ANIMAL PRODUCTS USED AS GEMS.—

CHAPTER I. ....CORAL	229—233
CHAPTER II..........PEARLS	234—246
CHAPTER III. ......COLORED PEARLS	247—248
GENERAL REMARKS UPON THE TERM "CARAT"...	249
INDEX	250—264

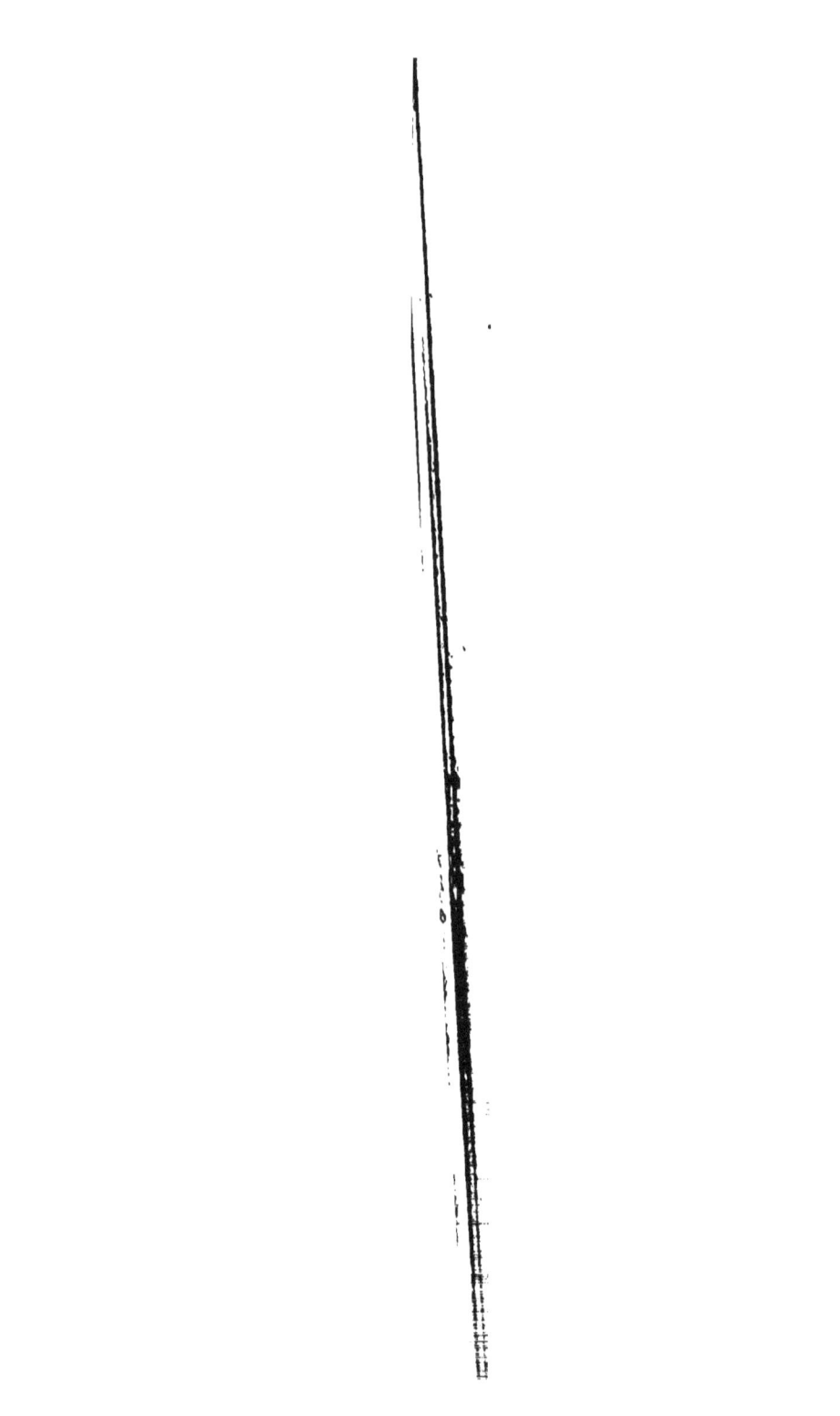

TO THE READER.

MANY pages have been written on the history of PRECIOUS STONES. Authorities on authorities, from remote antiquity to this our day, have been cited as to their value, their uses, their beauties, and their properties, and still one might venture to say that there are fewer judges of the genuineness and real value of Precious Stones, than there are treatises to guide people to such knowledge. Would it be altogether unwarrantable to express a grave doubt whether even in the trade there are very many skilled in detecting the real measure of difference between one stone and another, either by that most essential test, the specific gravity, or by minor tests of rarity and quality? Be this as it may, I have arrived at the deliberate conviction, as a merchant and dealer long versed in the purchase and sale of gems, that some practical and popular guide to those who have an interest in ascertaining and testing the genuineness and value of Precious Stones, is in demand and would be useful.

A Gem should be a real possession, capable of affording

pleasure to the wearer and the spectator, and, with fair usage, retaining an intrinsic and marketable value, undiminished by lapse of time. I have sometimes seen in wear, gems scratched so that their lustre has been seriously impaired, and a suspicion excited in the minds of both wearer and friends that there was a defect in the hardness of the stones, and consequently in their genuineness. It would be worth while to point out that a small sum expended in re-polishing such stones would restore their original lustre, revive the pleasure derived from the possession of them, and prevent them from being sold as paste or imitation jewelry.

A lady had bequeathed to her some family jewels, consisting of a Sapphire and Diamond suite. As they had passed probate several times, there was no doubt in the mind of the legatee of the genuineness of the Sapphires. On being applied to in relation to their value, I had to pronounce them to be only paste. Had they been genuine they would have realized from £30,000 to £40,000. One often sees the Spinel and the Balas—the one a lively poppy-red, and the other a violet-rose—usurping the dignity of the true Ruby, and yet the pure Ruby of ten carats is worth from £3,800 to £4,800, and the other stones, called by the same name, would be dear at one-twentieth of the sum.

The Chrysolite of the Ancients, though highly esteemed by them, has not retained its popular character. It is by us termed the Oriental Topaz, and is a Corundum formed of alumina, colored golden-yellow by oxide of iron. The ordinary Topaz of commerce, composed of silica and alumina, with hydrofluoric acid (hydric-fluoride), commonly of a pale orange, toning down to a straw color, is of comparatively little value.

It is quite pardonable, and of small consequence, that

the characteristics of such gems should be comparatively unknown ; but there are Precious Stones about which there should be no doubt in the minds either of the purchaser or the merchant, viz., the Diamond, Ruby, Emerald, Sapphire, Opal, Cat's-eye, Peridot, and Pearls.

A lady refuses to wear a gown composed of inferior material intended to represent silk, because its color, texture, and draping indicate, to every experienced eye, the substitution of the false for the real ; but she seems to ignore the fact that the color, brilliancy, and texture of a true gem, are as distinguishable from those of the false or mere imitation, as the cotton from the silk. We presume to believe that the gown, which in a few nights' wear loses its worth altogether, is of less consequence as to the genuineness of its material, than gems which should be heirlooms of value, not to be deteriorated by the lapse of years.

In the division of family jewels much injustice is done by persons incompetent to form a correct opinion of their relative values. A study of this hand-book may serve to demonstrate the difficulty of an accurate discrimination. In all cases it would be wiser to submit the jewels to a practised judge, both for valuation and probate. It is not right to leave the decision to some house agent or mutual friend.

Some study and attention will be required to attain a knowledge of the properties and appearance of gems, but the subject is by no means unattractive, and may be turned to good account.

The study of Pearls especially, is not so intricate as is generally believed. If a little attention be paid to the ascertained mode of their construction in fine concentric layers, this will readily supply the key to detect spurious fabrications. The peculiarities of these products of organised nature are not very difficult to understand; but if the specimens are large, and of supposed great value, it would not be undesirable to obtain the opinion of a skilled judge in such matters, especially in relation to colored Pearls.

With objects, such as those referred to above, I am publishing the present volume, the outcome of more than thirty years' experience, and of the united knowledge of many men of science, and of my contemporaries in trade. I hope that it may be of some service to us as merchants, to our customers, and to the public in general.

It must be borne in mind that this book is not intended to be a scientific treatise, but a practical work for those who, whether in the trade or among the public at large, desire to obtain some knowledge of the general characteristics of Precious Stones.

In conclusion, I trust that the Goldsmiths' Company, as fathers of the trade, will ere long throw open their fine suite of rooms in Foster Lane. To them we must look for aids to the more general appreciation of fine art jewelry, by affording favorable opportunities for exhibitions and prizes, together with gratuitous lectures, and the free use of their reading-room to members of the trade. This would give an impetus to study to those engaged in jewelry-work, and enable the public to obtain a more accurate knowledge of, and a deeper interest in, a subject which has hitherto remained the property of an exclusive few.

The legacies bequeathed to the Goldsmiths' Company by the famous jewellers of the 15th, 16th, and 17th centuries, which have since increased in value to an extent almost inconceivable, without doubt were intended for some such purposes as those to which we have referred.

I am in an especial manner indebted for the subject matter which forms the basis of this work, to the works of

Professor Kluge, translated by Mrs. Brewer; and also to Major Beaumont, M.P., and Mr. James A. Forster. These contributors are authorities in the departments of science in which they have conceded me their invaluable assistance.

EDWIN W. STREETER.

18, *New Bond Street*,
  London.

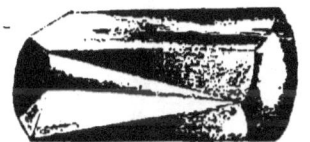

The " Shah " Diamond, *weight*, 86 *carats*.

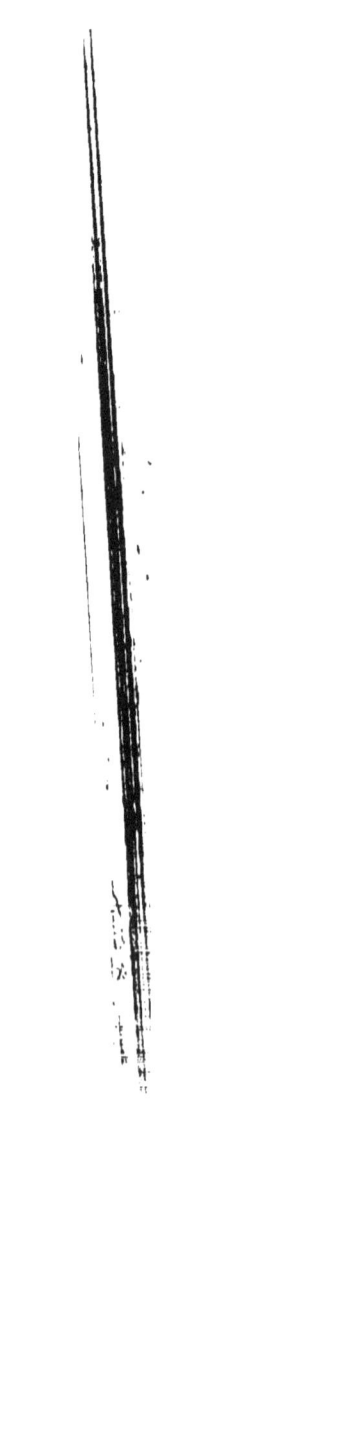

SECTION I.
PRECIOUS STONES IN GENERAL.

CHAPTER I.
DEFINITION OF THE TERMS GEM AND PRECIOUS STONE.

 GEM or Precious Stone, in its widest sense, is a mineral; hard, of beautiful color, or absolutely colorless; usually transparent, of great rarity, and of value in the manufacture of jewelry. Generally, minerals with these characteristics are divided into two classes: (1) Jewels, or Gems proper, perfectly pure. (2) half-pure Precious Stones, colored or tinted.

Included in the first class are those rarer minerals, distinguished by colors, at once bright and sparkling, soft and tender; distinguished also by transparency, high lustre, great density, and capability of polish.

The so-called half-pure Precious Stones of the second class have all the above peculiarities, but in a much less degree. They are found more frequently, and in greater abundance. This arrangement, however, is artificial. Many stones belong sometimes to one, sometimes to the other class.

Again, the money value does not allow of an infallible line being drawn between the two classes, as that depends very much upon accidental circumstances, such as peculiar beauty, rarity of color, perfection, and the demands of fashion. Hence it often happens the semi-precious Stones are preferred to the Gems or pure stones of the first class.

The Science of Precious Stones, taken in a wide sense, is a knowledge of them, and all their peculiarities and relationships. In a more limited sense, it is only the *scientific* knowledge of the stones. It is a department of Applied Mineralogy or Lithurgics.

The properties of Precious Stones are morphological (referring to their shapes), physical, and chemical. The science depends, therefore, materially upon Geometry, Physics, and Chemistry.

As the science has for its object to show the application of these minerals to the Arts and every-day life, Technology, or the explanation of terms used in the Arts, is essential in this field of study.

As aids to the study of gems, besides literary works and collections of jewels, several chemical and physical instruments are required, such as a blow-pipe and spirit lamp, a goniometer or instrument for measuring angles, scales to determine specific gravity, and files for testing the hardness of stones.

CHAPTER II.

WHERE PRECIOUS STONES ARE FOUND.

THE habitat, or native home of Precious Stones, will be specially indicated in the description of each individual Gem, or the class to which it belongs ; we shall, therefore, content ourselves with a very few general remarks upon the subject.

Precious Stones are found in the same perfection, as far as their quality is concerned, in very different parts of the world, although they do not all choose similar chains of mountains for their home.

Diamonds, however, in the *rough* state from India, are readily distinguished from the Brazilian, South-African, or Australian stones ; but the difference is only superficial, for, when polished, it has been found impossible to discriminate between the Indian, Brazilian, and South-African productions. Good and bad come from all these localities; and the terms "Old Mine Stones" and "New Mine Stones" are rather trade phrases than the expressions of actual facts.

The Emerald of Peru is much the same as that from the Red Sea. The Beryl appears in equal beauty in Siberia and in Brazil; and the Amethysts of the Palatinate fairly rival in beauty those found in Ceylon or Brazil. It is not the geographical position which determines the difference, although it is acknowledged that India, Brazil and Ceylon have produced larger Precious Stones, and in greater abundance, than other lands. The Ancients were wont to ascribe this pre-eminence to evaporation from the earth where Precious Stones are found—an evaporation obviously more intense in tropical countries. It is as if the sunburnt tropics were more favorable to the blossoms of the inorganic world, than the dark skies of the north.

But although Precious Stones are not limited to any defined geographical area, their distribution is in a measure circumscribed. They are not met with in all mountain ranges, nor in all formations of mountains. The most valuable are found in such ranges as are considered the oldest in the world; such as are composed of granite, porphyry, and mica-slate. Sometimes they occur imbedded in the mass of the rock; at other times, growing, as it were, on the surface. When they are thus found, in the very rocks where they were originally formed, they are said to be in their primeval bed. Many, however, are found far from their primal home, in a *derivative* or secondary bed, in diluvial or alluvial soils, and in the gravels and sands of river-beds. This last mode of occurrence is the most frequent for the finer Precious Stones. Far removed from their native home by the force of heavy rains and rushing torrents, they have been loosened and carried onwards, rounded by friction against the debris with which they have been accompanied in their course. It is by their hardness and density that they are preserved, and many even retain traces of their original crystalline form.

In Ceylon, India, Brazil, Australia, California, the Ural, Siberia and South Africa—from which countries the great majority of our Precious Stones are obtained—the most usual way in which they occur is in these derivative beds; and it is interesting to notice how various kinds of Precious Stones are found in the same locality, forming as it were a noble society of Gems, still more illustrious by their association with gold and platinum.

CHAPTER III.

PRECIOUS STONES AND THEIR USES IN BYGONE TIMES.

PRECIOUS Stones were valued and preserved by the Ancients thousands of years ago. In India, where the most costly were abundantly found, this was especially the case. Other Eastern lands, on the contrary, possessed Precious Stones, and handed them down from generation to generation without knowing anything of their worth or nature, valuing them simply for their transparency, their dazzling beauty, their hardness, their crystalline forms, all of which excited their wonder, and induced them to preserve them as amulets, or to use them as personal ornaments. We know that in the time of Solomon, the love of grace and luxury induced the rich to desire the possession of Precious Stones, and even to seek for them in foreign lands.

In Egypt, in ancient times, many half-precious Stones and scarabæan Gems were worked; and we learn from the Septuagint, and from Philo, that the robes of the High Priest were set with Precious Stones. The names the Hebrews gave these stones indicate that they derived their knowledge of them from the Egyptians, who undoubtedly, in common with other ancient races, knew little of what we understand by Mineralogy. As regards India, Strabo and Pliny tell us that gold and Precious Stones were used for personal adornment, and that drinking cups were formed of precious metals set with Emeralds, Beryls, and Rubies.

From the East the Phœnicians, in their universal traffic, exported costly stones as well as ivory, with Syrian purple and other stuffs, which were known as early as the Homeric period. The songs of Homer contain references to valuable bright stuffs and stones which served for ornament, without mentioning their special names or qualities. For instance—"the witch puts on her costly robe and brilliant earrings," but their nature is not defined. Eurymachus gives to Penelope an exquisitely worked necklace of gold, ornamented with light amber, bright as the sun. Eurydamas gives magnificent earrings, such as must have been worn by high-born ladies and princesses in Homeric times. But the precious Onyx and the Sapphire are mentioned by Job, with the Coral, Pearls, Rubies, and Topaz of Ethiopia; and the place in which some were found appears to have been known by that patriarch of Uz: "He putteth forth His hand upon the rock: He cutteth out rivers among the rocks, and His eye seeth every precious thing."

Six or seven hundred years B.C. the Greeks knew of many Precious Stones, and the rulers in Greece and neighbouring lands wore ornamental and signet rings made with cut stones. The famous ring of Polycrates (died B.C. 522) was doubtless as valuable to him for its costly stones and workmanship, as for any supernatural power which it is said to have possessed. Herodotus, and some later Greek authors, mention Theodorus of Samos, the first engraver of stones, as the maker of that ring.

In the beginning of the 5th century, B.C., we find

among the Greeks, a didactic History of Precious Stones; an indication that they had long had knowledge of them.

Onomacritus, a Priest and Founder of Hellenic mysteries, 500 years B.C., treated of Precious Stones and their mysterious power. Commencing with the bright transparent crystal, he says, "Whoso goes into the Temple with this in his hand may be quite sure of having his prayer granted; as the gods cannot withstand its power." Further, he states, "that when this stone is laid upon dry wood, so that the sun's rays may shine upon it, there will soon be seen smoke, then fire, then a bright flame." This flame was known among the Ancients as *holy fire*, and they believed that no sacrifice was so acceptable to the gods as when offered through its agency.

In like manner, Onomacritus sang the praises and supernatural power of the Agate, the Topaz, the springgreen Jasper, Amber, Chrysolite, Coral, and Opal. The superstitions attached to these and other stones were not confined to the Ancients. Even in this enlightened age, the Empress Eugénie of France, would not wear a precious Opal because it was said to bring ill luck to the wearer. Queen Victoria, on the contrary, having no such superstition, has presented each of her daughters, on their marriage, with a parure of Opals and Diamonds.

After the early Greek period the knowledge of Precious Stones advanced. Herodotus must have had accurate acquaintance with many of them. He mentions, besides the Emerald in Polycrates' ring, signet rings, such as that of Darius; and speaks of the so-called Emerald column in the Temple of Hercules at Tyre, which at night gave out a wonderful light. Plato mentions the Sard, Jasper and Emerald. The Adamant,—possibly our modern Diamond— Amber and Loadstone were not unknown to him; and he shows some knowledge of the origin of both common and

Precious Stones, and of their natural hexagonal, octagonal and prismatic forms.

It is certain that Aristotle had a knowledge of a still larger number of Precious Stones, and that he was acquainted with some of their special properties. His scholar, Theophrastus, has left us a small work on this subject. Diodorus mentions the Topaz found in the Serpent Island of the Arabian Sea; this is probably what we now call Chrysolite. Dionysius Periegetes mentions the clear and brilliant Diamond, the beautiful Astrios that glitters like a star, the Lychnis, with the color of fire, the blue Beryl, the dull Jasper, the pure bluish or greenish Topaz, and the lovely Amethyst with its soft, purple sheen.

In the time of Alexander the Great, and still more in the time of the luxurious Diadocheus, there was a great increase in the use of Precious Stones as articles of luxury. They were not only used for signet rings, but also in ornamenting many articles of use and luxury, particularly drinking vessels and candelabra.

After the Romans became possessed of the treasures of Asia and Africa, they probably gained a much fuller knowledge of Precious Stones. Pliny must have been better informed than his predecessors as to the places where gems were found. From him also we gain most of our knowledge of the views of the Ancients as to Precious Stones. During this period the luxury of Rome in respect to Precious Stones was enormous. The Emperors adorned their robes with jewels of immense value. Paulina, the wife of Caligula, covered her dress entirely with Emeralds and Pearls of untold worth. Pliny says "we drink out of a mass of gems, and our drinking vessels are formed of Emeralds." A little later they began to set their sacred pictures in frames adorned with gems. Constantine entered Rome in a chariot of gold, adorned with Precious Stones which sent forth brilliant rays of light, and in his time the royal crown was first set about with Precious Stones. This ornamenting crowns with gems has been a general custom to this day.

Passing on to the Christian Era, among writers upon Precious Stones, Sidorus, Bishop of Seville, in the year 630 A.D., takes a prominent place. He divided gems according to their color.

The number of properties attributed to Precious Stones at this time is wonderful. They were said to have the power of conferring health, beauty, riches, honor, good fortune and influence. Men and women carried them about their persons, and called them Amulets. They were thought also to have some connection with the planets and seasons. A special gem was worn for each *month*: thus—

In January	The Hyacinth.
„ February	„ Amethyst.
„ March	„ Jasper.
„ April	„ Sapphire.
„ May	„ Agate.
„ June	„ Emerald.
„ July	„ Onyx.
„ August	„ Carnelian.
„ September	„ Chrysolite.
„ October	„ Beryl.
„ November	„ Topaz.
„ December	„ Ruby.

The Twelve Apostles, also, were represented by gems, called Apostle-stones, viz :—

1.—The hard and solid *Jasper*, representing the rock of the Church, was the emblem of *Peter*.
2.—The bright-blue *Sapphire* was emblematic of the heavenly faith of *Andrew*.

3.—The *Emerald*, of the pure and gentle *John*.
4.—The white *Chalcedony*, of the loving *James*.
5.—The friendly *Sardonyx*, of *Philip*.
6.—The red *Carnelian*, of the martyr *Bartholomew*.
7.—The *Chrysolite*, pure as sunlight, of *Matthias*.
8.—The indefinite *Beryl*, of the doubting *Thomas*.
9.—The *Topaz*, of the delicate *James the younger*.
10.—The *Chrysoprase*, of the serene and trustful *Thaddeus*.
11.—The *Amethyst*, of *Matthew the Apostle*.
12.—The pink *Hyacinth*, of the sweet-tempered *Simeon* of Cana.

In later times, an Alphabet was formed of Precious Stones and Half-precious Stones.

	TRANSPARENT.	OPAQUE.
A.	Amethyst.	Agate.
B.	Beryl.	Basalt.
C.	Chrysoberyl.	Cacholong.
D.	Diamond.	Diaspore.
E.	Emerald.	Egyptian Pebble.
F.	Felspar.	Fire-stone.
G.	Garnet.	Granite.
H.	Hyacinth.	Heliotrope.
I.	Idocrase.	Jasper.
K.	Kyanite.	Krokidolite.
L.	Lynx-sapphire.	Lapis-lazuli.
M.	Milk-opal.	Malachite.
N.	Natrolite.	Nephrite.
O.	Opal.	Onyx.
P.	Pyrope.	Porphyry.
Q.	Quartz.	Quartz-agate.
R.	Ruby.	Rose-quartz.
S.	Sapphire.	Sardonyx.
T.	Topaz.	Turquoise.

Precious Stones and their uses in bygone times.

	TRANSPARENT.	OPAQUE.
U.	Uranite.	Ultra-marine.
V.	Vesuvianite.	Verd-antique.
W.	Water-sapphire.	Wood-opal.
X.	Xanthite.	Xylotile.
Z.	Zircon.	Zurlite.

If, for instance, you wanted the word *Alice* represented in a ring, you would choose Amethyst, Lynx-sapphire, Idocrase, Chrysoberyl and Emerald ; or any other group of stones whose initial letters spell the name.

CHAPTER IV.

THE WORKING OF PRECIOUS STONES.

A.—GENERAL.

HE qualities for which Precious Stones are most prized, viz., lustre, transparency, refraction, and dispersion of light, are to some extent visible even in their rough state; but in order to bring out these advantages to perfection, and make them objects of attractive ornament, the stones must be subjected to artistic cutting, slicing, and polishing.

The Art whereby this is accomplished is divided into two parts.

1. The Lapidary's Art, that is, the grinding, polishing, and manipulation of the rough stone, so as to produce regular and smooth surfaces, or facets.
2. The Engraver's Art consists in stone cutting, engraving and the working of the polished stone into certain designs.

B.—HISTORICAL.

The art of cutting and polishing stones for ornaments into shapes with many surfaces or facets, so as to develope all their valuable qualities, as it is understood by us, was unknown to the Ancients. They were content with rubbing down the angles, polishing the natural surfaces, and arranging them fancifully. The clasp of the royal mantle of Charlemagne (in the National Collection of France) was set with Diamonds, but the natural planes of the octahedron were only partially polished.

In the year 1290, a corporate body of gem-polishers and cutters was formed in Paris; and in 1373 there were Diamond-polishers in Nürnberg: but we do not know their method of polishing.

A little later, the so-called "table-cutters" at Nürnberg, and all other stone-engravers, formed themselves into a guild. So difficult was the acquisition of their Art, that one of their rules was that apprentices must serve for five or six years before they could be allowed to start in business for themselves.

In 1434, Guttenberg learnt gem-cutting and polishing of Andreas Drytzehen of Strasbourg.

In the year 1590, a Frenchman, Claudius de la Croix, went to Nürnberg, and carried on the cutting of Rose-garnets. As we have already seen, there were Diamond-cutters and polishers in Nürnberg in 1373.

On very old church ornaments have been found, from time to time, Diamonds having upper table-like surfaces with four polished borders, and the lower sides cut as four-sided prisms or pyramids.

In the inventory of the jewels of Louis, Duke of Anjou, exhibited in the years 1360—1368, the following cut Diamonds are mentioned. (1) a Diamond, of a shield shape, from a reliquary: (2) two small Diamonds, from the same reliquary with three flat-cut, four-cornered facets on both sides: (3) a small Diamond, in the form of a round mirror, set in a salt-cellar: (4) a thick Diamond, with four facets: (5) a Diamond, in the form of a lozenge: (6) an eight-sided, and (7) a six-sided plain Diamond.

In the beginning of the 15th century, there are traces of the art of Diamond-polishing in Paris. There still exists in Paris a cross-way called La Courarie, where the Diamond - workers lived two hundred and fifty years ago.

In 1407, Diamond-cutting made great strides under Hermann, a clever workman. The Duke of Burgundy gave a magnificent dinner at the Louvre to the King of France and his Court, and the noble guests received eleven Diamonds set in gold. Their value would be £117 18s. sterling. It is said that these Diamonds were cut, imperfectly perhaps, but still, enough to increase their play of color, and make them more worthy of presentation to such noble guests.

It was in Bruges, in 1456, that Louis de Berquem, who had lived long in Paris, made known his discovery of cutting the Diamond into regular facets. This increased the play of color considerably. So complete a revolution in the traffic of Diamonds was this, that his contemporaries looked upon him as the originator of Diamond polishing and cutting. In the year 1465 we find in Bruges a regular Corporation of Diamond Workers.

In 1475, Louis de Berquem made his first experiment with the "perfect cut" on three rough Diamonds of extraordinary dimensions, which had been sent to him by Charles the Bold, Duke of Burgundy.

No. 1 was a thick stone, which he is said to have cut over with facets, and which at a later period was known as the "Beau Sancy." I have had the stone examined, and many models made of it, and my firm impression is that the cut and work are Indian. It may have been retouched in Europe, but it is hard to believe that it was originally cut by Berquem.

No. 2 passed into the hands of Pope Sixtus IV.

No. 3, a badly proportioned stone, was shaped as a triangle and set in a ring, which, as a symbol of constancy, represented two hands clasped. Strange to say, it fell into the hands of that most faithless, inconstant of kings, Louis XI. It was presented to him by the Duke of Burgundy. Robert de Berquem relates that his grandfather Louis received 3,000 ducats for his work from Charles the Bold.

Of Louis' pupils, many went to Antwerp, some to Amsterdam, and others to Paris. In this last city the Art of Diamond Cutting did not succeed, owing possibly to want of encouragement and lack of raw material. It made some progress, however, under the powerful influence of Cardinal Mazarin. He ordered twelve of the thickest Diamonds of the French crown to be newly cut, and they received henceforward the name of "the twelve Mazarins." No one knows what ultimately became of these costly stones. In the inventory of the French Crown Jewels, in 1774, there is only one, under the number 349, with the name "tenth Mazarin." This was a four-cornered Brilliant, with somewhat obtuse angles, of pure water, weighing sixteen carats, and valued at 50,000 francs.

Owing to the patronage of the Cardinal, and the taste for Diamonds (cut Diamonds especially) which sprang up among the higher classes in France, the art prospered in the 16th century.

In the 17th century, Vincenzio Bruzzi, of Venice, as he was experimenting on the colored Diamond, came upon the form of the Recoupé Brilliant. At this time Paris possessed seventy-five Diamond cutters in full work, and amongst them not a few very clever masters. Jarlet cut a Diamond for the Russian Crown of 90 carats weight. Although a splendid prospect seemed to open at this time for Diamond working in Paris, gradually the art dwindled, until there were no workers left. The old stones were all re-cut, and rough ones came no more to Paris; so that in the year 1775 there were only seven masters left in that city, and they scarcely able to gain a livelihood.

In 1796 there were rough stones of 3,832 carats weight, absolutely sent *from* Paris to Antwerp, to be cut and polished as Brilliants. The trade was depressed more and more, until towards the end of the Colonne Ministry, a stranger, named Schrabracq, offered to the government to try and raise the art to its former degree of excellence. In the suburb of St. Antoine alone there were soon twenty-seven mills erected. Apprentices came in numbers, and all was going on satisfactorily, when suddenly, without notice, Schrabracq disappeared, and was seen no more. Since then the trade has been but limited in Paris.

Now-a-days, Diamond-cutting is a thriving trade in Holland; for although London has always owned artists of great ability in this line, and the "Old English cutting" (so termed in the trade) is looked upon as the type of the best workmanship, yet, as the competition of skilled hands in Holland vastly exceeds that of England, the labor is less expensive and in more general demand there than here.

It is curious how the Jews of Amsterdam have monopolised this branch of the Diamond trade. It is said that out of 28,000 Jewish inhabitants of Amsterdam, 10,000 are in some way or other connected with this business.

In India the stones are very imperfectly cut, often quite irregularly, and on one side only. The size of the stone is valued there rather than the artistic cut. In workman's language the stones cut in India are "lumpy." This was the fault of the Koh-i-noor, which was cut so clumsily by Hortensio Borgio, a Venetian, that it was reduced from 793 carats to 186, and rendered as dull as a piece of rock crystal. It was afterwards re-cut by

Mr. E. Coster, and reduced to 106 carats. Bad judgment was shown in its re-cutting. The stone still retained a vitreous lustre, the size having been preserved at the expense of its beauty. The two famous Diamonds belonging to the Shah of Persia, the *Dariainoor* (the brilliant sea), and the *Koh-i-noor* (the mountain of light),— which must not be confounded with the stone spoken of previously—are both specimens of irregular cutting.

Indian stones of such imperfect cutting are called *Labora*, and when sent to Europe are re-cut and polished.

C.—DIAMOND-CUTTING.

1.—DIAMOND DUST.

The Diamond, the hardest of all known bodies, can only be manipulated by means of Diamond in the form of a fine powder. This powder is prepared generally from faulty Diamonds and from the refuse in cleaving and cutting; which, being put into a mortar of hardened steel, is beaten until it is fine enough for use. The powder is worth from 8/- to 10/- a carat.

2.—CLEAVING OR SPLITTING DIAMONDS.

The cleaving or splitting of Diamonds serves a double purpose: firstly, that of removing faulty parts or spots from the stone; and, secondly, bringing out the facets in rough.

Some Diamonds cannot be brought to perfection without immense labor in grinding, especially such as have very convex facets, and such as are nearly as round as balls.

To get perfect facets in these would be endless trouble.. By splitting them, however, according to their natural cleavage, facets in the rough are obtained without much difficulty, and the pieces broken off are, as a rule, quite capable of being worked up as good stones themselves. To avail himself of the cleavage, the workman must have an intimate acquaintance with the structure of the crystal. Diamonds can only be split along certain definite lines of cleavage.

3.—CUTTING OF DIAMONDS.

There are three distinct operations in the cutting of Diamonds, namely, *splitting*, *cutting* and *polishing*. They form distinct branches of the trade.

a.—The stone is first given to the *cleaver* or *splitter*, who examines it carefully in order to ascertain how he can develope or bring out every property to the best advantage, with as little loss of weight as possible. He must discover every imperfection. His tool is a wooden baton, having at one end a little projecting ferule, containing cement of brick-dust and resin. He makes this cement soft, by warming it at a small fire or lamp, lays the Diamond in it, allowing the stone to remain there until the whole is quite cold, by which time the Diamond is firmly embedded in the cement. He then takes another Diamond with sharp edges, and cuts with it a mark or notch in the one he is going to cleave. This mark is generally in the shape of a V_1 and is a guide as to the direction of the cleavage-plane of the stone. This would be very difficult for an unpractised eye and hand. He catches every particle of dust in a box, with a sieve in it, which separates the dust of the cement from that of the Diamond. When the notch is made deep enough in the Diamond, the wooden baton is set upright in a block of lead. With one hand he introduces the blunt edge of a little steel blade into the notch that he has made; with the other hand he strikes the blade a quick, sharp blow with a steel rod, and the stone is split. This is always a serious operation, for if any want of skill were shown by the workman, the stone would be injured, perhaps irretrievably. The stone, now that it is divided, is taken out of the cement, and the process is repeated until the Diamond has received the rough form which the workman has decided upon.

b.—The stone then goes to the *cutter*, who has similar instruments for his work. Instead, however, of cutting notches in the Diamond, he grinds two together until both are quite smooth, and thus brings out the facets which were roughly produced by the splitter. He has to be very careful in grinding the stones that they do not get too hot. This would give them a faint surface and lessen their value. This process is very laborious, and the workman has to wear thick leather gloves to preserve his hands. From time to time the stones must be looked at, and the powder brushed from them with a fine camel-hair brush, and the facets touched with the tongue to keep them damp. The cutter gives the stone its definite form. If it is thick enough for a Brilliant, he forms the "table" first, and then successively all the facets.

Only highly skilled and very honest artisans are entrusted with the cutting of large Diamonds.

c.—POLISHING THE DIAMOND.

When the Diamond passes from the cutter's hand it is by no means perfect. The lustre and transparency for which it is so valued are only fully developed in the hands of the polisher.

The polishing rooms of great factories, such as those of Messrs. Coster, in Amsterdam, are well worthy of a visit.

The grinding and polishing of the Diamond are effected on flat wheels propelled by steam-power, which make about 2,000 revolutions in a minute. Before these silently revolving discs you will see workmen so intent upon their work that they have eyes for nothing else; for, notwithstanding the machinery, the skill of the workman is of primal importance. It is with their fingers and thumbs that they adjust the points, edges and facets of the Diamond with extreme accuracy, keeping it constantly moist with Diamond dust and olive oil. The thumbs being used continually, and with much force, sometimes become enlarged. It requires years of assiduous toil to acquire proficiency in this work.

d.—CUTTING OF PRECIOUS STONES GENERALLY.

This section embraces the cutting of all Precious and Half-precious Stones used for ornaments, except the Diamond. The lapidary arranges his work much in the same manner as the Diamond cutter, but he uses other means for the cutting and polishing, according to the nature of the stone to be worked. These special means will be noticed under each particular stone.

e.—THE FORMS OF PRECIOUS STONES.

The beauty of a finished stone depends so much upon the form and position of its facets, that a moderately fine stone, well cut and polished, is of far greater value than a large one less artistically worked. It happens sometimes that the lapidary receives a stone of very unfortunate shape. His duty will, therefore, be to take all possible care to preserve its size; and, hiding its faults, give it such a form as shall send it forth with the greatest worth and beauty.

In selecting Precious Stones you must mentally ask yourself the following questions: Is their transparency

THE PROPER SIZES OF WELL PROPORTIONED BRILLIANTS OF THE VARIOUS W

The Black Lines underneath show the relative thickness each Diamond should
and the round dots the size of the Culet.

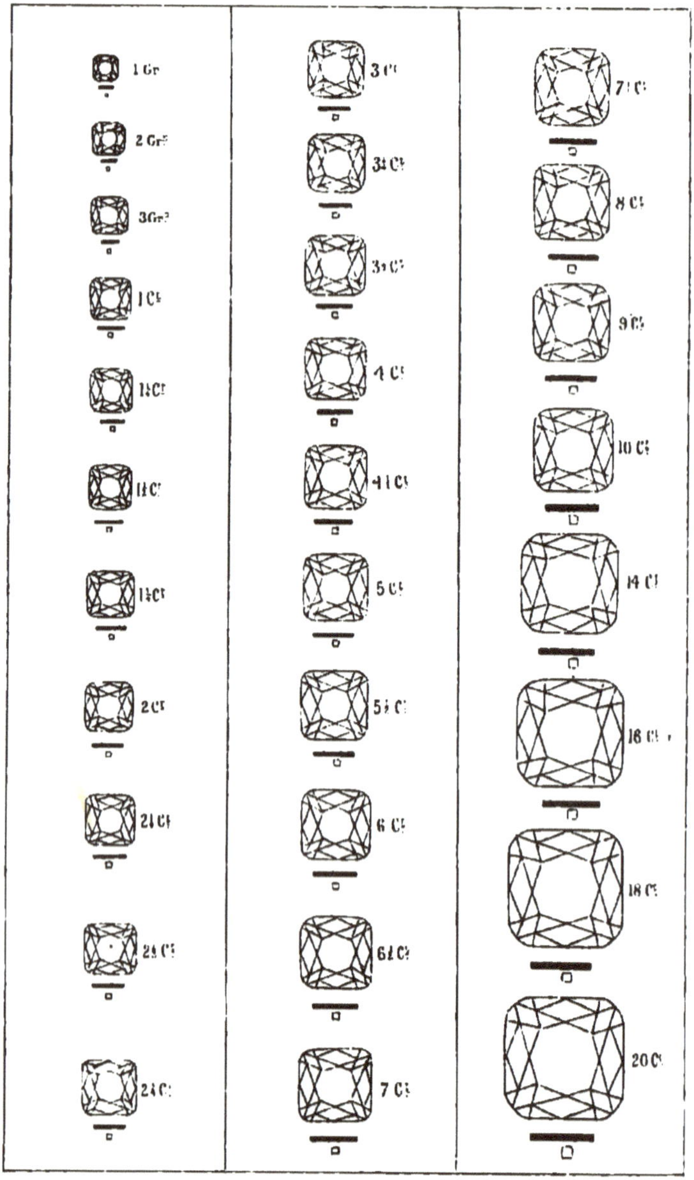

1 Gr	3 C!	7½ C!
2 Gr!	3¼ C!	8 C!
3 Gr?	3½ C!	9 C!
1 C!	4 C!	10 C!
1¼ C!	4½ C!	14 C!
1½ C!	5 C!	16 C!
1¾ C!	5½ C!	18 C!
2 C!	6 C!	20 C!
2¼ C!	6½ C?	
2½ C!	7 C!	
2¾ C!		

conspicuous? Are they like a dew-drop hanging from a damask rose leaf, that is, are they of pure water, and do they possess the power of refraction in a high degree? Or, are they transparent and colored; and, if the latter, have they a play of color? Lastly, have they notable imperfections?

Transparent stones must not be too thick; for either they will refract light too strongly, or impede the light passing through, and thus rob the stone of its brilliancy and fire.

In colorless and pure-water stones, the width and thickness which they must have are, as a rule, determinate; while the coloured ones are grouped according to the intensity and thoroughness of the color.

The workman is compelled sometimes to give the stone a form other than that intended by nature, in consequence of flaws and clefts, and in order to remedy irregularities in the stone. This is most frequently the case in large stones.

Different forms of cutting receive different names, which are often extended to the finished stone itself. For instance, if you hear of a "Brilliant" or "Rose" you know at once it is a Diamond, although many other precious stones receive the same form.

I.—THE BRILLIANT.

In the Diamond, as well as other stones, this is the most favorable form for enhancing the play of color and fire of the stone. It is said to be the crowning invention in the art of Diamond-cutting. It was due originally to Vincenzio Peruzzi, of Venice; which city was, in his time, the chief seat of the Diamond trade.

As a Brilliant, the Diamond has the form of two cones united by their bases the upper one being so truncated as to give a large plane surface; the lower one much less so, in fact terminating almost in a point. The stone being set with the broad plane uppermost has great depth of light; and the number of facets strengthens the refractive power and adds marvellously to the brilliancy. The plane surface at the top is called the *table*; the bottom plane is called the *culet* or *culette*; the junction of the upper truncated pyramid with the lower is the *girdle*; and the lower pointed portion is the *pavilion*. Between the table and the girdle are thirty-two facets, and below the girdle twenty-four. These facets receive their names from their forms. *Star* facets are those whose edges abut on the table; the others are generally triangular. According to the number of the facets, the Brilliant is said to be single, double, or, Old English, cut. The Brilliant depends greatly upon the facetting for its exceeding beauty.

The English make the girdle rather sharp; but the Dutch make it broader. The former method brings out the play of color better.

A form, called the "Star," was invented by M. Caire, to take advantage of the clear portions of rough Diamonds, which could not be otherwise used without great sacrifice of material. This star-cut Diamond, as it is now worn, must be cut with extreme exactitude, avoiding the very slightest irregularity.

Brillonètes are those stones which are cut as Brilliants on the surface, but have neither culette nor girdle. They are rare, and when a pair can be obtained exactly matching they are of very great value.

2.—THE ROSE.

This form has been in use since 1520, and resembles an opening rose-bud. It is chosen when the loss to the stone would be great if the brilliant cut were selected.

PROPER SIZES OF WELL PROPORTIONED ROSES OF THE VARIOUS WEIGHTS.

It should be understood that the back of the Rose Diamond is always flat.

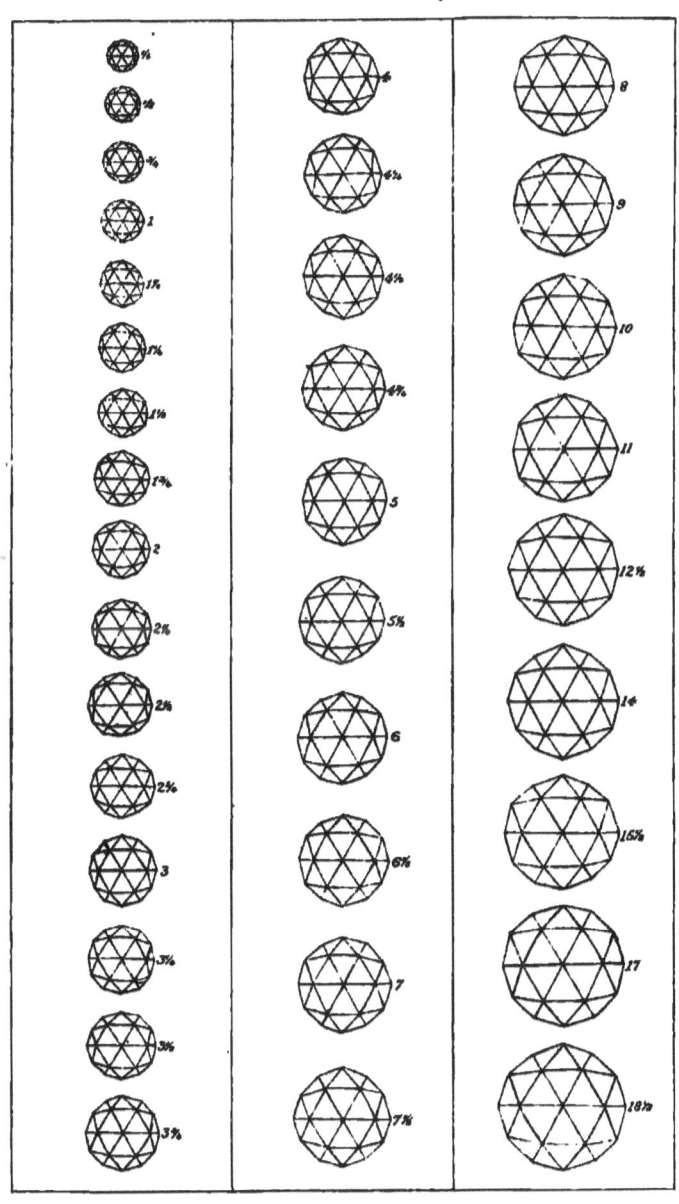

The characteristic of the "Rose" is that it is flat below, and forms a hemisphere or low pyramid above, covered with small facets. These facets are in two rows: those in the upper row are called *star-facets;* those in the lower, *diagonal-facets.* In the centre there are generally six facets of triangular shape. A circular stone is best for the Rose; the facets are more effectively brought out, and can be more easily polished in a stone of this shape.

Although the Rose gives out a strong fire and sends its rays as far as the Brilliant, yet in the latter the play of color is more beautiful, since here the facets exactly correspond, so as to increase the refraction and reflection, making the prismatic colors as bright as possible.

The number of facets, together with their position, decides the name of the "Rose." Twenty-four facets make a Dutch Rose; the same number, but less raised, a Brabant Rose; thirty-six facets, a Rose Recoupée.

3.—INDIAN CUT.

This has an upper part, lower part, and girdle. Its most frequent form is that of a single cut Brilliant. In consequence of the small effects produced by this form it is generally re-cut.

4.—POINT CUT.

Stones may be pointed naturally or artificially. Some Precious Stones may either be cut as four-sided pyramids, or are so formed by polishing the faces of the octahedron, and making them exactly true and regular. This style of cutting is only found in old ornaments; and was well-known to Kentmann, who wrote in 1562.

5.—PORTRAIT STONES

are very thin plates of Diamond, evenly polished on both

sides with little facets on the edges. They serve to cover portraits in rings, with good effect.

6.—STEP-CUT OR GRADUATED FORM

is where the facets gradually decrease as they approach the table and the *culasse*. It is a very good style for colored stones, because the light is more completely reflected, and the play of color increased.

7.—CONVEX CUT, OR CABOCHON.

A cut by which the stone receives one or two convex faces, with or without facets at the base. It is employed for Stones either somewhat transparent, as the Almandine Garnet, or for those that have a play of colors, as the Opal and Cat's-eye. In ancient times the Sapphire was always thus cut. The Emerald and Ruby are now frequently cut *en Cabochon*, but for this inferior stones are generally chosen.

E.—ENGRAVING.

a.—THE KIND OF STONE WHICH THE ANCIENTS USED FOR ENGRAVING.

Intaglios have the design sunk below the surface; in Cameos the subjects are in relief, or raised above the surface. The Intaglio and the Cameo can be produced on all kinds of stones. The smallest and hardest stones can be used in the production of them; brittle gems, however, being generally avoided. The stones selected are various: one-colored, many-colored, transparent, opaque, convex, flat, spotted, striped. The great master-pieces, however, in this department are on beautiful transparent stones. An artist does not care to expend his time and talent on a stone which does not show his work to the best advantage, and at its full worth. The stones preferred by the Ancients for this work were the Emerald, Beryl, Hyacinth, Amethyst, Topaz, Lapis-Lazuli, Opal, and Chrysolite; and among those of less value, the Carnelian, varieties of Jasper, Agate, Onyx, Sardonyx, Turquoise, Rock Crystal, Green Quartz, Malachite, and Serpentine.

There is a very beautiful specimen of a Turquoise Cameo in the Vienna Collection; and an Isis-head of the finest workmanship, in Malachite, in the Russian Collection of Jewels at St. Petersburg.

For Cameos it is desirable to select large stones, remarkable for beauty of color, with different layers; although beautiful works of art have been elaborated on gems of one color.

The more layers an Onyx or Sardonyx has, the more beautiful the colors, and therefore the more costly the stone. The best stones for this particular work are those with a white layer on a dark ground. They are still better where there is a third layer above, as white with a reddish or brownish tinge, which the artist can work into hair, wreaths, or dress. Entirely transparent Stones are very rarely used for Cameos.

b.—THE ART OF STONE ENGRAVING IN THE MIDDLE AGES AND IN MODERN TIMES.

Stone engraving seems to have been introduced into the West by Jews from Alexandria. In the middle ages, and even in later times, when there was no great master in the Art of Engraving, the cut stones of the Ancient Greeks and Romans were used as signet rings. King Pepin sealed with the Indian Bacchus, and Charlemagne with a stone representing Jupiter Serapis.

Later on, signet rings were engraved with the King's signature; and lovers were wont to exchange at their betrothal, rings, cut to represent wishes or allegories.

In the 15th century, when Constantinople fell under the dominion of the Turk, the Greek artists left their fatherland, carrying with them the secret knowledge of Stone Engraving into Italy. The first fruits of this immigration was seen during the Pontificates of Martin V. and Paul II. Lorenzo di Medici assisted this development by affording to Giovanni Bernardi the means of instruction by which he profited, so as to engrave Carnelian to such perfection that he received the cognomen of Giovanni delle Corniole. His work was so exquisite that it bore favorable comparison with the masterpieces of old classic times, and he has been regarded as the restorer of the art of Stone Engraving in Italy.

A contemporary of his, named Dominico de' Camei, cut beautiful Intaglios as well as Cameos. He sculptured on a pale red Ruby the likeness of Ludovico, the Moor, Duke of Milan. Clemens Birago, or Claude Briaque, of Milan, discovered in 1556 the Art of sculpturing the Diamond. According to Blum, Ambrosius Caradossa was the first to sculpture Diamonds. It is stated that he engraved the figure of a Father of the Church, for Pope Julius II., in 1500.

The earliest trace of Stone Engraving in Germany is found in Nürnberg and Strasburg, in the 15th and 16th centuries.

France, England, and in modern times, Rome also, produce most excellent artists in Stone Engraving.

Modern artists have so imitated the works of the Ancients that it is difficult to distinguish the old Jewels from the new, which are copies from the originals. The Ancients possessed very able workers in Stone Engraving;

but it would be unjust to modern artists to declare that all excellence in this department belongs to the Antique, as the originals have not only been equalled, but surpassed.

Many of the most beautiful of ancient gems are carefully preserved in Berlin, Vienna, Naples, Florence, in the Barberini Palace, in the Museum of Duke Odescalchi in Rome, and in St. Petersburg and Copenhagen. The Blacas Collection, in the British Museum, contains some of the most valuable "Gems" (engraved stones) in the world. Francis I. of France, made the first collection of engraved stones; and the Duke of Orleans' collection in Paris was of world-wide celebrity. When true copies of these works are required, impressions can be made of them in various kinds of material. Plaster of Paris, and sulphur, are most frequently employed for this purpose.

c.—BURNING OF PRECIOUS STONES.

Precious Stones are often burnt or subjected to a high temperature. Red heat exercises a very peculiar influence upon many stones, and acts in a strong degree upon the color.

The Oriental Carnelian owes its beautiful color entirely to burning. It is found in quartz sand, near Barotsch in the province of Hazarate, in Hindostan, and is cut and burnt at the place where it is found.

The Brazilian Topaz derives its beautiful pale-red color from burning. The facets of a naturally red Topaz reflect a purple light, and by candle-light the red is more deeply tinged with purple than violet: while, on the contrary, the burnt one, of less worth, is more deeply tinged with the violet color.

One way of burning Precious Stones, is to roll them up in a piece of sponge, and burn it: or, as is done with Sapphires, Hyacinths and Amethysts, place them in a crucible, with unslaked lime or iron-filings, and heat them until they are quite colorless. Occasionally where a faulty stone with dark spots is burnt with sand and iron filings, the spots are removed and the color equalized. This process requires great care.

Rubies are occasionally infected with white spots, but these are removed by burning. Crystal also, carefully burnt in a crucible with lime, sand or charcoal, will come out perfectly clear.

d.—DYEING OF PRECIOUS STONES.

The possibility of giving artificial colors to Precious Stones was not unknown to the Romans. Pliny relates: (1) that receipts were offered for sale which professed to turn Rock-crystals into Emeralds and other transparent gems: (2) that in India many Precious Stones were produced by dyeing Rock-crystal: (3) that the Ethiopians lay the pale Carbuncle in vinegar for fourteen days, after which, for the same number of months, it was to shine brilliantly. Respecting the artificial coloring of certain gems of the Quartz species, Pliny says that of certain Agates (Cochlides) more are probably produced artificially than naturally: and that in Arabia the Agate-almond, if cooked seven days and seven nights in honey, will, when prepared by the artist, present veins, stripes and spots, and serve admirably for ornaments. The cooking in honey is for the purpose of cleansing the whole stone from all impurity, and not its surface merely.

This notion of honey purifying the Agate seems to be the foundation of the following beautiful idea : " All kinds of Precious Stones, cast into honey, become more brilliant thereby, each one according to its color, and all persons become more acceptable in their vocation, when they join devotion with it: household cares are thereby rendered tranquil, the love of husband and wife more sincere, the service of the prince more faithful, and all kinds of business more easy and pleasant."—*Extract from the introduction to "The Devout Life," by S. Francis de Sales. Chap. III., par.* 13. 1708.

In the last century many attempts were made to dye Agate, Chalcedony and Carnelian, both on the surface and internally, with various colors, by means of metallic solutions.

EXPERIMENTS AT OBERSTEIN AND IDAR.

In Oberstein and Idar the artists have been most successful, not only in coloring the surface of the stones, but their inner depths. Both in polishing and coloring the stones, they have given such variety and beauty to their wares as to increase their value considerably in the market. The use of honey in the dyeing of stones was in early times the secret of a few Agate merchants at Idar. They either by craft or purchase obtained the secret from some Romans who came to procure every variety of Onyx from the stone-polishers at that place and Oberstein. It is impossible to say whether these Romans gained the knowledge by reading Pliny, or received it as a tradition in Italy.

This Art depends mainly upon the fact that the fine stripes of the Chalcedony, in the so-called Agate Nodule or Almond, no matter how faint their tints, can by application of a colored fluid be intensified and made to appear throughout the stone. This induced the stone-polishers to think it possible that they might change mean and insignificant looking stones into beautiful ones, suitable for Cameos and other purposes, and so materially increase their value.

The Agate merchants test the worth of the raw stone for dyeing by striking a thin piece off it, damping it with the tongue, and observing whether the drying of the stripes takes place quickly or slowly. If the stripes suck up the moisture quickly, then is the stone good for dyeing and especially for Onyx-dyeing. This test, however, cannot always be relied on, and they are sometimes obliged to color a small piece before buying the stones from the mines.

At Oberstein and Idar the Onyx is dyed in the following manner. The stone is twice washed, and then dried. It is next laid in honey and water (half-a-pound of honey to about sixteen or twenty ounces of water). The dish in which it is laid must be chemically clean. This is placed in a warm oven, and care must be taken that the water does not boil, and that the stone is always covered with the liquid. This treatment is continued from fourteen to twenty-one days. The stone is then taken out of the honey, washed, and soaked in another dish with sulphuric acid. The dish is then covered, and placed in hot ashes with burning coals on the cover. In a few hours the stone will be dyed. Some stones require a longer time; some will, despite all care, take no color. The last thing necessary is to take the stone out of the sulphuric acid, wash it, dry it in the oven, and lay it in oil for a day; thus the stone obtains a greater brilliancy. By this process it will have obtained light-grey stripes, and, according to the porosity of the stone, grey, brown, black, or red stripes will be brought out.

The so-called "Carnelian of Brazil" is worked in great quantities in Oberstein and Idar.

Of late, an exquisite blue dye has been found for the Chalcedony, of all shades of Turquoise. The method of producing it is a secret known to only a few of the stone-polishers; but in Egypt the Art is practised successfully.

CHAPTER IV.
PRECIOUS STONES AS OBJECTS OF COMMERCE.

a.—THEIR DISTRIBUTION.

HE trade in Precious Stones is much more important now than formerly. Before the discovery of America, India was the great emporium. Pegu, famous for its beautiful gems of all kinds, received yearly a very large sum for its exports. So also did Ceylon, from which island we even now obtain a large portion of our colored Precious Stones. During the dynasty of the Candian Rulers, the right of digging for Precious Stones was most jealously guarded as a royal prerogative, and the inhabitants of particular villages, under the supervision of hereditary overseers, were occupied in the search for gems. Under the British Government this monopoly was given up, and traders needed no "special permit."

A number of men are constantly occupied in this exciting and precarious business: and the idle and disorderly adventurers who visit the villages are the cause of great immorality among the inhabitants. The results of their labors they sell to the Malays who come to Saffragam with cloth and salt, which they exchange for Precious

F

Stones. At the yearly Bhudda Festival, there is a jewel market held in Ratnapura, whither those interested in jewels flock from all parts of Ceylon.

The position of the people in Saffragam is so much improved of late years that they are able to retain any stones they find of great worth for themselves. Now and then they are induced to exchange them for gold, which they can equally well conceal. The artificers who cut and polish the stones on the spot are generally Malays: but their work is so imperfect, and their knowledge of the Art so faulty, that the stone positively loses by passing through their hands. Stones of smaller value, such as Cinnamon-stone, Garnets and Tourmaline are cut and polished by ordinary workmen in Candia, Matura and Galla. Artistic and experienced workmen who cut Rubies and Sapphires live chiefly in Caltura and Colombo.

As a general rule, the rare gems are cheaper in Europe than in Colombo. Precious Stones are brought from all parts of the world to London, both in the rough and also to be re-cut. In Ceylon the stock is so uncertain, that the price is largely determined at the moment by the rank and wealth of the buyers. The small Malay dealers do not buy rare and fine jewels, knowing quite well that the best and finest specimens are carefully held back by the rich traders, who can always ensure a high price for the best Ceylon stones from the native princes of India, who have an ardent passion for Gems of conspicuous beauty or size.

It is quite impossible to judge accurately by the Customs' Register in Ceylon of the worth of the Precious Stones which are sent out of the island. Only a small part is sent to England. The rest are bought up by private hands; but these ultimately find their way into the English market. It is calculated roughly, however, that the value of the Precious Stones found in the Island is £10,000 yearly.

It is said that the Dutch East India Company formerly received the rough stones in packets, sealed with their special seal. Those packets were sold by auction, without being opened. Often from 20,000 to 30,000 florins were paid for one packet, and the buyer was very rarely wrong in his purchase.

It is more than a hundred years ago that Brazil became a powerful rival of India. The most beautiful stones were found in the nearly inaccessible wilds of Minas-Novas, by poor mulattos and negros, and sold to the merchants.

While Brazil belonged to the Portuguese Crown, Lisbon enjoyed the largest share of the trade in Precious Stones. The trade was a prerogative of the Crown.

In the trade of Precious Stones, the colored stones stand far behind the Diamond : insomuch, that this stone alone represents 90 per cent., and the others altogether only 10 per cent. of the quantity on sale.

b.—THEIR PRICE.

Apart from the kind of stone, the price of Precious Stones is determined by their beauty, the equality and play of color, brilliancy, purity, rarity, the art and perfection of cut, and above all, their size. This last quality increases the price considerably, as the most beautiful stones are generally found in small pieces.

In the case of Half-precious Stones, the size and color go for much in determining the price, but are not so important as the artistic working of the stones. Stones depend almost entirely upon this latter for their actual worth. The price of Precious Stones depends mainly on their rarity and quality, fashion occasionally exercising influence in a greater or less degree upon their market value.

Not long ago, at the Leipsic Easter Market, Diamonds

fell suddenly 50 per cent., owing to Don Pedro having paid the interest of the Brazilian State-Debt to England in Diamonds instead of money, and so caused a glut in the market. In 1836 the price rose considerably. In 1848, in consequence of the Revolution in France, Diamonds again fell in value.

c.—FAULTS IN PRECIOUS STONES.

In buying Precious Stones, the greatest precaution must be used. There are scarcely any wares with so many faults and imitations as these. The faults are such as materially lessen the value. In the rough stones they are not easily observed ; and in manipulated gems they may be hidden by clever workmanship.

Among the most frequent faults are: (1) *Feathers:* little rents or fissures in the inside of the stone ; they are found in all kinds of Precious Stones. (2) *Clouds:* gray, brown and white spots, very like clouds, which much increase the labor of working the stone. This fault is mostly found in Diamonds and pale Rubies. (3) *Sand:* or little seed-like bodies within the stone, of white, brown or red color : these are called *dust* when very fine and in large number in one stone. But of stones, it may be predicated as of animals, that there is no such thing as perfection known.

SECTION II.

CHAPTER I.
THE DIAMOND.

a.—FORM.

HE regular crystalline forms in which the Diamond is found belong to the Tesseral system, and are generally the octahedron and the rhombic dodecahedron. The former is assumed by the East-Indian Diamond, ánd the latter by the Brazilian Diamond. The peculiarity of the crystallization of the Diamond is that the surfaces of each side are more or less curved or convex, whilst those of other crystalline bodies, with few exceptions, are flat.

Most of the rhombic dodecahedra have, at the extremities of the *short* diagonals, the rhomb defective, whence results a very distorted pyramidal cube. When the defectiveness is at the ends of the *long* diagonals we get a bulging pyramidal octahedron. A combination of these gives a pyramidal rhombic dodecahedron, which, by the rounding of the faces approaches a ball or egg shape.

Groups of crystals (dodecahedra as well as octahedra)

are not rare. There is a very fine specimen of such a mass of coalesced octahedra in the Royal Mineral Museum at Dresden; and in the Vienna Collection there is a Diamond which has, enclosed within itself, another similarly crystallized Diamond of a yellow color. For further information on this topic, the reader is referred to the chapters on Cape, Australian, and Brazilian Diamonds.

b.—SURFACE.

The surface of the crystals is generally smooth; sometimes, however, it is rough and striated, in which case it resembles a poorly polished glass, and loses its lustre and sharp corners.

Very rarely is the Diamond found compact of fine-grained porous aggregates of brownish black color.

The Diamond has occasionally been found massive in Brazil, in small black pebbles, having a specific gravity of 3·0 to 3·4. These pebbles, nearly pure carbon, were sold on the spot at 75 cents. the carat.

c.—COHESION.

The Diamond has a perfect cleavage, parallel to the faces of the octahedron, which is its primary form. The Diamond cutter avails himself of this. He is thereby enabled to remove portions damaged by rough spots, without resorting to the weary work of grinding. The fracture is conchoidal, and here and there liable to split off in fragments. Notwithstanding the great hardness of the Diamond, it is so brittle that it can be pulverized in a mortar.

In addition to the property of cohesion, the Diamond possesses pre-eminently that of hardness; a quality in which it so exceeds other bodies that it can penetrate them all without itself being even scratched, and for this reason formerly it was only possible to polish it very partially, and to use it in its natural crystal form.

In early times there existed such an exaggerated idea of its extraordinary hardness that it was said a Diamond could not be broken by a hammer on an anvil, and that it was far easier to strike the anvil into the earth than break the Diamond.

It was upon this notion that the anvil test was applied for proving the genuineness of the Diamond. Many a good Diamond has been shattered and so lost because its brittleness was really tested by the hammer, and not its hardness which is a very different quality.

Pliny gives a detailed account of the Diamond in his "Natural History," xxxvii., 15. He says: "The most valuable thing on earth is the Diamond, known only to kings, and to them imperfectly. * * It is only engendered in the finest gold. * * * Six different kinds are known. Among these the Indian and Arabian, of such indomitable, unspeakable hardness, that when laid on the anvil it gives the blow back in such force as to shiver the hammer and anvil to pieces. It can also vanquish fire, for it cannot be burnt. * * * This power over steel and fire is broken by goat's blood, in which it must be soaked when the blood is fresh and warm, and then only after many blows, and when hammer and anvil have been both in pieces, will it yield. * * * Only a god could have communicated such a valuable secret to mankind. Even when it yields by means of the blood, it falls into such small pieces that they can scarcely be seen." This was the stand-point of the Ancients in relation to the Diamond.

Hardness is the best test of the genuineness of a Diamond. If a mineral cannot be scratched or cut by Ruby or Sapphire, it can only be a Diamond. The officers of the "Junta Diamantina," in Brazil, test the genuineness of two rough Diamonds by rubbing them together close to the ear, when, if they be real, they make a peculiar creaking or grating noise, which is easily recognized by the testers.

d.—OPTICAL PROPERTIES.

1.—*Refraction.*

The conditions which the Diamond presents in relation to light are very remarkable. It belongs to those bodies which refract light most strongly. The magnifying power of a Diamond is greater than that of glass: hence it is sometimes used for microscopic lenses; but owing to the great difficulty of making them perfectly accurate, their use is much restricted, and very few good ones are made.

Newton arrived at the conclusion that the Diamond must be a combustible substance; partly from the following consideration, viz.: the relative density of Quartz and Diamond is as 3 to 4, but the refracting power is as 3 to 8; therefore he concluded that the Diamond could not be an incombustible body.

2.—*Reflection.*

In addition to its property of strong refraction, the Diamond possesses the power, in an extraordinary degree, of reflecting the colored rays of light, and causing what is technically termed the "play of colors" observable on a well-cut Diamond.

As the value of a Diamond depends very materially upon this play of colors, many methods have been assayed from time to time for testing it. Babinet recommends the following plan, which he himself was in the habit of employing. In a sheet of white paper he bored a hole somewhat larger than the Diamond to be tested: he let a ray of sun-light pass through the hole, and holding the Diamond a little distance from it, yet at such an angle as to allow the ray to alight on a point of the flat facet, he found this facet to be forthwith represented on the paper, as a white figure, whilst all around little rainbow circles were delineated. If the observer found the primary colors, *i.e.* red, yellow, and blue, definitely separated one from the other in these little circles, and if their number were considerable, and they stood at equal distances from each other, then he pronounced the Brilliant to be well cut.

In the Rose the light reflects from the under-plane, and produces a similar effect to that seen in the Brilliant.

3.—*Double Refraction.*

The Diamond does not possess the power of double refraction, neither does it polarize light; although, according to Brewster, there are sometimes internal air-bubbles as in Amber, by which the course of the light is somewhat altered. Since on the outside of these air-bubbles light passes through perfectly unpolarized, it appears that the mass was originally so soft that the enclosed air could by expansion change the part lying nearest to it, just as one is able to produce similar results by pressure in glass and resin. Such compression on the mass close to the air-bubbles, Brewster declares to be nowhere found among minerals produced by the operation of heat; and he concludes, therefore, that the softness which the Diamond without doubt formerly possessed was that of a half-dried gum. This deviation in refraction has given rise to the erroneous belief that the Diamond possesses double refraction.

e.—LUSTRE.

The lustre of the Diamond is the peculiar, indescribable, but well-known *adamantine lustre*.

The refracting and reflecting properties of the Diamond are very trifling in the rough, compared with the cut and polished stone.

The surface of the native crystal is often rough with little rents and flaws, and has a peculiar leaden-grey semi-metallic lustre, somewhat like small lumps of gum-arabic.

f.—COLOR.

The Diamond generally, and in its purest condition, is colorless and transparent; yet at times it is found colored, but only slightly, with pale-yellow, ochre-yellow, light bottle-green, yellowish-green, blackish-green, blue, red, and from brown to black. Next to yellow, green Diamonds are most numerous; the blue are very rare, and not of a bright tint. When the Diamond is between brown and black its transparency entirely disappears, or is seen only at the angles.

Entirely colorless Diamonds come from the mines of India, Brazil, the Cape, and Australia. One-fourth of the Diamonds are colorless; one-fourth, of "pure water," with a stripe or spot of color; and the remainder colored.

The colored Diamonds preserve their lustre and clearness best when they are cut; especially the beautiful yellow ones, which, by candle-light, almost surpass in brilliancy the Diamonds of pure water.

Diamonds can be grouped according to their shades of color (*see chapter on "Blue and other Colored Diamonds"*).

Barbot, by means of chemical agents and a high temperature, is said to have succeeded in removing the coloring matter from the rough Diamond; green, red, and yellow stones becoming perfectly colorless; while the dark yellow, brown, and black, gave up very little of their color. It seems scarcely possible that this can be accurate. In many Diamonds the core is not pure, but shows blackish or greenish spots. This is particularly the case in the green stones. Many Diamonds show also "feathers" and fissures, which materially modify the passage of light.

Black Diamonds of great beauty are occasionally supplied by Borneo. These are so remarkably hard that the ordinary Diamond-dust makes not the smallest impression upon them; and they can only be cut or polished by using their own dust for the purpose.

g.—PHOSPHORESCENCE.

This is produced not only by great heat, but also by the action of light, even after subsequent isolation. The Diamond becomes phosphorescent under the influence of the sun's rays, and remains so for some time after removal from the sunshine, even when covered with cloth, leather, or paper.

This property is most striking after the Diamond has been exposed to the *blue* or more refrangible rays of the spectrum; under the red rays it is much weaker. In an experiment of Barbot's, it is said the Diamond showed phosphorescence when he placed it under cover of limewood two millimetres (one-twelfth of an inch) thick, after it had been removed from the influence of the sun's rays.

h.—ELECTRICITY.

The Diamond is a non-conductor of electricity: and this is the more strange as Graphite and Charcoal, substances absolutely identical with it chemically, are very good conductors. By *friction*, however, both in the rough and polished state, it becomes *positively* electric, but loses its electricity completely in the course of half-an-hour.

i.—CHEMICAL PROPERTIES.

1.—*The Composition of the Diamond, and the History of its Discovery.*

Chemically the Diamond consists of pure carbon. Newton concluded the Diamond must be a combustible body, in consequence of its high refractive power. Robert Boyle, however, strove in vain to consume it in the crucible. For the purpose of investigating this supposed combustibility, the Academy of the Cimento, at Florence, in the year 1694, induced by the Grand Duke, Cosmo III., fixed a Diamond in the focus of a large burning-glass. The Academicians found that it cracked, coruscated, and at length disappeared, without leaving a particle behind.

In the year 1750, the Emperor Francis I., at Vienna, subjected in the presence of the chemist, Darzet, Diamonds and Rubies worth 6,000 florins, for twenty-four hours, to the heat of a smelting furnace. The Diamonds were found to have totally disappeared; but the Rubies remained, and appeared much more beautiful than before.

Scientific men of France carried on these experiments; and in the year 1771, on the 26th July, a magnificent Diamond was burnt in the laboratory of the chemist Macquer. Hence arose a great discussion. The fact was undoubted; the Diamond had disappeared; but whither? Had it volatilized? Had it burnt? Had it exploded? No one could say. Upon this there stepped forward a celebrated jeweller of Paris, by name Le Blanc, who asserted the indestructibility of the Diamond in the furnace, stating that he often placed Diamonds in an intense fire to purify them from certain blemishes, and that they had never suffered the smallest injury (I have conducted similar experiments, and generally with the same good results.) The chemists, D'Arcet and Rouelle, then demanded of him that he should make the experiment on the spot in their presence. He took some Diamonds, enclosed them in a mass of coal and lime in a crucible, and submitted them to the action of the fire. He had no doubt that he should find them safe. But, alas! he had sacrificed his Diamonds; for at the end of three hours, on looking into the crucible, they had utterly disappeared. But the scientific men did not long enjoy their triumph.

Another jeweller, Maillard, in the presence of the celebrated Lavoisier, took three Diamonds and closely packed them in powdered charcoal in an earthen pipe-bowl, in a strong fire; and when the pot was taken out there lay the Diamonds in the powdered charcoal untouched.

It was, however, gradually discovered that it was only by entirely shutting out the air and therefore the oxygen, with which the carbon combines, that the Diamonds were preserved from burning; whereas, by the simple admission of air of which oxygen is a constituent part, Diamonds burn just the same as common coal. This fact Lavoisier proved in 1776; and Davy subsequently showed that the Diamond contains no hydrogen.

It is almost unnecessary to say that the gas formed from the combustion of Diamonds is carbon-dioxide (carbonic acid Co^2), the gas yielded by every fire and gas-burner, and by the combustion of our own bodies: these latter, in the combustion that attends their very living evolve carbon-dioxide by the lungs, so that the old fable of the maiden from whose lips fell Diamonds may have a really scientific basis after all.

2.—*The temperature at which the Diamond burns.*

The temperature must be very high for the burning of a whole Diamond. A much lower degree of temperature will be sufficient to burn Diamond dust, if the latter be spread out on a red-hot, thin platinum plate, and put over a spirit-lamp. Small Diamonds will burn in a very short time, if placed on a plate of the same metal, and the flame of a spirit-lamp be directed by a blow-pipe under the plate; upon raising the temperature to a very high degree, they will disappear entirely in a few minutes.

3.—*Appearance of the Diamond while burning.*

When a Diamond is subjected to the sun's rays in the focus of a burning-glass, or heated in oxygen gas, it gives out bright-red sparks while burning. In order to see in what direction the Diamond suffered during the process of combustion, Petzholdt took two sharp-angled pieces of Diamond, and placed them before the oxy-hydrogen blow-pipe. Whilst undergoing this fierce heat, he removed them from the flame once or twice to watch the action of the fire upon their form and substance; he then detected that the heat had acted on the sharp angles, rounding thus the Diamonds first; and on the re-application of the heat, he observed that the Diamonds soon split up into pieces, and lost both their transparency and lustre. He could not detect any evidence of fusion on the surface of the burning Diamonds; but, on removing them from the fire, they assumed a leaden-grey color, which is worthy attention as an indication that this precious gem darkens or blackens in process of combustion. Lavoisier also noticed that on exposing the Diamond to intense heat, black spots appeared on it, then disappeared, and re-appeared in the action of destruction by fire. Guyton de Morveau confirmed these statements. He consumed a Diamond in oxygen, by means of the burning-glass. First he saw on that corner of the Diamond which was in the exact focus of the lens a black point; then the Diamond became black and carbonized. A moment after, he saw clearly a bright spark, twinkling as it were on the dark ground; and when the light was intercepted, the Diamond was red (red-hot) and transparent. A cloud now passed over the sun, and the Diamond was more beautifully white than at first; but as the sun again shone forth in its full strength, the surface assumed a metallic lustre. Up to this point the Diamond had sensibly decreased in bulk, not being more than a fourth of its original size; of elongated form, without definite angles, intensely white, and beautifully transparent. The experiment was suspended for a day or two, when, on its resumption, the same phenomena recurred, but in a more marked degree; subsequently the Diamond entirely disappeared. At the conclusion of his treatise, in which these experiments are detailed, he says, "If it were possible, while the Diamond is burning, to collect the black substance which covers the surface, the Diamond would indisputably be shewn to be carbon:" that is, be recognized under the more generally known form of carbon, viz., charcoal.

Fourcroy corroborates Guyton de Morveau. He placed two small Diamonds in a capsule, under a muffler, heated them, arrested the burning, suffered the half-consumed bodies to cool, and on removing the muffler he found them quite black, as though they had a covering of soot, which he removed by rubbing with a piece of paper, on which was left a black mark.

Clark took an amber-colored Diamond, six times the size of that used by Guyton de Morveau, and subjected it to the action of the oxy-hydrogen blow-pipe. It was entirely burnt in a few minutes. The first action of the flame upon it, was to make it perfectly clear and colorless: it next became faint-white, and quite opaque in appearance, very like to ivory. In this stage its size and specific gravity were both lessened: next one of the angles of the octahedron disappeared, and the surface was covered with little bubbles, like blisters. Subsequently all the angles disappeared, leaving an elongated ball, with a strong metallic lustre; and after a short interval, there was no sign of a Diamond having been there.

The Brothers Rogers say that with potassium chromate and hydric sulphate (sulphuric acid) at from 180° to 230° the Diamond is oxydized into carbonic acid. Jacquelaine and Despretz used very powerful galvanic batteries, and found that a Diamond, in an atmosphere of carbonic acid, by means of the oxy-hydrogen-gas blow-pipe, or one fed with carbon-oxide and oxygen, gradually disappeared without any sign of softening. Gassiot also has experimented on the Diamond by strong galvanic currents between carbon points.

Summing up.

(1) In burning the Diamond, uncrystallized black carbon is produced. (2) Many rough Diamonds possessing a metallic lustre become leaden-grey. (3) The blackish spots, adhering to the surface of some, may be got rid of by great heat.

4.—*The Diamond in relation to other chemical agents.*

No solvents, not even acids, have the slightest power over the Diamond to dissolve or decompose it; in this it is distinguished from other Precious Stones, most of which, having silica in their formation, cannot withstand the influence of hydric-fluoride (hydro-fluoric acid H F.).

j.—THE ORIGIN OF THE DIAMOND.

All the many opinions as to the origin and formation of the Diamond can be collected under two heads: (1) The Diamond is formed immediately from carbon or carbonic acid by the action of heat: (2) It is formed from the gradual decomposition of vegetable matter.

(1) Leonard says that the Diamond is formed by

sublimation of carbon in the depths of the earth; Parrot, that it is produced by the action of volcanic heat upon small pieces of carbon; Göbel, that pure carbon has been separated from carbonic acid by electricity in the presence of reducing agents, such as magnesium, calcium, aluminium, silicon, iron; Hausmann, that it is by the action of electricity, especially in the form of lightning, upon carbonic acid, that its decomposition is effected; and he quotes the statement of the Ancients, that in those mines where the largest number of Diamonds were found were also found in large number the so-called thunder-bolts.

(2) Among those who support the *vegetable* origin or the Diamond, is Newton, who believed it to be a coagulated, fat, or oily body, having a vegetable origin: Jameson and Brewster advanced similar views: Petzholdt also decided for the vegetable origin; and Liebig, who undoubtedly made himself a great authority by his knowledge of the decomposition of organic bodies, says, "Science affords us no analogy, except that of decomposition and decay, for the formation or origin of the Diamond. We know that it does not owe its origin to fire; for a high temperature and presence of oxygen are incompatible with it on account of its combustibility: on the contrary, there is undeniable ground for supposing that it was formed in 'the wet way;' and the decomposition process alone satisfactorily helps us in attempting to solve the mystery of its origin. What kind of vegetable substance, rich in hydro-carbons, was the decomposition of which gave rise to the Diamond, and what particular conditions had to be fulfilled in order to crystallize the carbon, are not at present known to us; but this much is certain, that the process must have been exceedingly gradual, and in no way hastened by a high temperature; otherwise the carbon would not have become crystallized, but would have separated itself as a black powder."

Wöbler also is of opinion that the Diamond did not originate in a high temperature, at least not by fusion.

G. Wilson held the view that the Diamond might originate from Anthracite or steam-coal, without a change from the hard state.

Later opinions seem to incline towards the Diamond taking origin directly from some other form of the element carbon.

Opposed in some degree to all these theories, but ranging under class 1 rather than class 2, is the view of Simler of Breslau, that the Diamond is the result of the crystallization of carbon from a liquid solution. According to his theory, carbonic acid collected, in far away times, in a number of cavities, and liquefied under great pressure; that it dissolved some pre-existing form of carbon; and subsequently that the carbonic acid became gradually dissipated through fissures and clefts, and the cystallization of the dissolved carbon began. Where the pressure suddenly abated, and in consequence a quick evaporation of the liquid occurred, a considerable compact mass of Black Diamond would be formed, such as is known in commerce as carbonado or carbon. It is very probable also that the rough, scaly, lead-colored rind, coating the rough Diamond, may be due to vaporization thus suddenly induced. Many a puzzling appearance in the Diamond can be explained if Simler's theory be accepted: the enclosed splinters of Quartz; the occasional feathers; the peculiar form of that rough Diamond in the British Museum, which has a moderately large cavity, whence a small yellow Diamond projects, as if it most certainly must have been thrown out in a liquid condition; and finally there is that large Diamond alluded to by Tavernier, in the cavity of which was found a mass of black carbonaceous matter, weighing from eight to nine carats, which he designated vegetable mud.

Which of these theories will have most weight with future generations it is impossible to say ; if the last, there would at first sight appear no insuperable obstacle to our producing some day an adamantine crystal artificially, although the conditions requisite for its hardness, brilliancy, and purity, essential to its value, might then, alas! be as far off as ever.

k.—MODE OF OCCURRENCE OF DIAMONDS.

Occurring in alluvial formations, the Diamond, in common with other gems and the Pearl, has not until late years been found of extraordinary size.

The localities of the Diamond are India, Sumatra, Borneo, Brazil, and South Africa, some places in North America, the Ural, and the Australian mountains. Other localities have been pointed out, but confirmatory evidence is required. In 1833, it was reported that in the gold-sand of the river Gumel, in the Algerian province of Constantine, three Diamonds had been discovered. The idea that Algiers was a land of Diamonds seems to have been once entertained ; and Dr. Cuny, an African traveller, reported that a whole camel-load of Diamonds had come from West Africa to Darfur in 1859. According to Murray a Diamond was found in a brook in Ireland ; and Bowles insisted that Diamonds ought to be found at Capo de Gat, in the South of Spain, because of its geological formation. Further, Java, Celebes, and Columbia have all been pointed out as producing Diamonds. Sometimes recognized localities are forgotten in books: thus Pagen, in his book published in 1849, gives only India, Borneo, and Brazil, as localities for Diamonds, whereas they had been discovered in the Urals twenty years before he wrote.

CHAPTER II.
CAPE OR SOUTH-AFRICAN DIAMONDS.

S I am writing a book on Jewels, not for the year 1777, but for a century later, and in London, the greatest emporium and market of Gems and Precious Stones in the world, I do not follow the topographical order of my predecessors. They would commence by descriptions of the Diamond fields of India, and the bygone glories thereof: I begin with a chapter on the *Cape*, as South Africa is a richer field, and its produce is far more to the purpose of modern history, and to the supply of the Precious Stones which form our wealth of gems, than the old Diamond fields of the East or West. So with a belief in the future of Queensland as a Diamond field, I treat of the Australian Stones also before the Indian.

Rather more than ten years ago, it happened that a child of Mr. Jacobs, a Dutch farmer settled at the Cape, amused himself by collecting pebbles from the neighbourhood of the farm, near Hopetown. At first sight there might seem nothing remarkable in this circumstance, for pretty pebbles were to be had in plenty near the neighbouring river. One of the stones, however, was sufficiently bright to attract the keen eye of the mother, though she regarded it simply as a curious pebble, and gave it little more than a passing glance. Some time afterwards a neighbouring boer, named Schalk van Niekerk, visited the farm, and knowing him to be curious in such matters, Mrs. Jacobs called his attention to the bright transparent stone. So little heed, however, had been given to the pebble, that when wanted it was nowhere to be found; and it was only after diligent search that it was at last discovered outside the house, just where it had happened to fall when the child had last used it as a plaything. Van Niekerk was sorely puzzled with the stone, yet thinking that it might possibly have some value, he offered to buy it of Mrs. Jacobs. The good woman laughed at the notion of selling so common a stone, and at once gave it to the enquiring farmer. Just then it chanced that Mr. J. O'Reilly was returning from a hunting and trading expedition in the interior of the country, and to him Van Niekerk confided the stone, with a request that he would endeavour to ascertain its nature from any trustworthy mineralogist whom he might meet. By Mr. O'Reilly the stone was taken to the town of Colesberg, and there shewn to Mr. Lorenzo Boyes, the Clerk of the Peace of the District. Mr. Boyes knew that his friend, Dr. G. W. Atherstone, of Graham's Town, was an excellent mineralogist; and, anxious to get his opinion, he sent the enigmatical stone through the post, accompanied by an explanatory letter. Had it been suspected that the stone was of any exceptional value, the envelope would no donbt have been carefully sealed, and the letter duly registered. As a matter of fact, however, the envelope containing the stone was simply gummed, and despatched as an ordinary letter. When it reached Graham's Town, the good doctor had some little difficulty in deciding what the curious pebble could be; but after carefully examining its physical characters, after testing its degree of hardness, its density, and its behaviour when subjected to optical tests by means of polarized light, Dr. Atherstone was bold enough to pronounce it a genuine *Diamond*.

This was in March, 1867, and the Universal Exhibition in Paris was about to open in the spring. What more appropriate, the doctor thought, than to send this stone to Paris? Here was the greatest novelty the Colony could exhibit — the first African Diamond! *Semper aliquid novi Africa affert.* Dr. Atherstone accordingly communicated his suggestion to the Colonial Secretary, the Hon. R. Southey, and in consequence of this suggestion the Diamond was duly conveyed by steamer to Cape Town, where it was examined by the French Consul, M. Heriette, who having confirmed Doctor Atherstone's judgment and determination as to the stone, forwarded it in due course to Paris. There it stood during the whole of the summer, and having been examined by *savants* of all nations, it was purchased at the close of the Exhibition, by His Excellency the Governor of the Colony, Sir Philip Wodehouse, for the sum of £500. The weight of this Diamond was $21\frac{3}{16}$ carats.

Such is the history of the discovery of the first Cape Diamond; a discovery, which being soon followed by others, led to the developement of the great Diamond-fields of South Africa. These fields are situated chiefly in the Colony of Griqualand, West, which was proclaimed British territory in 1871. The new Colony is intersected by the river Vaal, and it is in the Vaal valley, and in that of some of its tributary streams, such as the Modder and the Vet, that most of the Diamonds have been found. Drawing its head-waters from the Drakenberg or Quathlamba range of mountains, far away in the East, on the borders of Natal, the Vaal river, or the Ky Gariep, flows in a sinuous course, generally in a westerly direction, until it joins the Orange river, or the Nu Gariep. This, the greatest known stream in South Africa, runs for more than 900 miles in a westerly course, and finally rolls its burden of waters into the Atlantic. The Diamond-fields are situated in the neighbourhood of the Middle Vaal, about 60 miles above the confluence of the two streams. But though the chief productive localities are situated there, Diamonds have also been found in the valley of the Orange river, at least 50 miles below its junction with the Vaal. In fact the area from which Diamonds have already been obtained is of vast extent. To the north, it certainly reaches as far as Blomhof, near Pretoria, the capital of the Transvaal ; and it is reported that Diamonds have been found at least a hundred miles nearer the sources of the Vaal. On the south side of the Orange river, they occur some miles to the north-west of Hope-town. Jagersfontein, 96 miles south of the Vaal, is a well-known locality ; and a stone of 70 carats has been found at Mamusa, 75 miles beyond Jagersfontein.

Until the discoveries of Diamonds directed attention to this district, scarcely anything was known of its geological characters. Even now it is far from easy to co-ordinate the scattered notices which have been published in various journals, and thus obtain a clear notion of the structure of the country. Stripped, however, of all superficial deposits, the solid framework of the country appears to consist of rocks belonging to that great geological series which, from its conspicuous occurrence in the "karoos," or vast plains in the interior, has received the name of the *karoo-formation*. This formation is developed to a vast extent in South Africa, occupying indeed by far the larger portion of the country, and covering at least 200,000 square miles, whilst its thickness approaches to something like 5,000 feet. For the most part it consists of shales and sandstones, which represent old deposits of mud and sand, now hardened and altered, but originally thrown down as sediments in a vast fresh-water lake. Africa is still famous for its large sheets of inland water; but the lakes in which the karoo beds were deposited are of great geological antiquity, probably corresponding roughly in time with the period at which the new red sandstone of this country was formed. Although for the most part destitute of fossils, the karoo strata are in places rich in organic remains, the most notable being the relics of extinct reptiles, which must have lived near the margin of the waters that deposited the ancient sediment. Some of these triassic reptiles were furnished in the upper jaw with a pair of tusks, not unlike those of the walrus, whence they were called by the late Mr. Bain, who discovered them, *Bidentals;* and by Professor Owen, who scientifically described them, *Dicynodons.* In addition to these remains of extinct animals, we find in many of the karoo-beds numerous vegetable relics, in some places in the form of fossil-wood, while elsewhere the wood has been converted into coal. The coal seams of the karoo series occur especially in the upper part of the formation, and notably at the Stormberg. By the action of heat, some of the Stormberg coal has been converted into Anthracite or steam-coal, a variety of fossil-fuel peculiarly rich in carbon; whilst the occurrence of graphite, or "black-lead," in some of these beds, has been regarded as the result of further alteration of the coal. As graphite is but an impure variety of carbon, whilst we know that the Diamond is simply a pure crystallized form of the same element, some geologists have been tempted to speculate as to the possible effects of further metamorphism upon the graphite, and have thus dimly seen in the vegetable fossils of the karoo formation the ultimate origin of the South-African Diamonds. If this metamorphic action has been found sufficiently potent to transmute vegetable matter into coal, then to convert this bituminous coal into anthracite, and possibly afterwards to transform the anthracite into graphite, why should its potency be arrested at this point? Let the same kind of action be continued, and we are brought to the logical conclusion that the ultimate term of the series will eventually be reached; and that ultimate term is assuredly represented by the Diamond. Fascinating as such speculation unquestionably is, it must be admitted that we are at present far too ignorant of the conditions under which Diamonds have been formed, to regard such speculation as anything but the vaguest hypothesis.

In some places the lacustrine shales and sandstones of the karoo formation are cut through by long dykes or veins of various eruptive rocks, known popularly as "trap;" whilst in other places similar igneous rocks are spread out in sheets which are intercalated between the sedimentary strata. It is in the neighbourhood of these old lava-like rocks that the coal is locally converted into anthracite. But the "traps" associated with the karoo beds have other points of interest in connexion with our present subject. Varying considerably in their characters in different localities, some of them exhibit a vesicular texture, and contain in their bubble-like cavities kernels of Chalcedony, Agate, Jasper, and other siliceous minerals. By the disintegration of such rocks, the hard Agates and kindred stones are set free, and carried down as pebbles by the rivers. Indeed the shingle of the Orange and Vaal Rivers has long been famous for the beauty of its Agates and other pebbles. In addition, however, to these attractive Chalcedonic pebbles, the shingle contains fragments of a great variety of other minerals and rocks, of which comprehensive lists have been published by Prof. Rupert Jones, F.R.S. But among these constituents of the alluvial gravels, there is one mineral of paramount interest: the Diamond itself. It is in the Agate-bearing gravels of the Vaal and Orange Rivers that the Diamond washer has successfully established his "river-diggings."

How the Diamonds got into the gravels is a moot point, which has puzzled many a geologist. The rounded character of the pebbles, and the frequent presence of fragments of fossil wood, much rolled and water-worn, seem to indicate that the materials of the gravels must have travelled from a great distance. Zones of similar fossil wood are known to occur in the karoo beds of the Stormberg and the Draakensberg ; and it has been suggested that the materials of the Vaal gravels have been brought down from the head waters of the river. From the appearance of many of the Diamonds, and from the large proportion of broken gems, it has been argued that they must have travelled from afar, and the eyes of some geologists have been turned towards the distant hills of the Draakensberg as the possible home of many of these gems. It seems equally probable, however, that the Diamonds may have been introduced into the gravels at some other part of the course of the river. In fact, Mr. Tobin, the pioneer of my Diamond Expedition Party, in 1870, has shewn that the source of the Vaal is in sandstone, and that the Agate pebbles are not to be found in the stream until after it has traversed a distance of several miles.

It should be remarked that it is not only in the present bed of the river that the Diamond-bearing gravels are found. Terraces of similar gravels run along the margins of the river, at a considerable elevation, and many of the larger Diamonds have been found in these old high-level gravels. Such gravels unquestionably owe their origin to the former action of the river, when it flowed at a much higher level. Running water in the form of rain and rivers has indeed effected a vast amount of denudation in the valleys of these South-African rivers: and in some places the karoo-beds have been completely worn away, and the underlying older rock laid bare.

In addition to the deposits along the margins of the river valleys, there are superficial accumulations of gravel, sand, and clay widely spread over a vast area of the country. Diamonds have been obtained from these deposits, at localities many miles distant from any river. It has been suggested by Mr. Stow that such deposits of "drift," or unstratified materials, owe their origin to the action of ice; and in support of such an explanation, he points to the fact that the drift contains irregular accumulations of boulders, many of which are smoothed and polished, while a few are even scored and scratched, just as we know to be the case with fragments of rock which have been subjected to the grinding action of a glacier. Mr. Stow's opinion as to the glacial origin of this drift has been endorsed by several other geological observers. It, therefore, seems not unlikely that a large proportion of the South-African Diamonds, whatever their ultimate origin may have been, have at some period of their history been subjected to glacial conditions, and possibly brought into their present position by the agency of moving ice. This conclusion, however, in no way affects our former statement that the river-gravels—deposits distinct from those to which we are now referring—were formed by the action of running water.

The wide-spread accumulations of drift conceal the surface of the country over which they are spread, rising up the sides and covering the summits of the little hills which form so marked a feature in the scenery of the Diamond districts. These hillocks, which in some cases attain to a height of upwards of 100 feet, are known locally as *kopjes*, and many of them have become famous for their yield of Diamonds. Such, for example, is the Colesberg Kopje, now called the Kimberley Mine, on the north side of the Vaal, where "dry diggings" have been prosecuted with remarkable energy and success. But the most celebrated group of dry diggings is that around Du Toit's Pan, De Beer's, and Bultfontein, situated about twenty miles south-east of the missionary station of Pniel.

A photograph on the opposite page shows the workings at the Colesberg Kopje. No. 1, taken in 1872, gives a view of the roads running through the "claims." The mounds in the background are the remains of the earth carted away by the diggers for sorting. No. 2 represents the Colesberg Kopje as seen in 1876. The photograph is an illustration of the various "claims" in which the owners are seeking for Diamonds. Each claim is in connexion, by means of wires, with a portion of the wooden staging seen at the top of the picture. Up these wires buckets are drawn, filled with the earth dug out from below.

The origin of these diggings is curious. A Dutch boer, named Tan Wyk, who occupied a farmhouse in this locality, was surprised to find Diamonds actually embedded in the walls of his house, which had been built of mud from a neighbouring pond. This led to examination of the surrounding soil, which was soon found to contain Diamonds. On continuing to dig lower and lower, Diamonds were still brought to light; nor did they cease when the bed-rock was at length reached. Such was the origin of the now famous Du Toit's Pan. The "Pans" are local depressions in the flats—basin-like hollows, frequently of large size, reaching in some cases to a length of two or three miles. They receive the drainage of the surrounding district, but

No. 1.

No. 2.

having no outlet, the water as it evaporates acquires a brackish taste, and in dry seasons the pans exhibit a whitish saline incrustation—"natron."

All the dry diggings appear to possess certain common features. Each site is a more or less circular area, generally surrounded by horizontal shales, the edges of which are slightly turned upwards round the margin of the circle. This evidently suggests that the shales, which were originally horizontal, have been pushed aside by the intrusion of matter forced from below. Indeed, many geologists whose opinions are entitled to much weight, maintain that the Diamond-bearing rock is of eruptive origin, and has been brought up in the form of columnar pipes thrust through the surrounding shales. Thus, Mr. Dunn regards the pipes as "merely the channels that connected ancient volcanic craters with deep-seated reservoirs of molten rock." On the other hand, there have not been wanting observers who take an entirely opposite view of the origin of the deep deposits in the dry diggings.

The upper portion of a pipe generally consists of a reddish, sandy soil, accumulated no doubt by the action of wind. Below this comes a layer of calcareous tufa, or a light deposit of carbonate of lime; and it is by no means uncommon to find Diamonds adherent to this tufaceous rock. At a still lower depth, we reach the main contents of the pipe. This consists of a strangely modified rock; in places much broken up, and passing into a breccia. Its exact nature has puzzled petrologists; but the rock has been most carefully examined by Prof. Maskelyne, F.R.S., and the component minerals analyzed by Dr. Flight. The base of the rock is a soft mineral, soapy to the touch, and of green or bluish color: it contains angular fragments of shale, more or less altered, associated with various distinct minerals; including crystals of a bright-green bronzite; of a hornblendic mineral resembling smaragdite; of a new species of vermiculite, called *vaalite;* with Garnet, Ilmenite, &c. Veins of calcite, and nodules of iron-pyrites, are occasionally present. But the only minerals that attract the miner's attention are the Diamonds. These are sprinkled pretty freely through the "stuff;" sometimes as beautifully formed crystals, but frequently as mere fragments and splinters. They are said to be most abundant in the neighbourhood of dioritic dykes, but their distribution is very irregular; in one claim they may be richly disseminated, whilst in a neighbouring claim they are but sparsely scattered through the rock. The Diamond-bearing stuff has been worked in some cases to depths exceeding 200 feet. Each pipe is said to yield Diamonds easily distinguished from those of other pipes, so that buyers on the fields can generally tell on looking at a stone from which locality it has been obtained. These local peculiarities suggest that the stones have been formed in, or near the centres where they are now found. Indeed, it has been maintained that the rock, now filling the pipes, was, in its unaltered state, the original home of the Diamond—that the gems are in fact in their proper matrix. In support of this view, it should be mentioned that most of the crystals are sharp at the edges, and exhibit no signs of abrasion, such as we might expect to find had they been transported far from their original site. On the other hand, a large proportion of the crystals have evidently been shattered, and exist now as mere fragments, shewing that the rock has suffered great disturbance, though it may only have been during its projection to the surface from some deep-seated source. It is a curiously significant fact, well worth noticing, that many of the crystals of Diamond in these pipes exhibit, on their octahedral faces, regular triangular depressions, strongly suggestive of the triangular striations which the late Gustav Rose produced on Diamonds, by heating them in a muffle, so as to undergo incipient combustion.

According to the views just explained, the South-African Diamonds were originally developed in an igneous matrix, belonging, probably, to that large series of eruptive rocks which have burst forth through the Karoo strata at so many points in South-Africa. In the dry diggings these Diamonds are probably not far removed from their original position; but by denudation of the diamantiferous rocks, the gems have been carried far and wide over the country. In the river diggings they have been transported to their present position by the action of running water, whilst in some of the superficial deposits elsewhere they may have been distributed by means of moving ice. Such, at least, are the several hypothesis which have been advanced to explain the origin and present distribution of the Diamonds. Our aim has been to explain all these hypothesis fairly, without committing ourselves to any, and without preferring one to another.

Dismissing so vexed a question as that of the genesis of the Diamond, we tread upon firmer ground when we pass to a description of the gems which have been discovered in the South-African fields. Scarcely a decade has passed since these fields were first known, and during that brief space of years a large number of stones of unusual size have been brought to light. The high proportion of large-sized Diamonds is indeed a notable feature in the South-African discoveries. The "Star of South-Africa" weighed in the rough, 83½ carats; and, after cutting, 46½ carats. A Diamond of pale yellow tint, weighing 112 carats, was brought to Prof. Tennant by an old student, and yielded a brilliant of 66 carats. Again, a stone of 124 carats was found at Du Toit's Pan, by Messrs. Stevens and Raath, on July 21, 1871. But the largest South - African Diamond yet discovered is the famous " Stewart," which was consigned to Messrs. Pittar, Leverson & Co. (See Sketch opposite.) It weighed in its rough state 288⅜ carats (nearly two ounces troy), was by far the largest ever found in South-Africa, and according to the best authorities, was only exceeded in size by three others in the world. It is of a light yellow color, beautifully crystallised.

The following history and particulars of its discovery are extracted from the *Port Elizabeth Telegraph*, of the 22nd of November, 1872. " The claim from which this gem was taken was originally owned by a Mr. F. Pepper, by him sold to a Mr. Spalding for £30, and handed over by the latter to one Antonie, to work on shares. The claim was quite an outside one, and not thought much of by the owner, but as others were finding near him, he thought it was just possible he might find something. He persevered until, first, the so-called 'Fly Diamond' (also in Messrs. Pittar, Leverson & Co's. possession for sale), and, a few days after, this gem rewarded his labour. Antonie's feelings when he first obtained a glimpse of the treasure may be better imagined than described. He says that he was working in the claim, when he told his boy to leave off picking in the centre and commence at the side. Not being understood, he took a pick and began himself, when he was suddenly spell-bound with the sight of a large stone, looking like a Diamond. For some minutes he could not speak or move for fear of dispelling the apparent illusion, but, collecting his energies, he made a dart forward and clutched the prize. Even then, however, he did not feel quite safe, and it required a grand effort to reach Mr. Spalding, a cart having to be called

The "DUDLEY" Diamond

The "TWIN" Diamond

into requisition. For two days afterwards he was unable to eat anything, so excited were his feelings."

The "Dudley" Diamond is another important Cape stone, weighing about forty-six carats; triangular in shape, of great brilliancy, perfectly colorless, and cannot be distinguished from an old Indian stone. It was sold by Messrs Hunt & Roskell, to the present Earl of Dudley, and was mounted by them, with other Diamonds, as a "head ornament." (See Plate opposite.)

While South-Africa has thus been remarkable for yielding stones of large size, it should also be borne in mind that the new supplies are equally satisfactory as to quality. True, a large number of the Diamonds are "off-colored" stones, generally exhibiting a delicate straw-tint, but nevertheless extremely beautiful when properly cut. At the same time, a very fair proportion of the South-African Stones are Diamonds of the first-water, rivalling in beauty and purity the finest Brazilian and Indian stones. It has been estimated that about 20 per cent. of the Cape Diamonds are of the first quality; 15 per cent. of the second; and 20 per cent. of the third quality, whilst the remainder is "bort." All Diamonds which are too impure for cutting are now known under the general name of *bort;* and these possess a certain market value, as they may be turned into Rose-Diamonds, and the powder which they yield, when crushed, is used for cutting Diamonds, and for engraving hard gems.

An interesting specimen in my possession exhibits several octahedral crystals of Diamond grouped around a central nucleus of dark-colored bort. This specimen weighs 19 carats, and was obtained from the Diamond-fields by my own explorers.

During the time the expedition was working at the Cape, I was so convinced of the superiority of the river stones over those from the dry diggings, that I contemplated giving orders for machinery to be made with the object of turning the course of the Vaal River. Thus I hoped for some months my Diamond Party might have worked in the river-bed. This project was abandoned in consequence of the ill-health of the leader of the expedition. I was none the less convinced from my knowledge of Indian Diamonds, that the finest stones were to be found in the river-bed. Time has proved the correctness of my anticipations; for Diamonds rivalling Indian stones have been found in the river-bed of the Vaal. A "drop," mounted by me (see preceding Plate), with a twin of clear cinnamon color (also from the Cape), was declared by several Diamond merchants, of the greatest experience, to be an Indian, and not a Cape stone!

Although immense numbers of Diamonds have been brought to light during the recent workings in South-Africa, it is notable that not a single piece of *Carbonado*, now known only as carbon—the black, impure variety of Diamond common in Brazil—has yet been discovered. In fact, while certain points of resemblance have been traced between the occurrence of Diamonds in Africa and that in Brazil, there are other points in which such a comparison entirely breaks down. It may be said, indeed, that in many respects the Diamond-fields of South-Africa are unique.

CHAPTER III.

AUSTRALIAN DIAMONDS.

ALTHOUGH three, at least, of our Australian Colonies have yielded Diamonds, it is only in New South Wales that they have been found in sufficient quantity to invite systematic exploration. As far back as the year 1851, Mr. E. H. Hargraves and the Rev. W. B. Clarke, in a report dated from Guyong, referred to some specimens of gold, and to a number of gems, including what they call, rather vaguely, "a small one of the Diamond kind," found in Reedy Creek, near Bathurst. But it was especially the Rev. W. B. Clarke, a gentleman well-known for his researches in Australian geology, who first attracted public attention to the Diamonds of New South Wales. Four specimens had been brought to him from the Macquarie river, near Sutton's Bar, in September, 1859, and a fifth, the following month, from Burrendong. In the meantime, he had received Diamonds from Pyramul and Calabash Creeks. These discoveries were considered by Mr. Clark so significant, that he wrote a description of the occurrence, boldly heading it with the startling title, "New South Wales, a Diamond Country." This announcement was not commercially justified till seven or eight years later, when occurred the gold-rush at the Two-mile Flat, on the Cudgegong River, about nineteen miles north-west of Mudgee. As soon as the gold-diggers had set to work they detected Diamonds; and in July, 1869, operations were conducted by the Australian Diamond Mines' Company of Melbourne. The Cudgegong empties itself into the Macquarie, which is an affluent of the Darling.

At the Mudgee workings, gems were found in an old river-drift, distributed in local patches, which appear to be remnants of deposits once widely-spread over the district, but now partially removed by denudation. These ancient river-gravels occur at various distances from the actual channel, and at elevations of forty feet or more above the level of the river. They are generally covered by a protective layer of basalt, sometimes columnar; and shafts have been sunk through this basaltic cap, so as to reach the under-lying Diamond-drift, which rests either on vertical strata or on massive greenstone. The gravels contain pebbles and boulders of Quartz, Tin, Crystals, Jasper, Agate, and other siliceous minerals, mixed with coarse sand and clay. Many of the boulders are remarkable for their peculiar polish. In some places the materials of the drift are united by a siliceous cement, into a compact mass, colored pale-green by silicate of iron. Among the pebbles of the gravel, the diligent seeker may find many of the rarer minerals, including crystals of Topaz, Sapphire, Ruby, Zircon, Spinel, Garnet, a peculiar vesicular variety of Pleonaste, &c.; and even this catalogue might be extended to include all the varieties of minerals already discovered, but for my present purpose I need only add that it includes two of the most prized substances in nature—gold and the Diamond. The Diamonds are sparsely and irregularly distributed through the gravels;

but, nevertheless, when large quantities of the drift are sifted and washed, the gems are brought to light, but hardly in sufficient numbers to pay for working : for example, during the first five months' washings no fewer than 2,500 Diamonds were picked out; but unfortunately most of the stones were extremely small, the largest of the Mudgee Diamonds being a colorless octahedron weighing 5⅝ carats.

We find them in a deposit of gravel, but they have probably been washed out of the older drift. Occasionally, too, they have been found in "water-holes" in the present river-bed ; but their origin may then generally be traced to the "tailings" washed into the river at such points from the gold diggings, and therefore we expect to track the Diamonds back to the old drift. When found in the river-bed, the stones are frequently scratched and fractured.

Within the last two or three years, a Diamond-field has been opened up near Bingera, in New South Wales. This town is about 400 miles north of Sydney, on the River Horton, popularly known as the Big River. How the Diamonds occur at this locality, has been well described by Professor Liversidge, of Sydney. The Diamond-bearing deposits are situated in a kind of basin, about four miles long and three miles wide, hemmed in by hills on all sides save on the north. An old river-drift, probably an ancient bed of the Horton, rests upon rocks of Devonian or of the Carboniferous age, and is associated with basalt, by which it appears, indeed, to be overlain. On some places the materials of the drift are compacted together into a conglomerate; so that the mode of occurrence of the Diamond at Bingera, strikingly resembles that at Mudgee. The minerals composing the gravels are also generally similar in the two cases, though points of difference are not wanting. One of the best indications of the presence of the Diamond, according to the Bingera miners, is a black Tourmaline, known locally as "Jet-stone." Some of the Diamonds are clear and colorless, others have a pale straw-tint, and all are of small size, the largest weighing only eight grains. According to an examination of some of the Bingera drift, by the Gwydir Diamond-mining Company, a ton of "stuff" yields on an average twenty Diamonds. Up to August 26th, 1873, the Eaglehawk claim had produced 1,680 Diamonds; but as the aggregate weighed only 803 grains troy, the very small size of the average stones is sufficiently apparent. It has been roughly estimated that at least 10,000 Diamonds have hitherto been found in New South Wales; although it must be remembered that the workings have not been vigorously prosecuted.

In addition to the prominent Diamond-bearing localities described above, we might readily point to several other spots in the Colony where the gem has occasionally been found. Thus the Borah Tin and Diamond Mining Company obtained upwards of 200 Diamonds in the course of a few months, from their Mine near the junction of Cope's Creek with the Gwydir. Most of the stones were either of light straw colour or of very pale green tint. The largest weighed 5 grains. The Bengover Tin Mine, about two miles below the Borah workings, has yielded several Diamonds, including one of $7\frac{1}{2}$ grains. A stone of 9 grains has been found at Bald Hill, Tambaroora, Hill End; and it would be easy, were it necessary, to multiply our notices of the Diamond-yielding localities of New South Wales.

Compared with the Diamond discoveries of this Colony, those of other parts of Australia sink into insignificance. South Australia is rich in mineral treasure; but this treasure mostly takes the form of ores of copper and iron.

Yet the Colony is not without its gold fields, and with the gold a few Diamonds have been found. In the year 1852 Diamonds were discovered in alluvial gold washings in the hills, near Echuca, about twenty miles south-east of Adelaide. It is said that more than a hundred Diamonds have at different times been found in this neighbourhood.

Whilst Victoria is pre-eminently the "Golden Colony," and its gold-fields have for many years been actively explored, it is only now and then that a solitary Diamond has been discovered. In 1862 the discovery of a Diamond in the Ovens district was announced by Mr. George Foord. It was a transparent yellow crystal, with perfect edges, weighing about 2 grains. The Rev. J. J. Bleasdale, who has paid great attention to the study of Australian gems, described three Victorian Diamonds—two from Beechworth, and the third from Collingwood Flat. There appears, however, to have been for several years, some little doubt hanging over the reputed discoveries of Diamonds in Victoria; but in 1865 an Exhibition of Gems was held in the Hall of the Royal Society of Victoria, and, from the specimens then exhibited, and the information accompanying them, the matter was set at rest. "The results of this exhibition," said Dr. Bleasdale, "have now placed this important truth beyond impeachment." Altogether about sixty Diamonds have been found in the Beechworth district, but they have not been of good color, nor of large size, most of them weighing less than a carat each.

The first Australian Diamond ever brought to this country was presented by Sir Thomas Mitchell to the Museum of Practical Geology, in Jermyn Street, where it may now be seen. This small crystal weighs ¾ of a carat, and was found near Ophir, west of Bathurst, New South Wales.

To sum up our knowledge of Australian Diamonds,

New South Wales, which is rich in coal, in oil shales, and in various carbonaceous products, is by no means poor in Diamonds, although those already discovered are, for the most part, extremely small; South Australia, with its vast wealth in copper and iron, possesses a limited Diamond-producing area; Victoria, the great centre of the gold fields, has furnished only an occasional Diamond as a mineralogical rarity; and the other Australian colonies, so far as we know, have not hitherto yielded a single Diamond. But I dare to prophecy, and that I may prophecy, I will begin by regretting, that if, instead of searching for Diamonds in the gravel drifts and old river beds, geological researches had been instituted in the gorges of the Australian Alps, in those of the rocky rivers and snowy mountains, it is very likely the matrix would have been discovered, whence the Diamonds already found have been washed. The geological formation of the whole of the New England district in New South Wales resembles closely that of the district of the Baggage Mines in Brazil, and sooner or later will be found to yield Diamonds in paying quantities. Another Diamond field will be found ere long in Queensland, either on the Palmer River or its affluents,—where very remarkable and rich gold mines have lately been discovered,—or, on the Gilbert River and its affluents, and in the country extending from the Gilbert to the Gulf of Carpentaria.

CHAPTER IV.

BRAZILIAN DIAMONDS.

a.—PRIMARY, OR ORIGINAL DEPOSITS OF THE DIAMOND.

IN Brazil it was first discovered that Itacolumite was the matrix of the Diamond. This was suspected by Dr. Gardner, who observed that the matrix of the stone is not the diluvial, gravelly soil, but the metamorphic quartzo-schist rock.

The Grammagoa mountain, on the left bank of the Corrego dos Rois (43 miles north of Diamantina), consists of thick and slightly inclined arenaceous schists, passing at times into Itacolumite. To this mountain above 2,000 people flocked in the beginning of the year 1839 to search for Diamonds. For many years the result was successful, but only with much labor. The matrix or mother-stone had to be blasted, and the fragments broken by the hammer, and washed in the Batea. This method, however, had to be abandoned, as the deeper they went, the harder the stone; and the extraction of the Diamond out of deep strata, at so much labor, was not so profitable as washing the gravel-beds for them.

In the museum at Rio de Janeiro is a large rounded Diamond which retains the impressions of sand-grains.

It is said that the Diamonds obtained from the

Itacolumite sandstone have rounded angles and corners, whilst those from the sandy schist are perfect crystals. If this be a fact, we must believe that the agency which changed the sandstone into Itacolumite acted also on the Diamond.

b.—SECONDARY DEPOSITS.

These Diamonds occur not only embedded in the primary strata (living rock) but are also found in the gravels composed of the débris of the decomposing rock. The most important district of these secondary deposits lies between 16° and 26° south latitude, including the Provinces of Minas and St. Paulo, the conditions of which are almost identical with the gold bearing alluvium of Borneo and the Urals.

In the north of Minas is diamantiferous sandstone, covered with a limestone, which again is overlain by a gypsum formation. No sooner are the valleys cut deep enough to expose the sandstone, than everywhere Diamonds are found in the river beds of this region, as on the Rio Acary, and at other places.

From the defiles of Itambé, the loftiest mountain of this district, the Copivary and Jequitinhonha, rich in Diamonds, take their rise. In the first of these, a Diamond was found a few years ago of about 9 carats weight. There occur in this district, in constant companionship with the Diamond, rounded fragments of clear transparent quartz, also fragments of a very hard, thick, red ironstone, or of black Lydian stone, from the size of a hazel nut to that of a pigeon's egg. The natives give to this last the name of " Feijão," from its likeness to the common black bean, and always hail its presence in the gravel with pleasure, as with it are found other precious stones than the Diamond, such as White and Blue Topaz, Spinel,

Garnet, and Lazulite. Some wonderfully beautiful specimens of Chrysoberyl are also found in the Diamond-sands of Brazil, of yellow, parsley-green, and sky-blue colors, together with beautiful specimens of rose-colored and sea-green quartz. In the Diamond-sand of Bahia is found impure, black, grey, or brown, crystallized carbon, known in commerce as *Carbonado* or *Carbon*.

c.—PRODUCE OF DIAMONDS IN BRAZIL.

The sparkling stones found in washing gold were thrown away, or used as card-markers in early times. It was not until 1727 that Bernardino Fonseca Lobo, an inhabitant of Serra do Frio, in the gold district of Minas Geräes, accidentally discovered the true nature of these stones. He had seen rough diamonds in India ; and the likeness to these was so striking, that he took a number to Portugal for sale, and thus drew general observation towards the new Diamond mines.

The European merchants, who up to this time had obtained their Diamonds from India, were frightened lest this discovery should cause a fall in the price of the gems in their possession. They spread the report that the Brazilian Diamonds were only the refuse of the Indian stones, forwarded to Goa, and thence to Brazil.

The Portuguese however, turned the tables, and sent the Brazilian Diamonds to Goa and thence to Bengal, where they were offered for sale as Indian stones, and obtained Indian prices. The supply was greatly increased in the early part of this century, by the discovery of new and richer mines in the province of Bahia, the stones of which are called in commerce *Bahias*. They rival in beauty the Indian stones ; are roundish, of medium or small size, of a brilliancy and fire not surpassed by those of any other rough Diamonds in the world.

The profit made in Minas-Geräes was very considerable. In the first twenty years, 144,000 carats were found annually.

In 1772 the Government first worked the mines on its own account. Rich as the find was, the cost was enormous, for every carat cost the Government from fifteen to eighteen shillings.

Up to 1850 the Province of Minas-Geräes had yielded about 5,844,000 carats of Diamonds, value about £9,000,000.

If in addition to this, we consider the contraband trade at the beginning of this century, valued at £2,000,000, the worth of the Diamonds found in Minas-Geräes would be about £11,000,000. The yield of these mines differs from that of the Bahia mines in shape and color. The form of the stones is more regular, many having the filed crystallization which is noticeable in Cape stones, while their color is more uniform in its greenish tints without any yellow reflection.

Diamonds were found also in other parts of Brazil, especially in the inland provinces. It was soon easy to recognize the sand containing the Diamond, by the presence of certain stones called by the natives "Cativos." These are Agates, Tourmalines, and Sandstones.

In the dry season of the year, the sand is washed in large basins under water, until the practised eye discovers the Diamonds. Formerly, as many as fourteen or fifteen Diamonds were often found in a single basin.

The Paraquay and its many tributaries carry down gold and Diamonds. During the dry season, from April to the middle of October, when the depth of the river is much dimished, the water is drawn off into a canal, and the mud of the river bed is dug out from six to ten feet, and carried to a place, where it can be washed by the negroes during the wet season. In digging out the mud, large holes are often found containing many Diamonds and much gold. When the wet season stops the digging of the "Cascalho," the scene of action is the "washing huts."

Washing troughs (canoes), are placed side by side, and the overseer has a raised seat, so as to be able to observe all the negroes at work.

Every trough has its little stream of water, and a negro keeps the contents in constant motion, until the mud has been washed away, and the water is quite clear.

Then the sand and fine gravel are taken in the hand and searched for Diamonds. If one is found, the negro stands upright and knocks, as a signal for the overseer, who takes the Diamond from him, and lays it in a vessel filled with water, which hangs in the middle of the shed. When the day's work is over the contents of this vessel are taken by the overseer, and their weight entered in a book.

Large Diamonds are very rarely found. It has been estimated that in *ten thousand* specimens, rarely more than *one* weighing *twenty* carats is met with, while possibly eight thousand of one carat, or less may be encountered. At the works of the Jequitinhonha River during a year's labor, only two or three stones are found of from seventeen to twenty carats, and in the whole of the works in Brazil, for the space of two years, not more than one of thirty carats was found. In 1851 a Diamond weighing 120¾ carats was discovered at the source of the Patrocinho River in the province of Minas-Geräes.

Somewhat later, on the Rio-das-Belhas, the laborers came upon a stone of 107 carats weight, and in Chapada upon one of 87½ carats.

The largest, however, which has been discovered of late years is that called the "Star of the South," which weighed 254 carats before it was cut. There are many laws and regulations to prevent the negroes concealing and smuggling Diamonds. As a means of encouraging honesty, if a negro finds a stone of 17½ carats, he is crowned with a wreath of flowers and led in procession to the manager. Then his freedom is bestowed upon him, plus a suit of clothes and permission to work for wages.

If a negro finds one from eight to ten carats weight, he receives two new shirts, a suit of clothes, hat, and a handsome knife. For smaller, but valuable stones, other rewards are given.

For unfaithfulness, the negroes are beaten with sticks, or have iron bands fastened round their throats; and for repetition of the fault, they are not admitted to the works again. Notwithstanding all these rewards and punishments, one-third of the produce is supposed to be surreptitiously got rid of by the laborers.

Manifold are the tricks used by the negroes to appropriate and dispose of the stones. In the very presence of the overseers they manage to conceal them in their hair, their mouths, their ears, or between their fingers; they will throw them away, and come to seek them in the dead of night.

The discovery of these Precious Stones proved in 1746 a great curse to the poor inhabitants of the banks of the Diamond rivers. Scarcely had the news of the discovery reached the Government, ere they tried to secure the riches of these rivers for the Crown. To effect this, the inhabitants were driven away from their homes to wild, far away places, and deprived of their little possessions; nature herself seemed to take part against them: a dreadful drought, succeeded by a violent earthquake, increased their distress. Many of them perished, but those who lived to return on the 18th May, 1805, were benevolently reinstated in their rightful possessions. Strange to say, on their return, the earth seemed strewn with Diamonds. After a shower the children used to find gold in the streets, and in the brooks which traversed them. Often the little ones would bring in three or four carats of Diamonds. A negro found a Diamond at the root of a vegetable in his garden.

Poultry in picking up their food took up Diamonds constantly, and their refuse was never thrown away save after careful examination.

The profit of the Diamond seeker is a very uncertain quantity. While *one* person may find at one spot in a river 1440 carats, another, like the Spaniard Simon, may seek for four years with the help of 200 slaves and obtain only 7000 carats. In consequence of the large wages demanded by laborers, the number employed has greatly diminished.

When Diamonds were first discovered in Bahia, the old capital of Brazil, a densely populated and fruitful province, the observant and intelligent Portuguese minister, Marquis de Pombal, forbade further search, as he feared agriculture, which he justly regarded as the blessing and health of the land, would suffer.

A very strange history is connected with the discovery of Diamonds in Bahia. A cunning slave from Minas-Geräes, keeping his master's flocks in Bahia, thought he observed a similarity between the soil of his native place and that of Bahia. He sought therefore in the sand, and soon found 700 carats of Diamonds. Fleeing from his master, he carried these with him, and offered them for sale in a distant city. Such wealth in the hands of a slave caused him to be arrested, but he would not betray himself. The master to whom he was given up tried to get at his secret by cunning, but without avail, until he thought of restoring to him his former occupation in Bahia, and watching him. As soon as the secret was known, numbers flocked from Minas-Geräes and other parts of Brazil to Bahia, so that the following year as many as 25,000 people were occupied in seeking Diamonds there, and the amount daily obtained for some time rose to 1,450 carats.

The number of Diamond seekers gradually diminished to between five and six thousand; but up to the end of the year 1849 there were as many as 932,400 carats of Diamonds obtained from the Chapada of Bahia. This rich field is about eighty miles long and forty miles broad. The total produce from the entire Brazil Diamond district was, up to the year 1850, over 10,000,000 carats. In the year 1851, the produce increased; but in 1852 it diminished very seriously.

The total value of Brazilian Diamond produce from 1861 to 1867 was about £1,888,000. Some very interesting information has been afforded us by Herr von Tschude concerning the produce of the Brazilian Diamonds; and we may consider it as authentic, as he himself visited the Diamantina, in the province of Minas-Geräes, in February, 1858. He observes, "The pivot on which Diamantina turns is Diamonds. I was present during the unexampled commercial crisis which extended from town to town, and country to country, with such disastrous consequences and which fell with the weight of an avalanche on the inhabitants of Diamantina. All business was stopped, and Diamonds fell to one-half the price they reached only the year before. I have taken much trouble to obtain an accurate statement of the present position (1859) of the Diamond trade in Brazil, and for that purpose have consulted the best authorities. The Diamonds of Brazil are known in commerce as (1) Diamantina Diamonds, and

(2) Cincora Diamonds. The latter are of less value than the former, because they are not of such pure water, nor of so good a shape. In Matto-Grosso, the Diamonds are small, but of the purest water, and in their rough state have a peculiar lustre, which is seen in none other of the Brazilian Diamonds."

The panic alluded to by Herr von Tschudi was severe, but it is very doubtful whether in those remote times any panic was ever equal in extent and importance to that caused by the discovery of the riches in the Transvaal, Africa, which occurred in the year 1868, and which in 1870 caused the great revolution in the Diamond market. For some time after the discovery of the South-African riches, the Brazilian Diamonds held their ground well in the market; but the great gains that accompanied the introduction of the Cape stones soon diverted the attention of the trade to the latter, and traders and speculators were completely fascinated by the Cape stones. The lapidaries of Amsterdam for a long time would cut none other.

No country was more incredulous about the prodigious yield of the Transvaal mines than Brazil, and thus it was that the loss became disastrous to the Brazilian merchants, who refused to receive the warnings sent in perfect good faith. The favoritism bestowed on the Cape Diamonds, the great margin of profit which they yielded through being brought to market by all kinds of holders, ignorant of the ways of the Diamond trade, and of the value of the stones, could not fail to cause the Brazilian Diamonds to be more and more neglected; and as the difficulties created by the Amsterdam lapidaries increased, so the neglect was heightened, causing a greater depreciation than the prices demanded for the Cape stones really justified.

There were speculators who had been hoarding up Brazilian Diamonds, so that when the supply from the

Cape rose above the market value, these hoards were resorted to for easing the market, and bringing back prices to a more uniform scale. This manœuvre finally proved successful.

The Cape yield of large stones enhanced the difficulties of influencing the Amsterdam lapidaries. They, finding a superabundance, refused to cut small ones, and these Brazil furnished in every parcel with which the merchants supplied the market. The merchants of Brazil had, therefore, to exclude all small stones, and contrive to compose their parcels so as to enter into competition with Cape gems. They have not succeeded yet, not because in beauty and quality the Brazilian Diamonds had deteriorated, but because of the exorbitant price at which they have been offered for sale. These high prices are mainly owing to the increasing scarcity of stones, as the working of the mines has become less remunerative.

The future appears to be decidedly unpropitious for the importation of Brazilian Diamonds, so long as the prices of Diamonds generally remain at their present level. A very considerable rise would alone induce a resumption of the working of the mines in the Diamond districts of Brazil, where none the less untold treasures are still hidden.

CHAPTER V.

INDIAN DIAMONDS.

HE Diamond fields of India have been celebrated from remote antiquity. The extent of the Diamond-alluvial formations has suggested to Karl Ritter to divide the formation into five groups. He explains not only the topography of the several districts, giving a history of the Diamond-mining as far as he could from careful study of ancient and modern literature, but he has also collated the opinions entertained upon the origin of the Diamond, and notices its geological condition.

From his writings we select some passages. Thus, referring to Heyne and Voysey, Franklin and Adams, he says, "They are agreed that there is everywhere only a superficial layer of alluvial soil, a conglomerate of rounded pebbles, a sandstone-breccia, which contains the Diamonds. Further, that the Diamonds are by no means scattered throughout this conglomerate (breccia), but occur only in one particular stratum, harder than the rest, and, at most, only one foot thick, and this is so throughout the whole of India, wherever the Diamond is found. Voysey, who calls this rock a sandstone-breccia, says it lies under a firm sandstone bed, and consists of a fine mass of fragments of Red and Yellow Jaspers, Quartz, Chalcedony, and

Hornblende of different colors, bound together by a silicious cement. This passes into a looser pudding-stone, with pebbles cemented with clay or marl, and this is characteristic of the Diamond bed."

This rock has been erroneously called Amygdaloid or Wacke, whereof certain conical hills of the plateau are formed, but never the flat-topped and gravelly hills, in which Diamonds are seen.

The same kind of formation of conglomerate spreads southwards from the Pennar, on the east side of the tableland, through Mysore, from Arkote westwards to Chittledrug and Flurrihur, but this track contains no Diamonds.

In the time of Mohammed Ghori, who in 1186 was the real founder of the Mohammedan dominion in India, the quantity of Diamonds in that continent was so great, that he left in his treasury at his death Precious Stones to the weight of 400 lbs. These, it is reported, he obtained exclusively by plunder. Since the beginning of the thirteenth century these have been scattered ; and at the finding of the celebrated stone called " The Great Mogul," Diamonds began to fetch a high price.

The discovery of the Diamond regions in America had little influence in depreciating the gems of the Old World ; but the discovery of the rich Brazilian Diamond deposits could not be ignored.

GROUPS.

1.—*The Cuddapah Group Diamond Beds on the Pennar River.*

The most southern group of the Diamond strata begins at the environs of Cuddapah, on the Pennar. Here for many hundred years Diamonds have been met with in greater or less abundance. They are found in many places near to each other: at Cuddapah, on the Pennar, and at Condapetta and Ovalumpally; also, at Landur and Pinchetgapadu; and still further beyond the Pennar Valley as far as Gandicotta, and according to Rennell, even to Gutidrug.

Near Cuddapah (475 feet above the sea), the conglomerate is superficial, and from ten to twenty feet thick. The mountain rises 1,000 feet higher than this stratum, and its foot is everywhere covered with loose pebbles. The beds follow each other in the following order: uppermost a foot-and-a-half of sand, grit, and loam; then a tough blue or black muddy earth, without any stones, four feet thick; under this comes the Diamond bed, characterized by the numerous large round stones embedded in it. It is from two to two-and-a-half feet thick, and consists of pebbles and grit bound together by loam.

In the neighbourhood of Ellore, this layer is covered with a thick calcareous tufa. The stones are of various kinds, and the Diamond seekers give them special names: 1st, "Tellœ Bendu," white, earthy, subangular; 2nd, Transparent quartz, yellowish; 3rd, Pistazite; 4th, "Gajja Bendu," red, blue and brown Jasper pebbles; 5th, " Karla," basaltic pebbles; 6th, Sandstone, with ochreous crust; 7th, "Kanna," rounded ironstone, about the size of a hazel nut, which constitute the most important pebbles in the Ovalumpally Mines; 8th, Corundum. In the more northern Diamond pits, at Pastal, near Ellore, on the Lower Kistna, pebbles of Chalcedony and Carnelian also occur.

At Cuddapah, blocks of Hornblende as big as one's head, and mostly derived from the neighbouring mountain chain, constitute the chief mass of the Diamond bed.

The Ovalumpally mines, also on the right bank of the

Pennar, are a few hours' journey only west of Cuddapah. The Diamond bed here seems to follow the course of the river, and is of varying width. Here the Diamonds always occur rounded. Those found still further west are the best.

The Hindoos divide Diamonds into four classes, according to their castes. 1st, *Brahma*, of clear and "pure water." 2nd, *Chedra*, clear and of the color of honey. 3rd, *Vysea*, cream-colored. 4th, *Sudra*, a greyish-white. The Sudras are the Diamond-seekers who carry on their work without inspection, and pride themselves on their honesty. The pits which they dig are square holes, not more than sixteen feet deep.

2.—*The Randial Group between the Pennar and the Kistna, near Banganpally.*

Only fifteen miles north of the foregoing, at the north end of the same table-land, extending on the west side of the Nalla-Nalla hills, as far as the town of Randial, (672 feet above the level of the sea), lies the second group, under similar climate and condition to those of the former. The Diamond beds here are only about a foot thick, and both the over and underlying beds are more pebbly than in the first group.

Most of the Diamonds of this district lie loose, and have the crystallized forms of the double pyramid and of the dodecahedra. In the rainy season the miners work in the Diamond pits on the heights, and when the floods are over, on the low-lying mines by the Kistna.

3.—*The Ellore Group on the Lower Kistna, or the Golconda Group.*

To this group belong the celebrated Diamond mines

of "Golconda," famous for their antiquity, no less than their valuable yield. The name "Golconda" is scarcely correct, as the locality is at a considerable distance from the hill-fort of Golconda.

Formerly there were many mines here. There were, when Tavernier visited the spot in 1669, as many as twenty; but now all except two or three have been forsaken, and the names Tavernier gave them so obsolete that it is with great difficulty their very situations can be traced. They were partly west of Golconda, towards the middle tributary of the Kistna, where stood Raolconda. Other mines were to the eastward, on the Lower Kistna. The most famous of these, named "Gani" by the natives, but "Colore" by the Persians, was about fifteen miles north-west of Masulipatnam; and, in Tavernier's time, employed 60,000 workmen. The Diamonds found here were distinguished for their number and size; but, except in rare instances, they were deficient in purity and clearness. The largest and most celebrated found in this mine is described by Tavernier as the "Great Mogul." In its rough state it weighed 787½ carats. It was reduced by cutting to 297 carats.

Near Colore, or Gani, a locality is mentioned by Tavernier as having produced *inadamantine* Diamonds, whose brittleness led to great disappointment, and eventually induced the King of Golconda to close the mine.

The mines still open are between six and seven hours' journey W.S.W. of Ellore. They were visited by Heyne in 1795, and are known as the "Mallivully," so called from one of the seven villages of that name; where the miners live. In the neighbourhood of these villages, on the north bank of the Kistna, is the Gani Mine, which has in our times received the name of "Partala."

Golconda itself has no mines. The fort was the

storehouse of all the great Diamonds in the Nabob's dominions.

The plain on which the villages lie round about Mallivully, is on all sides surrounded by granite rocks. The average depth of the alluvium in which the Diamonds are here found is twenty feet. This alluvial deposit extends along the banks of the Kistna for the distance of about two or three hours' walk.

The change from a grey to a red soil, consisting of weathered granite gravel is here distinctly seen, The upper layer consists of the black "Cottonsoil," brought down from the higher grounds by floods. This quickly changes before the blow-pipe into light porous lava, or even into a glass bead. Beneath this layer lies a mass of fragments of sandstone, quartz, jasper, flint and granite, with great amorphous masses of calcareous conglomerate, without any indications of having been rolled there by water. It is in this stratum that the Diamond is found, together with other Precious Stones.

4.—*The Sumbulpoor Group, north of the Godavery, on the Central Tributary of the Mahanuddy, in Gondwara, (between 21° and 22° north lat.).*

This Diamond district extends to the immediate vicinity of Sumbulpoor only, in its fruitful alluvial plain, (385 feet above the level of the sea), and between the rivers Mahanuddy and Brahmini.

The Precious Stones which are found at the mouths of the little tributaries of the Maund, flowing from the north-east, are of various sizes and of purest quality.

In Sumbulpoor the Diamond seekers are of two

castes, but their origin is unknown. They resemble Negroes rather than the Hindoos. They go by the names Ihara and Tora. Sixteen villages of the poorest kind are given up to them as free Jaghirs. Ten are occupied by the Iharas and four by the Toras, the remaining two being devoted to their gods.

These Diamond seekers with their families, numbering from 4000 to 5000 persons, migrate yearly; and from November to the commencement of the rainy season search the bed of the Mahanuddy River from Chunderpore to Sonepore, a distance of twenty-four geographical miles, scrutinizing every cleft and corner for the Precious Stones. They carry with them only three tools, the pickaxe, a board five feet long, hollowed in the middle and provided with a raised border three inches high, and a second board about half the size.

With the pickaxe they scrape the earth out of the clefts and holes, pile it in heaps on the bank, when their women lay the earth on the larger board, slightly inclined, wash it with water, and remove all but the rougher sand and pebbles; these are subsequently placed on the smaller board, spread out, and searched for Precious Stones and gold dust. They find the Diamond mostly in a mass of tough, reddish clay, pebbles, a little sand, and some iron oxide. This is, indeed, the material chiefly looked for; it seems to be the debris of the same stone "breccia" as that which Voysey supposed to be Diamond rock in the Pennar and the Kistna groups.

The second method of obtaining the Diamond in India is to form a flat surface in the neighbourhood of the place where the Precious Stones are to be sought, and build round it a wall two feet high, leaving here and there openings for the water to run off. The earth which has been worked out by means of the pickaxe, is thrown into this extemporized well, and after two or three washings the large stones are removed, the remnant dried, and the Diamonds sought for. From time immemorial the Diamonds found in this district have been claimed as the Ruler's right. The finder of large Diamonds is rewarded by the royal grant of one or more small villages. For smaller Diamonds there are other rewards; but for the concealment of Precious Stones, the natives are punished by having their villages taken from them, and are subject also to be beaten. In spite of this, and threatenings of severer pains, smuggling and concealment go on.

Since the year 1818, Sumbulpoor has been under British rule. In this year a Diamond was found which weighed 84 grains, and although of only the third quality it was sold for 5,000 rupees.

5.—*The Panna Group in Bundelcund, between the Rivers Sonar and Sone (25 N. Lat.).*

The fifth and last group of Diamond beds is near Bengal, Bahar, and Allahabad, on the south bank of the Ganges. South of this mighty river there runs almost in the same direction a vast range of lofty tableland, sandstone on granite, extending 150 miles from east to west. In the eastern third of the lofty tableland there have not yet been discovered any signs of the existence of the Diamond, although a mine mentioned by Tavernier, must have been at some spot south of this range. In a second division of this sandstone belt, at its west extremity, and limited to an area of a very few miles, is a spot famous since the time of Ptolemy for its Diamonds : it lies very near to Panna.

In the small rivers which have their rise in the tableland, and take their course through valleys furrowed in rock, forming on their way wild cataracts, Diamonds are not infrequently found, carried along with soil violently dislodged.

It is not to our purpose to pursue many of the undoubtedly interesting geological and geographical topics which lie before us at this juncture. We will allude briefly to the points which complete our particular relation, and state that Diamonds are found under the cascade of the river Bagin, from 700 to 900 feet below the present Diamond strata; and the only explanation of it is that the Bagin has brought these Precious Stones down from the tableland, with other matter torn from its native bed.

As a rule, Diamonds are found 1,200 or 1,300 feet above the level of the sea, and, as Franklin observes, "when Diamonds are discovered 1,100 feet away from their native bed, they must have been borne there by water."

The most productive Diamond mines in this fifth group were in 1860 at the village of Sukariuh, about twenty miles from Panna. Here the upper stratum, from fifteen to twenty feet thick, had to be broken through in order to reach the rich Diamond bed.

Four kinds of Diamonds were found at Sukariuh. They are termed, 1st, *Motichul*, clear and brilliant; 2nd, *Manik*, verging in colour to green; 3rd, *Panna*, with a faint orange tint; 4th, *Bunsput*, dark colored.

6.—*Borneo.*

In the south-eastern point of Borneo, Tanah Laut (or Lake Land) ends the chain of mountains which runs parallel to, and on the east of, the large River Bangermassing.

The most southern portion of the mountain is known by the name of the Ratoos Range. Its highest point, 3,168 feet above the sea level, is for the most part composed of Serpentine, Diorite, and Greenstone. The Diamond mines are all on the west side of the Ratoos. The soil, mostly red clay, is thirty or forty feet deep; below that, for about six feet, is a gravel or shingle of Serpentine, Diorite, and Quartz, interbedded sometimes with Marl, in which are found fossils of the *Ostrea Cardium*, a still existing Mollusc in the neighbouring ocean. The Diamonds, accompanied by Magnetite, are found in a sand-bed resting on serpentine. The surest indications of the presence of Diamonds are little pieces of black quartz, containing Iron-pyrites, and flakes of Platinum. In this south-eastern province alone, 400 people are occupied in Diamond washing; in the north-west of the island, in Landak, Diamond industry is also carried on, but under what conditions and with what means is not known.

7.—Sumatra.

About the year 1840, in the district of Doladoulo, in the island of Sumatra, some moderately rich Diamonds beds were discovered.

CHAPTER VI.

COLORED DIAMONDS.

GENERAL.

THE collection of Colored Diamonds in the Vienna Museum, which was brought together by Herr Virgil von Helmreicher, a Tyrolese by birth, but long resident in Brazil, is undoubtedly the most complete in Europe.

The following is the order in which I think these gems should be arranged, having regard to their rarity and value.

1 Blue, 2 Red, 3 Green, 4 White, 5 Olive. 6 Black, 7 Fire-colored, 8 Yellow; the remaining need not be classified.

BLUE DIAMONDS.

Diamonds occur of every hue, and according to Mandeville, "seem to take pleasure in assuming in turns the colors proper to other gems." The Blue, or Sapphire tint is, with the exception of the Ruby Red, the rarest of colors met with in Diamonds, and ranks among the most beautiful of Precious Stones.

Diamonds of a faint bluish tint are not infrequently found, but are usually more or less opalescent, and therefore rank as stones of inferior quality; whereas the dark Blue Diamond is of extreme rarity.

Although writers describe these stones as possessing in an eminent degree the beauty of fine Sapphires, no comparison can really be instituted, their blue color being peculiar to themselves, dark, verging on Indigo, possessing a fierceness in their tint, which differs materially from the mild, soft hue of the Sapphire; and above all, they possess the exclusive irradiance and fire of the Brilliant. It is indeed a gem, which for its intrinsic beauty no less than its extreme rarity challenges the foremost place among "Precious Stones." The only Blue Diamonds known were found in the old Indian mines, probably those of Gani or Colore, visited by Tavernier in 1642.

The Brazilian mines, although yielding many colored Diamonds, are not known to have produced a single example of the dark blue variety. The same remark applies to the South-African, which have not as yet given to the world either a green or a blue specimen.

The first mention we have of a Blue Diamond in Europe, refers to a stone then considered unique. It weighed in the rough 112¼ carats, was bought by Tavernier in India in 1642, and was sold to Louis XIV., in 1668. It is described as "d'un beau violet." It would appear to have been somewhat flat and ill-formed. The figure in the plate, (see Frontispiece), to my mind, represents faithfully this stone in its then condition, and is a copy from an old French engraving. After its purchase by " Le

Grand Monarque," it was apparently cut; as we find in the French regalia a century later a faceted Diamond, triangular in shape, and of the identical color, weighing 67⅛ carats, which would be about the weight of Tavernier's celebrated purchase, after cutting.

This, the only recorded Blue Diamond, was, with the rest of the French Regalia, seized in August, 1792, and deposited in the Garde-Meuble. From this insecure place it was surreptitiously abstracted in September of the same year. What became of it remains a mystery: that it should have really been lost is incredible; and from the sudden appearance of a stone of similar character, the extraordinary rarity of which is acknowledged, I strongly incline towards the belief that it is Tavernier's recut, and so altered in form as to render its identification very difficult. This hypothesis, which I offer, receives additional probability from the fact that a Blue Brilliant about the year 1830 was in the hands of Mr. Daniel Eliason, which stone came to light without a history, without any account being rendered as to whence it came, and what had been its travels and fortunes. Subsequently I trace it as the property of the late Mr. Henry Thomas Hope, under the name of the " Hope Diamond." The difference in weight between the original stone of 67½ carats, and this actual stone of 44¼, forces upon us the interrogation, "Was the weight lost simply in the cutter's hands in manipulating the stone, or were one or more pieces removed by simple cleavage, and preserved?" *I* incline to the latter alternative, viz., that the Diamond abstracted in 1792, was reduced by cleavages, and formed into two Brilliants. This deduction is more probable, as Tavernier's Diamond evidently had one of the crystallographic faces *largely produced* on the one side, which gave the stone a "drop form." (see Frontispiece). This formation is frequently seen in rough Diamonds, especially in colored stones (excepting always the yellow varieties), leading us to infer that the cleavage plane must have run as in the diagram, from A to B. In the first cutting of the stone this original shape was to some extent preserved, which left an ill-formed, triangular-shaped Brilliant somewhat thin on one side. From this it would have been easy for an expert to cleave a triangular piece of about 10 or 11 carats, thus leaving the stone weighing about 56 carats; the re-cutting of which as a perfect Brilliant, well-proportioned, would reduce it to its present weight of 44¼ carats. It is observable that the "Hope Diamond" is even now straighter on one side than the other, and this strengthens the presumption of the stone having been cleaved as suggested. The late Emperor of the French ordered a model of the Blue Diamond in question to be made while it remained in the Paris Exhibition.

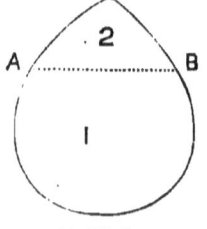

Ideal Outline.

It would confirm my hypothesis still further could the piece or pieces split off be discovered. The piece must at first have been triangular, having a straight side corresponding with the side of the Hope Diamond, as described above. If then we find a Blue Diamond of drop shape, of the same color precisely as the "Hope," having its base to correspond with the straight side of the latter, proportionate in substance, and weighing from 6 to 7 carats, we have a strong presumptive evidence that the two stones are parts of the same original, and that the smaller is a cleavage of the larger. Such a stone did actually come into the market in April, 1874. It was purchased in Geneva at the sale of the late Duke of Brunswick's jewels. The purchaser put the stone for a short time into my hands, and I examined it in juxtaposition with the "Hope Diamond." It is identical in *color* and *quality*. I know not how to avoid the conclusion that the Duke of Brunswick's "Blue Drop Diamond" once formed the triangular salient gibbosity which formerly appears to have characterised the stone now known as the " Hope Brilliant."

Besides the Hope and Brunswick Diamonds, there are only three Diamonds known in Europe that can justly be termed " Blue," and these all differ from the " Hope," and from each other in color. Of the three, the most important is the Brilliant, also sold at the Duke's sale, a Blue Stone with a dash of jet in it, weighing 13¼ carats. It is of an octagon shape with " flat top and thick back," not unlike a Rose Diamond.

I am myself in possession of a very fine, but small, dark Blue Brilliant, weighing about five grains, which at one time formed part of the Vienna collection. The only remaining Blue Brilliant, beside those described, is in private hands. This stone weighs about 4½ carats, is somewhat square in form, and is paler in hue than its famous congeners.

RED DIAMONDS.

The true Red Diamond is valuable " according to the glorious beauty of its perfection ;" to use a quaint phrase of good old Thomas Nicols, writing to the dons of Cambridge in 1651, " It feeds your eyes with much pleasure in beholding, and hence are discovered to us the excellency of super-celestial things."

The only specimen known to us is the gem bought by Mr. Joseph Halphen, of Paris, from a London firm. It came last year into my hands, and passed thence into into those of a great connoisseur, who would hardly be induced to part with it.

There are Rose colored Diamonds,—not a few,—but, the Blood or Ruby Red, such as the specimen to which I have alluded,—a gem on fire as it were,—is so rare, that I know of no second.

GREEN DIAMONDS.

The history of the finest specimen of a Diamond of this color may be not uninteresting. Twenty years ago this stone was obtained for £200. Some years after it was sold for £300. Subsequently it passed into the possession of a jeweller in Bond Street, who parted with it to an American gentleman for £600. Mr. Charles Drayson is now its owner; should he consent to take a £1000 it would undoubtedly be purchased for the regalia of one of the great European courts.

CHAPTER VII.
BORT AND CARBONADO.

a—BORT.

ERTAIN Diamonds are found of inferior quality, and so imperfectly crystallized, that they are useless as ornamental stones. These are called "Bort," and are crushed to form Diamond-dust, or are used for engraving. The Diamond-powder formed by the crushing of these inferior stones, and the Diamond-powder produced as the result of the cutting and cleaving of rough stones, possessing, of course, the property of intense hardness are, after mixture with oil, employed for polishing Diamonds.

b.—CARBONADO

or, as Major Beaumont, M.P. calls it, "Carbonate, or Carbon," resembles in color and appearance fragments of Hematite. Both these names, Carbonado and Carbonate are clearly misnomers, as, chemically, the body referred to is like Diamond, Graphite and Charcoal, a form of the element Carbon. It was at first introduced for the purpose of cutting Diamonds, after the same fashion as the "Bort" referred to above. Of late years however, a new and most important application of this material has been made. It is employed for the purpose of drilling holes in rocks, and with most remarkable success, so that the value of "Carbonado" has risen from 1/- to about 18/- a carat.

The stones are fixed in an annular ring of steel, and by means of a superincumbent weight of from 400 to 800 lbs., are pressed downwards into the rock, while at the same time the crown in which they are set, is made to revolve 250 times in a minute. Over the cutting faces water is constantly passed to keep the Diamonds cool, and to wash away all the debris that is formed.

The Diamond-drill works not by a blow but by rotation. Its action is an abrading one, not percussive or cutting. So adamantine is this "Carbonado," that a mile of sandstone or of granite can be bored through by the Diamond-boring apparatus before the stones are seriously worn. The loss from friction is quite trifling. Sometimes indeed, the Carbonado may be so set in the "head" as to present an angle of the "Carbonado," at which cleavage is practicable. Then of course, the use of this particular part is destroyed. The other loss which may be sustained, which far exceeds the former, results from some of the stones being violently torn out from the bore-head.

Before concluding our notices of the advantages of Carbonado in rock boring (as adopted by the Diamond Rock-Boring Company), we must refer to the drawback in this admirable apparatus, viz., that it is practically useless when the workmen come upon a soft stratum, but the advantages generally far exceed the drawbacks.

(1). The most important, from a practical point of view, is the evenness of the solid core produced by the boring machinery, which core gives full information as to the nature of the strata passed through.

(2). The apparatus works as well in water as in dry solid rock.

(3). It accomplishes in months what could only be effected by other known means in years.

(4). Finally, it is undoubtedly more than any other method of rock-boring, economical of money as well as of time.

c.—THE BORON DIAMOND.

The subject of Diamonds must not be concluded without some notice of a new chemical discovery which possibly may exercise great influence upon the commerce of Diamonds, and upon the use of them for personal adornment. The discovery treats of nothing less than a formation of bodies akin to the natural Carbon-Diamond, but consisting of the element Boron.

It is well-known how Wöhler and Deville, while trying to produce, in large quantities, pure aluminium, discovered a method of crystallizing Silicon and Boron. The crystallized Boron shewed in so remarkable a manner the properties of the Diamond—its hardness, transparency, and fire—that there must be an intimate relation between the two. This element, Boron, in combination with oxygen, forms boracic acid, as carbon with oxygen forms carbonic acid.

There is a surprising similarity between the elements Boron and Carbon. They both exist in three conditions: 1st, amorphous—as Charcoal; 2nd, graphitoid—as Graphite: 3rd, crystalline—as Diamond. They agree, also, as far as known, in the modes of origin of these three forms. To form artificial graphite an excess of charcoal is heated in contact with iron.; as the whole cools, such charcoal, as does not combine with the iron to form steel, crystallizes out as graphite.

The crystalline form of the carbon-graphite coincides with that of the boron-graphite; but as to color, the boron-graphite is red, and the carbon-graphite pure black or blackish grey.

The natural Carbon-Diamond crystallizes in the regular form, and in octahedra. The crystalline form of Boron is tetragonal—an elongated prism whose corners are somewhat blunted, or else foliated crystals. The foliated crystals are harder than the elongated prism and are almost always black. The large crystals are mostly transparent and sometimes colorless; and not infrequently they are tinged with Garnet-red, Hyacinth-red, or honey-yellow.

Possessors and purchasers of Diamonds need not be alarmed at the prospect thus dimly shadowed forth. It has only been possible to produce Boron-crystals of small size, and therefore of no value as ornamental stones. The Boron-Diamond will never replace—never in any way approach in value—the true carbon-stone. It is, however, a matter of great interest to scientific men generally.

CHAPTER VIII.

CELEBRATED DIAMONDS.

THERE are a few well-known and costly Diamonds which have received world-wide attention, and attracted ever since their discovery, hundreds of years ago, peculiar interest. Of these gems each has, so to say, its own special history; in many instances signallized by deeds of violence and crime. I purpose calling attention to a few of the most important.

(1.) The largest Diamond is known by the name of "Braganza," and was discovered in the year 1741, in Brazil. It is now among the Portuguese State Jewels. It weighed in its rough state, 1,680 carats, was the size of a hen's egg, and valued at £58,350,000. But as it has never been cut, its genuineness is naturally doubted, and it is believed to be a White Topaz.

It is supposed that the Portuguese Government suppressed information regarding it, out of a supreme care for their finances.

(2.) The largest known Diamond, at present, is that of the Rajah of Mattan, in Borneo. It was found on the island about 120 years ago, and weighs 367 carats; is a pear-shaped stone, with a small hole or crevice at its short end. Notwithstanding many battles have been fought for it, it still remains in the possession of the Rajah's family.

It is said that the Governor of Batavia offered 150,000 dollars, and two men of war, with guns and ammunition for it, but the Rajah refused to part with it on any terms, saying that he regarded it as a "talisman, upon the possession of which both his own and his family's happiness and success depended."

(3.) The Diamond known as the *Great Mogul*, has received an amount of attention beyond any other. Under the name of the *Koh-i-noor* (Mountain of Light), it played an important part in the Exhibition of 1851. The history of this stone dates back to 56 B.C., but there is nothing known with certainty about it until the beginning of the 14th century, when it was held by the Rajah of Malwa. Later it fell into the hands of the Sultans of Delhi, after their conquest of Malwa.

Tavernier gives a description of it as one of those he saw among the jewels of Aurengzebe, affirming that it exceeded all the others in size and worth. He speaks of it as a Rose in form, like the half of an egg; of 186 carats weight; but in its rough state it weighed $793\frac{5}{8}$ carats. The Schah Jihan sent the rough stone to a Venetian lapidary, named Hortensio Borgio, but was so angry with the manner in which this artist dealt with it, that he not only refused the payment for cutting it, but fined the unfortunate Borgio 1,000 rupees, all, in fact, that the man possessed.

There hangs some doubt about this gem, as Tavernier seems to have given two varying accounts of it. This has led to the belief that the Great Mogul and the Koh-i-noor are not one and the same stone, but two separate ones: there can, however, be really no doubt as to their being identical. It is not likely that there would be two stones in the same collection, with the same characteristics, and varying in size only half a carat.

It remained in the Treasury of the Mogul dynasty in Delhi until the wild outbreak of the Tartars, when they passed over the Affghan mountains, and poured in upon the north-west of India. Then the Mahommed Schah, great-grandson of Aurengzebe, became possessor of the jewel. He valued it so much, that he wore it hidden in his turban. When the conqueror Nadir Schah came to take possession of Delhi, Mahommed had to give up everything of value to him in the Treasury, but he kept this stone back. It was one of the women of his harem, however, who betrayed him to Nadir Schah.

A grand festival was held in Delhi, at which the two rulers swore love and friendship, and to Mahommed's astonishment, the Nadir, at the close of the feast, declared he must exchange turbans to cement the love and friendship they had just sworn to each other.

Mahommed had no time to consider, and indeed, the Nadir gave him no time, for he snatched off, his own and subsequently the turban of his friend.

The self-command of Eastern rulers is proverbial. Mahommed showed neither by word nor sign his sense of the loss, or his astonishment, and Nadir began to think he must have been deceived by the woman as to the hiding-place of the Diamond.

As soon as he was alone he untwisted the turban, and within its folds found a packet, which he opened. There lay the Diamond which he was the first to greet with the name Koh-i-noor, or Mountain of Light.

So the Persian Nadir carried it with him to Corassan,

gifting it with every kind of fabulous property. It passed at his death into the hands of his son who, having none of the strength of his father, possessed it but a short time. From him it went to Ahmed Shah, the founder of Cabul or Abdali dynasty; thence, to his descendant Shah Shuja, whose wild romantic life made him a fit possessor of this stone of many fables. When driven from Cabul the Diamond was his companion, and in his subsequent imprisonment his only companion. Although deprived of his eyes, and unable to gladden his sense of sight by its brilliancy, he still contrived that it should accompany him in his exile to Peshawur, to Cashmere, and to Lahore. He was nominally the guest, but really the prisoner, of Runjet Sing. Runjet Sing was no judge of Diamonds, but he set a high value upon the possession of this particular stone, and tried every means in his power whether by menace, entreaty or cunning to obtain it. He sent for the wife of the unlucky king of Cabul, demanding it of her, but she assured him she had it not. He commanded all her possessions to be brought to him, by which means he obtained many valuable stones, more costly than any he had ever possessed before. He naturally thought the Koh-i-noor must be amongst them. Shawls, carpets, and a score of other things he retained, so that the poor Begum had in the end but very little restored to her. Ere long he discovered that *the* stone was not there, and he had the Begum watched closely. Nothing now would satisfy him but its possession. He tried by starving her and her family to obtain news of it, but failing in this he tried the effect of promises. She stipulated that the Koh-i-noor should be placed in his hands if he released her husband from his imprisonment in Cashmere, gave a guarantee that his life should be spared, and conceded other minor matters which she named. The result of this was that Runjet Sing released Shah Shuja at once, relying on the honor of the Begum to fulfil her part of the contract. She thereupon declared that she had not the Diamond in her possession, but had pledged it to a merchant in Candahur. The Runjet resorted to his old experiment of starving her, but neither this nor any other plan was successful. At length Shah Shuja himself gave a promise to Runjet Sing, that on a certain day the Koh-i-noor should be his.

It was on the first of June, 1813, that Runjet Sing, together with some faithful friends and a few good judges of gems went to Shadera, the residence of Shah Shuja. On arriving they were greeted and seated. An hour passed in dead silence, and at length the Runjet whispered one of his attendants that he should remind Shah Shuja why they were there. The Shah thus reminded, beckoned to a slave, who retired, and soon returned with a packet which he placed on the carpet, midway between Runjet Sing and Shah Shuja. Again a dead silence fell on all, till Runjet Sing, able to bear no longer delay, beckoned to one of his people to open the packet. It contained a gem, which, according to the judges there present, was the *genuine Koh-i-noor.* The silence was broken by Runjet Sing asking, "At what price do you value it." " Good Fortune," answered the Shah, "and that is always the property of those who have vanquished their enemies." The manner and bearing of Shah Shuja were so dignified, that they made a great impression upon the assembly, and no one left the house without paying tribute to the honor and dignity of the deposed prince. The Diamond was set in a bracelet, and worn by Runjet Sing on every great occasion. On his death-bed there was an attempt made to induce him to bequeath the stone to the idol Juggernaut. It remained, however, in the hands of his successors, who wore it occasionally.

After the murder of Shu Sing, it was deposited in the Lahore Treasury until the boy Rajah Dhulip Sing, acknowledged by the English Government, was stationed at Lahore with an English Regent.

After the annexation of the Punjaub by the English Government, the crown jewels of Lahore, and among them the Koh-i-noor were confiscated to the East India Company, a stipulation being made that the Koh-i-noor should be presented to the Queen. Lord Dalhousie sent two officers in charge of the gem to England, and it was delivered to the Queen on the 3rd June, 1850. Its weight on arriving here was $186\frac{1}{16}$ carats. It was of an irregular egg-like shape, and so unskilfully cut that it did not look better than a crystal. It was exhibited in the 1851 Exhibition, and was valued at about £140,000. Prince Albert asked the opinion of Sir David Brewster as to the manner in which it could be most advantageously cut, and about the stone generally. He found in it, as in so many other large Diamonds, several little caves, which he declared (according to his theory), to be the result of the expansive force of condensed gases. This, together with the flaws already noticed, he considered would make the cutting of it, without serious diminution, a very difficult thing. Messrs. Coster, however, of Amsterdam, thought that in the hands of skilful workmen, the difficulties might be overcome. Several patterns of cuts were laid before the Queen, from which she selected the form it now has, that of a regular-cut Brilliant.

Herr Voorsanger was the workman selected from Amsterdam to cut it. His labors were conducted in the Atelier of the Crown Jewels in London. To assist his object a small four horse-power machine was erected, and the cutting commenced by the Duke of Wellington placing it on the cutting mill, on the 6th July, and it was completed at the end of thirty-eight days of twelve hours each.

In order to remove one of the flaws, the number of revolutions of the cutting wheel had to be increased to 3,000 in a minute, and then the object was attained, but very slowly. This process decreased the weight of the Koh-i-noor from $186\frac{1}{16}$ to $106\frac{1}{16}$ carats. King, in his *Natural History of Precious Stones*, regrets it being cut at all, thinking it preferable that it should have remained specimen of a monster Diamond.

4. *The Orloff*, or Amsterdam Diamond weighs 194¾ carats and is set in the top of the Russian Imperial Sceptre It is of pure water, but not cut to advantage; the upper surface having concentrated rows of three-cornered facets, and the lower surface, four-sided facets. Its size is about that of a pigeon's egg.

It came originally from one of the old mines of India, and tradition reports it to have been one of the eyes of the idol Sheringham, in the temple of Brahma. Later, with many others, it graced the throne of the Shah Nadir, of Persia. When he was murdered, it was stolen by a French grenadier, who had served there. He fled with it to Malabar, and sold it to an English sea-captain for £2000. It was brought to England, and sold to a Jewish merchant for £12,000. He, in his turn, sold it to the Armenian merchant, Shafras, at great profit; and in the year 1775, Catharine II. bought it of Shafras, in Amsterdam, for £90,000; giving him at the same time a title and a pension of £4000 for life.

Dr. Beke relates that in 1832, at the siege of Coocha in Corassan, a fragment of Diamond was found weighing 132 carats, by means of the Abbe Mirza, who said that a poor man living in his family had used it as a flint. Its form gave rise to the supposition that it was a piece of the Koh-i-noor.

5. The Diamond, well-known under the name of *The Shah*, (see page vii.), is about half the size of the Orloff, and was given to the Emperor of Russia by Prince Cosroes, younger son of the Abbe Mirza, when he was in St. Petersburg. It weighs only 86 carats, but is perfectly pure, without a flaw or cloud; and it is interesting, inasmuch as it is only partly cut; many of its *natural* octahedra being preserved. The cut facets contain Persian inscriptions, and there is a little groove round the top of it, to which a cord was fastened, in order that it might be worn round the neck.

6. The most perfect Brilliant in existence is the celebrated *Pitt* or *Regent*, which is among the French Crown Jewels. It weighs 136¾ carats. The Duke of Orleans, Regent of France, bought it of Pitt, the English Governor of Fort St. George for £135,000. It was said Pitt had obtained this stone in Golconda in the year 1702. It came from the mines of Parteal, forty-five leagues south of Golconda. It was found by a slave, who, in order to hide it, wounded himself in the thigh, and hid the stone beneath the bandage. He at length acknowledged this to a sailor and promised him the stone, if only he would secure him his freedom. This sailor enticed the slave on board, took from him his Diamond, and then threw the slave into the sea. The murderer sold the Diamond to Pitt for £1000, spent the money quickly in excesses of all kinds, and from a murderer became a suicide.

Another story is, that Pitt bought the stone in 1701 of the far-famed Jamchund, the greatest Diamond merchant in India for £12,500. A Commission consisting of all the most experienced French jewellers valued it at £480,000. It disappeared when the Tuileries were plundered in 1792 with the other Crown Diamonds, but in some mysterious way came to light again later on. The Republic then pledged it to the merchant Treskon, in Berlin. Again redeemed, it ornamented the sword of Napoleon I. Before it was cut it weighed 410 carats. In the cutting it was reduced to nearly one-third of its original size.

7. *The Florentine Diamond*, among the Crown Jewels of the Emperor of Austria, weighs 139½ carats. It is of pure water, of beautiful form, and, notwithstanding that its color is somewhat of a citron tint, it is valued at £105,000. It is supposed that this is the largest and most costly of those Diamonds which Charles the Bold lost at the battle of Granson. Charles the Bold is known to have valued the largest of those he lost at the worth of a Province. It was found by a Swiss in a little box accompanied by a costly pearl. The man regarded his find with contempt, and threw it under the wagon again, thinking they were merely bits of glass. He thought better of it however, picked it up again, and sold the two gems to a priest in Montagny for a guilden, who re-sold them for three francs.

At this time there lived in Berne, a rich merchant named Bartholomew May, who partly by relationship, and partly through business, was connected with Italy. He bought this Diamond for £200 and a small present to the man through whose instrumentality he had been enabled to purchase it. He sold it to a Genoese for a large sum, but Ludovico Sforza bought it of the Genoese for twice the amount he had given. It afterwards came into the possession of Pope Julius II., who presented it to the Emperor of Austria.

(8). *The Sancy Diamond* weighs 53½ carats. Its early history is very doubtful. According to Karl Emil Kluge, it came originally from India and entered Europe about the fifteenth century. It fell into the hands of Charles the Bold, Duke of Burgundy. It was either lost by or stolen from him, and came into the possession of the King of Portugal. His finances not being in a flourishing condition, *he* sold it with other stones to a French merchant for a large sum of money. In the sixteenth century it fell into the hands of a Huguenot nobleman, Mons. le Baron de 'Sancy, of whom Henry III. borrowed it, for the purpose of pledging it to the Swiss Government. The servant who was trusted (according to the Baron's own account) to carry it to the king, was waylaid and murdered. On hearing of his servant's death, he remarked "My diamond is not lost." He was right. The faithful servant had swallowed it, and on opening his body, it was found in his stomach. After this, through what means is not known, it came into the possession of James II. of England who, when he fled into France in 1688, carried it with him. Wanting money, he made it over to Louis XIV., for 625,000 francs. It passed from him to Louis XV. who wore it in the clasp of his hat at his coronation. In the Revolution of 1792 it disappeared, (as did also the famous Blue Diamond of 67½ carats), but came to light again in the time of Napoleon, and was sold by him to the Emperor of Russia for 500,000 silver roubles (£75,000).

(9). Tavernier's Table-Diamond. (For a representation of this famous Diamond, the reader is referred to the sketch on the title page.)

(10). The largest Diamond found in Brazil weighs 254 carats, and is called, *The Star of the South*. It is a Brilliant of purest water. Its general form is a Rhombododecahedron, with a very blunt point upon each of its faces.

On one of the faces of the Diamond a moderately deep hole is noticeable, and by help of a lens stripes were seen in the interior of the hole. It is evident that the Diamond belongs to the group of Diamond Crystals which have their bed in rocks of crystallized ore, and which probably are to be numbered among the metamorphic mountains of Brazil.

The *Star of the South* was found in July, 1853, in one of the mines of Bogagen (a district of the province of Minas-Geräes), by a poor negress who was engaged in the works. It was purchased by M. Halphen, and displayed in the Paris and London Exhibitions, and was conspicuous for its brilliancy, owing to its purity and perfect cut. About one-half of its weight was lost in cutting. Its form is an oval-round Brilliant, thirty-five millimètres long, ($1\frac{2}{5}$ inch), and twenty-nine broad, but only nineteen thick; its purity is extraordinary, and under light it shows a rose-tint, not unpleasant to the eyes.

(11.) Another celebrated Brazilian Diamond, weighing 138½ carats, is among the treasures of the King of Portugal. It was found in 1775 by a negro, a few miles north of the Rio Plata, and as a reward, he obtained his freedom, and a yearly income of £50.

An anecdote is told for which Mann is answerable, that three men, guilty of great crime, were banished to the interior of Brazil for life. They were never to approach either of the towns, or to mix with other people, upon pain of life-long imprisonment. These men went into the most unfrequented places in the land, searching for valuable matter. They wandered up and down for six weary years by the shores of the rivers, always in danger of becoming the prey of man, or beast. At length they came to the River Abaité, and at a time when, through a long season of dry weather, a part of the bed was exposed. Here, while seeking for gold, they came upon a Diamond nearly an ounce in weight. They had now to take into consideration the strict law against the unauthorized seeking for Diamonds, and the great desire they had to obtain their freedom. They, therefore, consulted a priest, who not only did not betray them, but advised them to trust to the goodwill of the government; and he himself accompanied them to Villa Rica, and obtained an audience for them of the Governor. The Governor was so astonished at the size of the stone that he would not trust his own eyes alone, but called together his officers, who declared it to be a genuine Diamond. The Governor thereupon bestowed upon the finders the rights of citizenship. The priest was sent with the stone to Rio de Janiero, and thence to Lisbon, when the King confirmed the pardon of the criminals, and their restoration to the rights of citizenship. To the priest he gave a good preferment. This stone remains likewise in the Treasury of the King of Portugal.

(12.) The *Pacha of Egypt* is cut on eight sides, weighs 40 carats, and cost 700,000 francs.

(13.) The *Pigott/* Diamond, brought from India by Lord Pigott, weighs 82¼ carats. In 1801 it was sold in a lottery for 750,000 francs; and in 1818 it passed into the possession of Messrs. Rundell & Bridge.

(14.) The *Nassac*, formerly in the possession of the East India Company, weighed 89¾ carats; but since Lord Westminster had it cut anew it weighs only 78⅝ carats. Its value is about £30,000.

(15.) The largest Diamond in the Green Vaults of Dresden is 48½ carats in weight. It is nearly as large as the Sancy. There are also here some parures of Diamonds, marvellously beautiful; and four very valuable yellow Brilliants, the largest of which is 117¼, and the smallest 52½ grains respectively.

THE CROWN JEWELS OF ENGLAND (COMMUNICATED BY PROFESSOR TENNANT.)

The Imperial State Crown of Her Majesty Queen Victoria, was made by Messrs. Rundell and Bridge in the year 1838, with jewels taken from old crowns, and others furnished by command of Her Majesty. It consists of Diamonds, Pearls, Rubies, Sapphires, and Emeralds, set in silver and gold; it has a crimson velvet cap with ermine border, and is lined with white silk. Its gross weight is 39 oz. 5 dwts. troy. The lower part of the band, above the ermine border, consists of a row of 129 Pearls, and the upper part of the band of a row of. 112 Pearls, between which, in front of the crown, is a large Sapphire (partly drilled), purchased for the crown by His Majesty King George IV. At the back is a Sapphire of smaller size, and six other Sapphires (three on each side), between which are eight Emeralds.

Above and below the seven Sapphires are fourteen Diamonds, and around the eight Emeralds, 128 Diamonds. Between the Emeralds and the Sapphires are sixteen trefoil ornaments, containing 160 Diamonds. Above the band are eight Sapphires surmounted by eight Diamonds, between which are eight festoons consisting of 148 Diamonds.

In the front of the Crown, and in the centre of a Diamond Maltese cross, is the famous Ruby said to have been given to Edward Prince of Wales, son of Edward III., called the Black Prince, by Don Pedro, King of Castile, after the battle of Najera, near Vittoria, A.D. 1367. This Ruby was worn in the helmet of Henry V. at the battle of Agincourt, A.D. 1415. It is pierced quite through, after the eastern custom, the upper part of the piercing being filled up by a small Ruby. Around this Ruby in order to form the cross, are seventy-five Brilliant Diamonds. Three other Maltese crosses, forming the two sides and back of the crown, have Emerald centres, and contain respectively 132, 124, and 130 Brilliant Diamonds.

Between the four Maltese crosses are four ornaments in the form of the French fleur de-lis, with four Rubies, in the centres, and surrounded by Rose Diamonds, containing respectively 85, 86, and 87 Rose Diamonds.

From the Maltese crosses issue four imperial arches composed of oak leaves and acorns; the leaves contain 728 Rose, Table, and Brilliant Diamonds; 32 Pearls form the acorns, set in cups, containing fifty-four Rose Diamonds and one Table Diamond. The total number of Diamonds in the arches and acorns is 108 Brilliant, 116 Table, and 559 Rose Diamonds.

From the upper part of the arches are suspended four large pendant pear-shaped Pearls, with Rose Diamond caps, containing 12 Rose Diamonds, and stems containing 24 very small Rose Diamonds. Above the arch stands the mound, containing in the lower hemisphere 304 Brilliants, and in the upper 244 Brilliants; the zone and arc being composed of 33 Rose Diamonds. The cross on the summit has a Rose-cut Sapphire in the centre, surrounded by four large Brilliants, and 108 smaller Brilliants.

Summary of Jewels in the English Crown.

1 Large Ruby irregularly polished	1,363 Brilliants
1 Large broad-spread Sapphire	1,272 Rose Diamonds
16 Sapphires	147 Table Diamonds
11 Emeralds	4 Drop-shaped Pearls
4 Rubies	273 Pearls

THE WEIGHT AND VALUE OF THE DIAMONDS OF THE FRENCH CROWN, MADE IN 1791.

	Carats, Total	Worth in Francs
The Regent	136	12,000,000
Blue Diamond (see frontispiece)	67	3,000,000
Sancy	53	1,000,000
Golden Blies	51	300,000
The Crown	28	250,000
The Ebenda	26	150,000
Pear-formed	24	200,000
Mirror of Portugal	21	250,000
The Crown	20	65,000
The Ebenda	20	48,000
3, each one of about 18 carats	55	180,000
3, each of about 17 carats	51	118,000
The 10th Mazarine	16	50,000
3, each about 14 carats	43	205,000
2, ,, 13½ ,,	27	95,000
4, ,, 11 ,,	46	50,000
4, ,, 10 ,,	41	94,000
6, ,, 9 ,,	56	130,000
35, ,, 7 ,,	249	472,000
17, ,, 5 ,,	90	164,000
21, ,, 4½ ,,	92	113,400
29, ,, 3¾ ,,	98	92,500
88, ,, 2¾ ,,	207	88,050
94, ,, 1½ ,,	149	60,800
13, ,, 1 ,,	13	2,160
37, ,, 3 grains	27	5,027
433, ,, 2 ,,	229	39,737
679, ,, 1½ ,,	79	13,277
229, ,, ¼ ,,	16	2,560

SEMI-BRILLIANTS.

	Carats, Total	Worth in Francs
2, each piece about 7 carats	14	14,000
1,	6	8,000
2, ,, 4 ,,	8	10,000
4, ,, 3⅜ ,,	13	14,000
1,	2	1,200

ROSE DIAMONDS.

	Carats, Total	Worth in Francs
2, each piece about 21 carats	42	50,000
1,	4	1,200
5, ,, 3½ ,,	17	14,400
1,	2	2,000
5, ,, 2 ,,	11	4,900
2, ,, 13/16 ,,	1	400
95, ,, ½ ,,	33	3,375
340, ,, ¼ ,,	67	6,725
1,	50	8,100

Semi-Brilliants and Roses without statement of weight.

4 pieces, worth	...	40,000	473 pieces, worth	...	25,000
10 ,,	...	394,000	Set ,,	...	1,064,000
478 ,,	...	12,000	2 ,,	...	300,000

In the year 1810, Napoleon commanded a new Inventory to be taken, of which the following is a copy.

Statement of Object.	Name of Stone.	No. of Pieces.	Weight, Carats.	Value in Francs.	Cents.	Total Worth.	
Crown	Brilliants	2506	1872	11,686,504	85	14,702,788	85
	Rose ...	146		219	0		
	Sapphire	59	120	16,065	0		
Sword	Rose ...	1659	308	...		261,365	99
Another Sword ...	Brilliants	410	135	...		71,559	30
Sword	Brilliants	1576	330	...		241,874	73
Plume of Feathers and Bird ..	Brilliants	217	341	...		273,119	37
Epaulette ...	Brilliants	127	102	...		191,834	06
Mantle Clasp ...	Brilliants	197	61	30,605	0	68,105	0
	Opal · ...	1	...	37,500	0		
Shoe Clasp & Garter	Brilliants	120	103	...		56,877	50
Hat Button ...	Brilliants	21	29	...		240,700	0
Rosettes on Hat and Shoe ...	Brilliants	27	83	..		89,100	0
Order of the Holy Ghost ...	Brilliants	443	194	...		325,956	25
Order of Legion of Honor ...	Brilliants	393	82	34,525	95	44,678	75
	Rose ...	20	...	40	0		
Cross of Legion of Honor ...	Brilliants	305	43	10,080	0		
	Rose ...	15	...	30	9		
Ornaments of Rubies and Brilliants ...	Rubies ...	399	410	211,336	68	393,758	59
	Brilliants	6042	793	181,925	41		
	Rose ...	327	...	496	50		
Ornaments of Brilliants and Sapphires ...	Brilliants	3837	558	129,051	0	283,816	09
	Sapphires	67	768	153,865	0		
Ornaments of Turquoise and Brilliants ...	Brilliants	3302	434	87,920	63	130,820	63
	Turquoises	215	...	42,900	0		
Parure of Pearls	Pearls ...	101	5912	1,164,123	0	1,165,163	0
	Rose ...	2320	...	640	d		
Collar	Brilliants	26	106	...		133,900	0
Ornament	Brilliants	9175	1033	..		191,475	62
Comb	Brilliants	250	92	...		47,451	87
Girdle Buckle ...	Brilliants	480	49	...		8,352	50

THE FIRST KNOWN APPLICATION OF DIAMONDS FOR ORNAMENT.

The adaption of the Diamond to personal ornament is grounded on its glorious lustre, its beautiful play of color, and its great hardness; all of which are brought prominently forward by cutting the stones in a variety of forms. This is a process by which the rough stone loses about one-half of its original weight.

The Syrians seem to have been the first to apply the Diamond to personal ornament, although it was an article of commerce much earlier among the peoples of the East. They valued it highly, carried it as amulets, and gave to it many medical virtues. It was regarded also as a safeguard against madness.

In early times, the *rough* stone was worn, or polished only on its upper surface. It was in this form that it was used to ornament state goblets, reliques and crowns.

It was not until the time of Charles VII. that the French ladies began to adorn themselves with Diamonds. The well-known Agnes Sorrel seems to have been the leader of this fashion. Under Francis I. the ladies indulged to such an extent in Diamond ornaments, that it gave rise to the saying, that "the ladies of France carried mills, forests, and lands, on their shoulders." The Luxus or Sumptuary Laws, in the reign of Charles IX. and Henry IV., were aimed at this extravagance.

It was not until after the time of Ludwig van Berquem that Diamonds were used so much for the hair, throat, ears, shoulders, arms, wrists, and fingers.

The original cut of the Diamond was that of the table-form, with a row of facets above; and it was not until the year 1520 that the Rose-cut was introduced, and the form of the Brilliant was not known until the reign of

Louis XIII. of France. It was Cardinal Mazarin in 1660 who first had the Diamond polished. Among the Diamonds of the French Crown is one of the twelve which received the form of the Brilliant, and is known as the Tenth Mazarine.

The Diamond is very rarely engraved : up to the time of Pliny it never appears to have been attempted. The Duke of Bedford has, however, a Diamond with the head of the philosopher Posidonius engraven on it; and although Kluge believes this to be an isolated example, yet there are others in existence. Last year I had one placed in my hands for sale. It was a thin stone, the size of a fourpenny piece, engraved with the head of an emperor. The price was £1,000, and had the owner consented to take less I could have found a purchaser. This stone was exhibited in the last Paris Exhibition.

PRICE OF CUT BRILLIANTS.

In consequence of the unsettled state of the Diamond market arising from causes given, it would be unwise to define other than an approximate list of values.

Diamonds below two grains

Inferior from	... £4 to £6	per carat
Medium ,,	... £6 ,, £8	,, ,,
Good ,,	... £8 ,, £10	,, ,,
Fine ,,	... £10 ,, £12	,, ,,

If over half a carat

Fine from ...	... £12 ,, £15	,, ,,
Over three-quarters	... £15 ,, £20	,, ,,
Stones of one carat	... £20 ,, £23	,, ,,

But the inferior qualities of these sizes would be in similar proportion to Diamonds of two grains.

Inferior stones from one to five carats £6 to £10 per carat.

Medium from	...	... £10 to £20 per carat
Good „	...	... £12 „ £30 „ „
Fine „		... £23 „ £60 „ „

Above these weights it is impossible to fix even an approximate price, each stone varying according to its quality. It must be understood that any one stone of exceptional character will, irrespective of the weight, rise to abnormal value.

CHAPTER IX.
ROUGH DIAMONDS.

THE valuing of Rough Diamonds requires much technical experience.

Although the Diamonds of all parts of the world possess similar characteristics and general appearance, yet have the stones from different places special peculiarities by which good judges are at once in a position to declare the locality whence they have been obtained, although they cannot always define the grounds of their judgment.

In valuing Rough Diamonds it is of primal importance to consider the following points: firstly, the form and proportions of the crystal, on which mainly must depend the loss of weight in cutting, as an irregular or broken piece naturally requires a greater sacrifice of weight to turn out a perfect Brilliant than a well-proportioned crystal; secondly, heed must be taken to distinguish the degrees of color, and purity of the specimen. The best forms to choose are the octahedral and the rhombo-dodecahedral.

It must not be forgotten, in estimating large Rough Diamonds, especially those from the Cape, that certain tints of color may be brought out in the cutting, which do not appear in the stone in its rough state; perfect polish, and the power of reflection natural to the Brilliant, intensify any tint of yellow existing in the stone. This observation does not apply to river stones, but rather the converse.

It is difficult, nay impossible, to quote a standard price for Rough Diamonds, as from what has already been stated, it will be easily understood that the value must vary immensely according to size and quality.

SECTION III.

CHAPTER I.
CORUNDUM.

THE term "Corundum" is used to denote the class of aluminous stones generally; or secondly, to particularize a species or sub-division of that class. It includes in the general term Sapphires, Rubies, Emery, Corundum (proper), and other species or varieties.

The primitive form of the crystals is a six-sided prism, but a common form is the dodecahedron, with faces formed after the figure of isosceles triangles. The crystals are very rough, and often deformed. Twins with rhombic faces are not infrequently met with.

Besides the crystalline form, Corundum appears in compact masses, and in aggregates of grains varying in their size.

PHYSICAL PROPERTIES.

Cleavage, more or less perfect. Fracture, conchoidal and uneven. Structure, brittle. Hardness, 9. It is scratched by the Diamond, but by no other mineral. All imperfect sorts are broken up into polishing material for other stones.

The Blue Sapphire is of equal hardness with the Ruby, and both exceed in hardness Emery or Corundum (proper). Its specific gravity is about 4.

For Rubies and Sapphires 4·6 to 4·8
„ Corundum ... 3·6 „ 4·9
„ Emery ... ... 3·7 „ 4·3

Corundum is sometimes colorless, and then it is very brilliant. As a general rule, however, it is colored blue: (Sapphire), red (Ruby), or else grey, yellow, brown, or green. The streak is white. Its lustre is vitreous, sometimes pearly on the basal planes, occasionally exhibiting a bright opalescent star of six rays in the direction of the axis. The Corundum is transparent. Its refractive index is 1·77, and therefore higher than that of glass, which is 1·5. By friction electricity is developed in it, and in polished specimens the electrical condition remains for a considerable time.

CHEMICAL PROPERTIES.

The characteristic constituent of Corundum is alumina, ($Al^2 O^3$), with a slight admixture of oxide of iron, chromic acid, or some other pigment. Acids have no effect upon it. It fuses not without difficulty with Borax, if in fine powder. Alkalis have no effect upon it.

WHERE FOUND.

Corundum is found (1) associated with sand or detritus with other Precious Stones. (2) In crystalline rocks, such as granite, mica slate, granular limestone or dolomite. (3) In the beds of rivers, either in modified hexagonal prisms, or in masses accompanied by grains of magnetic-iron-ore.

VARIETIES.

SAPPHIRES AND RUBIES.

The prominent forms of crystallization are the six-sided prism and the hexagonal pyramid. The predominant colors are Blue and Red.

SAPPHIRES.

Azure Blue, Indigo, Duck's-neck color, Violet-Blue, Poppy-Red, Cochineal, Carmine, Rose-Red to Rose-White, Milk-White, Yellow-White, French-White, Lemon-color and Green. As a rule, the colors are pure and high. Sometimes a crystal is found exhibiting a variety of colors. The Asteria or Star Sapphire shows, under the microscope, thread-like shafts directed towards the faces of the six-sided prisms, said to be spaces left at the moment of crystallization, and it is the reflection of light from these which give to the stone its star-like brilliancy.

The Blue variety is called Sapphire in its limited sense. The Red variety is the Ruby.

Other varieties deserve notice, such as Spinel, Garnet, Zircon, etc.

WHERE FOUND.

Asia.

The finest Rubies and Sapphires are found in largest quantities in Burmah, at Mo-gast and Kiat-pyan, five days' journey from Ava.

The small Sapphires of Ceylon are well-nigh all of a rose-red. They can be obtained easily from old collections, as they were formerly used officially. They are so clearly crystallized that they are easily distinguished from Spinel, which often accompanies them. Those found in Ceylon, Siam, and other Eastern countries, are remarkable for their colors. They are found like rolled pebbles in channels of rivers, and the colors run through green, red, yellow, and black. Bertolacci affirms that "the brilliancy and beauty of those in Pegu far exceed that of those found in Ceylon."

At the foot of the Capelan Mountain, near Sirian, a city of Pegu, and in the vicinity of Candy, Corundum is also found in the detritus of Granite, Magnetic-iron, Zircon, &c., all having been probably washed down from the granite mountains.

In Ceylon the Sapphire is common, the Ruby very rare; but the converse is the case in Pegu.

There are famous mines of Rubies at Badakshan in Usbekistan, a part of Tartary. The mines were known to the Emperors of Delhi. They are near the Oxus, near Shunan. There is a belief among the natives that two large Rubies are always near together: thus it is that the fortunate finder of the one hides it until he has found the twin like it; failing this, they will often break a large one in two. There is a belief also that the Ruby is the product of the transformation of limestone, and that it is found in the form of pebbles. Near to the Ruby mines a great quantity of Blue Felspar is obtained.

America.

It is affirmed that in North America, the Sapphire is found of a beautiful blue, with Hornblende, Mica, Felspar, Tourmaline, Ironstone, Talc and Calc-spar, and also well-formed six-sided prisms or rhombohedra of good size.

Granulated limestone, accompanied by Spinel and Rutile, with pale-blue Crystals and Kyanite, are found in Connecticut and Pennsylvania, with a greyish Corundum in fine crystals; also in Chester County, crystals are found with Tourmaline. In Margarite and Albite some of the masses are said to weigh 4,000lbs. A boulder of massive Corundum affording broad cleavage surfaces was found in North Carolina.

South America.

A fine Red Sapphire, in company with the Diamond, is said to have been found.

South Australia.

At Ballarat, in Victoria, the Blue and White Sapphires are found with some specimens highly crystallized, and exhibiting beautiful dichroism; and it is affirmed that in the hanging-rock caves, by the Pearl River, in New South Wales, blue and white striped six-sided prisms of beautiful Rubies and Sapphires are found.

Europe.

In Bohemia, from the Iser Mountains, small rounded crystals of Sapphire have been found, mostly in the quartz sand and detritus of granite. The land about the Iser table-land is in part marshy, and in part covered with forests. The little Iser rushes through, its rapid current carrying the detritus in which the minerals in small quantities and size are found. But the Sapphires found in the Giant Mountains often exceed in beauty and color those of Ceylon. The beds of the Iser—bed and meadow—appear to have been much, although irregularly, worked.

Small crystals are found in Saxon Switzerland, in alluvial soil, and are said to occur at St. Gothard, of a red or blue tinge, in Dolomite.

Corundum (proper) and Diamond Spar.

The mineral generally termed Corundum, is found in crystals with rough planes as a rule, and in individualized masses of a particular cleavage. The Rhombohedral form occurs as in the former varieties, but here only in combinations. The fracture is uneven. The colors, generally dull, are of Greenish-grey, Greenish-white, Asparagus tint, Oil, Pearl Grey, Flesh or Rose Red, sometimes of a Chestnut Brown. It has only an inferior degree of transparency. The last named variety comes from China, and because a peculiar bluish light, occasionally plays upon it, Werner called it "Diamond Spar." It is said that some crystals found near St. Gothard, exhibit two colors, and that some of these are in Dolomite, but more commonly they are found in mass. Some in Styria have grown in with the granite, and so firmly that it is difficult, if not impossible, to remove them without damage. The crystals may be from the size of a pea, to that of a hazel nut, of a greenish-blue or duck's-neck violet. Some pieces display several colors. In Bohemia they are found embedded in pebbly masses of Hercinite. In Rhodes, Sweden, and the Urals, they may also be found with Tourmaline in schist, with Platinum and magnetic iron ore. In Ceylon, China, and India, they are found in beautiful green crystals, possessing characteristic stripes, with black Hornblende.

3.—EMERY.

It is found in small, compact, and fine-grained conglomerate varieties, in color varying from bluish-green to indigo blue, generally deriving its impurity from magnetic iron ore. For ages past Emery has served as material for polishing other minerals. The Jews called it *Shameer.* "The sin of Judah is written with a pen of iron and with the point of a *Diamond.*"

Emery is also found in large boulders in Naxos, which has long been famous for this stone. This island has, running through it from north to south, a chain of mountains, partly formed of granite. In the granite is granulated lime with deep fissures, enclosing Emery with layers of Mica. Of late years, the quantity annually produced on this island, for the Government, has been 50,000 centners. The Emery which is sought for technical purposes is a mixture of greenish-white Corundum and magnetic iron stone. Sometimes indeed, though rarely, in the middle of a mass of Emery, a regular prism of dark Blue Corundum is found. The best place for finding Emery in the island of Naxos, is Bothri. Its usual color is ashy-grey, which at times gets a reddish-brown tinge from the oxide of iron. Emery acts powerfully upon the magnet. Of late years we have obtained an important quantity from Asia Minor (twelve miles east of Ephesus), but it is not so good in quality as that obtained from the island of Naxos. For its discovery here, as well as in Kula, Adula, and Manser, this last being twenty-four miles north of Smyrna, we are indebted to Dr. Lawrence Smith. According to Dr. Smith, Emery is a combination of Corundum, magnetic iron oxide, and iron-mica. This last can be clearly seen by means of a microscope.

CHAPTER II.

THE ORIENTAL RUBY.

THE Oriental Ruby is a Corundum, and is sometimes found loose in sand or débris in company with other Precious Stones, but more often it is embedded in Granite, Basalt, Gneiss, Talc, Syenite, and Hornblende. It consists of alumina with a little coloring matter. The specific gravity of the Oriental Ruby is 4·6 to 4·8, and its hardness 9. It will cut Sapphire, Emerald, Topaz, Rock Crystal, and all other stones, save the Diamond. It possesses double refraction, though in a small degree, and the electric condition obtained by friction remains for hours. Its color is Carmine, Cochineal, or Pigeon-blood, and Rose-red, often with a play of Violet. It is frequently asserted that the white spots often detected on the rough stone, may be removed by careful appliance of heat; but this is not true, and it is certainly a dangerous experiment, for if heat be recklessly applied, it will split the stone into pieces. Kluge says "that before the blow-pipe it shows a remarkable change of colors, which is the more striking in the small pieces. If small crystals are made red hot and allowed to cool, they become colorless, then after a time green, and lastly they regain their beautiful red color." I cannot vouch for this from my own experience, but if true, this experiment would be most valuable, as the means of ascertaining the genuineness of the Oriental Ruby: crystals of Red Spinel never become green in the process of heating and cooling.

The so-called Brazilian Ruby is a Pink Topaz, and differs entirely in its characters from Rubies. Its specific gravity is 3·4 to 3·6. Hardness 8. It cuts Rock Crystal, but less easily than the others; possesses double refraction, and retains electricity for twenty-four hours. Broken pieces when heated show a phosphorescent blue light. The original color of most of these Rubies is yellow, and it is by means of heat they receive the beautiful bright red or dark cochineal; they are found mostly in the débris of Mica-schist, in brown iron-stone, or in quartz veins.

There are some very famous and remarkable Rubies on record. For example, there was an Oriental Ruby of the size of a pigeon's egg in the crown of the Empress Catharine of Russia, which is said to have been presented to her by Gustavus III. of Sweden, when on a visit to St. Petersburg, 1777. One in Paris, seen by Farctière, weighed 406½ carats, and Chardin speaks with admiration of a Ruby cut "*en cabochon*," of great beauty, and of the size and form of half an egg, having the name of "*Thelk Lephy*" engraved on the point.

There are two very large Rubies in the possession of the King of Awakan, in India.

The King of Ada has a perfect Ruby of the size of a small hen's egg, which he wears as an eardrop.

The slippers of Chinese and Indian women are ornamented with Rubies cut *en cabochon*, that is, with convex, non-faceted tops; vases, armour, scabbards and harness, are also graced by the same stone in India and China, These stones, however, are of little value. Bags of them are, indeed, laid beneath the foundations of buildings, the idea prevailing that good fortune was thus secured to the structure.

It is reported that the King of Burmah has a Ruby of the size of a pigeon's egg and of extraordinary quality, but no European has seen it.

The two most important Rubies ever known in Europe, were brought into this country during the year 1875. One was a dark-colored stone, cushion-shape, weighing 37 carats, the other a blunt, drop-shape, of $47\frac{1}{16}$ carats.

It was deemed advisable to have these stones re-cut; and the work was entrusted to Mr. James N. Forster, of London, who re-cut the stone of 37 carats to $32\frac{3}{16}$, and the one of 47 carats to $39\frac{3}{16}$. They were much improved by the re-cutting, and competent judges pronounced them the finest stones of their size yet seen, their color being truly magnificent. I have reason to believe that the smaller stone of the two was sold abroad for over £10,000; the larger one likewise found a purchaser on the continent. The fact of two such fine gems appearing contemporaneously is unparalleled in the history of Precious Stones in Europe. It is questionable, however, if the London market would ever have seen these truly royal gems, but for the poverty of the Burmese Government, which is said to have been the cause of their disposal. In Burmah, the sale of these two Rubies caused intense excitement: a military guard being considered necessary to escort the persons conveying the package to the vessel. No regalia in Europe contains two such fine and important Rubies.

The most beautiful Rubies come from the kingdom of

Burmah, about five days' journey east-south-east of Ava. The inhabitants believe that they ripen in the earth; that they are at first colorless and crude, and gradually as they ripen become yellow, green, blue, and last of all, *red*, this being considered the highest point of beauty and ripeness. There is a law in force in Burmah, which deprives the market of the most beautiful Rubies. Whoever finds a Ruby of a certain weight (100 Ticals), is bound, under pain of losing his life, to deliver it up to the Financial Department of the Government. In order to avoid this loss of life and property the finder breaks it up into small pieces, thereby causing infinitely greater loss to the Government than he gains. Surely this is a traveller's tale. It was thought that when Pegu, the "Fatherland of Rubies," was annexed to England in 1852, Europe would be the richer in these beautiful stones, but it has not proved so. It appears that certain dangers exist, or are said to exist, in the lands where Rubies are found, such as wild beasts and reptiles. It is possible that these may be exaggerated by the Ruby merchants in order to hinder competition. The King of Burmah is known to be excessively fond of these stones. He jealously prohibits the export of them, so that, save through the agency of private individuals or by stealth, scarcely any Rubies pass out of his country.

Very beautiful Rubies have been found in a part of Tartary called Badakshan for many years. They are found also on the slopes of the Oxus, near to Shushan and Charan. The inhabitants believe that Rubies always occur in "pairs." When one of the seekers has fortunately discovered one, he will frequently hide it till its mate is found.

The Oriental Ruby is indisputably one of the most valuable of Precious Stones. Theophrastus speaks of it as incombustible, and as having the appearance of a burning coal when held up to the sun. He is said to have given forty gold pieces for a very small one. The price paid for this stone by the Ancients was very high. According to Benvenuto Cellini, in his time a perfect Ruby of a carat weight cost 800 Ecus d'Or, whilst a Diamond of like weight cost only 100.

In this our day fine Rubies under half-a-carat—

If English cut, cost from	£4 to £10
If Indian cut	,,	£1 ,, £4

Those over a carat in weight are, according to the quality, from £20 to £100 per carat; but no definite price can be given as a guide to the purchaser. No stone increases so much in value, in relation to size,—all excellencies being the same,—as the Oriental Ruby. One of less than twenty-four carats weight, the property of an Indian prince, has been bought for 156 lbs. weight of gold. It ranks first for price and beauty amongst all colored stones. When a perfect Ruby of five carats, is brought into the market a sum will be offered for it ten times the price given for a Diamond of the same weight; and if a Ruby reaches the weight of ten carats it is almost invaluable.

Rubies with flaws, or with specks of a milky appearance on the table or beneath it, and Rubies of too deep or too light a color, are now much depreciated in value. In former years, when the inferior stones could be sold in the foreign markets, they were worth at least fifty per cent. more than they are at the present time.

There are, it is true, many large Rubies to be met with in the market, and this statement may seem to contradict the above assertion, but these are by no means of the same value as the Burmese Rubies. They come from

Siam, and have a distinctly dark brown tint, marring the true "pigeon's blood" hue. This variety does not realise above half the price obtained for Rubies of the same size of the true color.

For a representation of the Ruby in its native, or rough state, see colored illustrations.

CHAPTER III.

THE SAPPHIRE.

NO Precious Stone is more interesting to the general reader than this. In old Arabic it was termed "Sappeer," to scratch; and in Syriac and Hebrew, by verbs cognate and of similar signification. The Chaldean characters of the alphabet and ancient books were called by the same "word," probably because of the great hardness of the Sapphire, and the ease with which stones and rocks could be scratched or engraven by it. This gem is known to almost all nations by the one name Sapphire. It is a Corundum, and is found most frequently in secondary deposits, loose in sand, or in debris, with other Precious Stones. Occasionally, however, it is found embedded in primary deposits, in Granite, Syenite, Basalt, Gneis, Talc, and Hornblende, strata of specular iron, and magnetic ironstone.

The type of its crystallization is the six-sided prism, and the hexagonal pyramid. Its specific gravity is 3·9 to 4·2. In color it is a beautiful blue, like to that of the blossom of the little weed called the "corn-flower;" and the more velvety its appearance, the greater the value

T

of the stone. The Oriental Sapphire retains its exquisite color by gas-light, while that of the less valuable becomes black, or like to an Amethyst in color. Pliny knew this gem well, and speaking of its color compares it to the same flower as we do. It can now be imitated, but the Ancients had no idea of the possibility of such a thing; and yet the dark-blue glass of the antique vase, with its dazzling white bas relief, in the British Museum, is world-renowned for its color and exquisite beauty. No doubt the color of the Sapphire depends upon a small *ingredient* of chrome. Strange to say, up to quite modern times it was regarded as a medicine, and very extraordinary powers were attributed to it. It was dedicated by the Greeks to Apollo, because, when consulting his oracle, they thought that the possession of this gem, from its heavenly nature, would secure them an early and favourable answer.

In consequence of its hardness, its beautiful color, and its bright, vivid lustre, it is one of the most prized as well as one of the most fashionable of gems. It will always be an article of luxury from its comparatively high price.

The Ancients knew and made use of the Sapphire, but rarely for outward adornment, possibly because of the difficulty of manipulating so hard a stone. For personal ornaments it receives the form of the Brilliant, which shows to best advantage the lustre of the stone.

Sapphires were originally obtained from Arabia and Persia; but now the finest stones are imported from the kingdom of Burmah. The same laws are in force, regarding the finding of Sapphires, as noticed in the chapter on Rubies. In Ceylon, Sapphires are not rare; they are found in the debris of the mountains. In North America, Sapphires are found in rhomboid crystals, or six-sided prisms, of a beautiful blue, in combination with Hornblende,

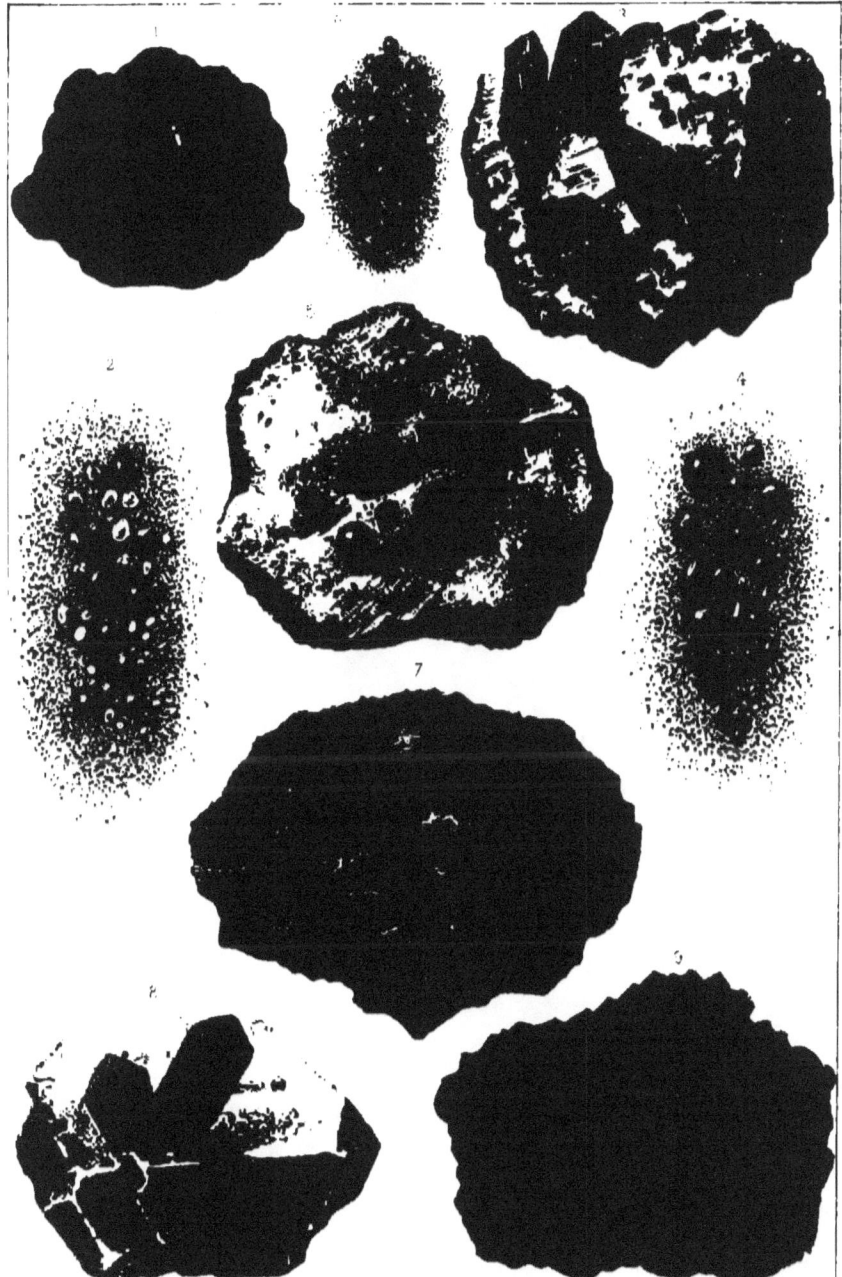

Glimmer, Felspar, Iron-pyrites, Talc, and in Granular Limestone ; this is specially the case in Newton, New Jersey. In South Australia (Ballarat, in Victoria), blue and white Sapphires are found so worn away that no trace of crystallization is left. Sapphires are also obtained from the clefts of the hanging rocks on the pearl rivers in New South Wales. Sapphires are found in many parts of Europe ; on the tops of the Iser Mountains in Bohemia. The river Iser having a very rapid current carries with it, in the soil, Sapphires and other Precious Stones, and often deposits them on its shores, far away from their original home. In the Sieben-Gebirge, small Sapphires are found with gold in the sand. In Saxony they are embedded in alluvium ; specially is it so in Saxon Switzerland.

Amongst the celebrated Sapphires is that which was seen by the English ambassador, who was sent to Ava. It was said to be 951 carats in weight, of a beautiful blue, and without a flaw. In the collection of minerals in the Jardin des Plantes, in Paris, is one of the most beautiful Blue Sapphires, weighing $132\tfrac{1}{16}$ carats, without spot or fault. This stone was originally found in Bengal by a poor man ; it subsequently came into the possession of the House of Rospoli, in Rome, who, in their turn, left it to a German prince, who sold it to the French jewel merchant, Perret, for 170,000 francs, a sum much less than its real value.

Notwithstanding the extreme hardness of the Sapphire, there are some beautifully engraved specimens still in existence. In the Cabinet of Strozzi, in Rome, is a Sapphire, a masterpiece of art, with the profile of Hercules engraven on it by Cneïus. A very remarkable and famous Sapphire, belonging to the Marchese Rinuccini, weighing fifty-three carats, has a representation of a hunting scene engraven on it, with the inscription, Constantius Aug. Among a number of old family jewels recently in my possession, I found a Sapphire beautifully engraved with the crest and arms of Cardinal Wolsey.

The value of these stones is very much determined by special circumstances, and like the Diamond, its color, purity, and size are taken into consideration when fixing the sum to be paid. Fine Sapphires under the carat in weight, if English cut, vary from £4 to £12 ; if Foreign cut, £2 to £5 ; those of a carat weight, £12 to £25. Sapphires, do not, like the Ruby, rise in price as they increase in size.

The Oriental Sapphire is the most highly valued; and a perfect stone, weighing about three carats, is even more costly than a Diamond of like weight and similar quality. Those imperfections which appear at times in the Sapphire, and which lessen its value, are clouds, milky half-opaque spots, white glassy stripes, rents, knots, a congregating of colors at one spot and silky-looking flakes on the table of the stone. Not only are other stones of like order sold for the Sapphire, but even glass, (technically called flux).

Varieties of "Doublet," (that is counterfeit stones, composed of two pieces of crystal, with a color between them, so that they have the same appearance as if the whole substance of the crystal were colored), are passed not infrequently for Sapphires. They may be distinguished from the genuine stone partly by their color, but more especially by a careful examination of the girdle, when, should the Sapphire have been joined to an inferior stone, the attempted deception will be detected.

⁎ *For a representation of the Sapphire in its native or rough state, see colored Illustrations.*

CHAPTER IV.

THE EMERALD.

OPINIONS differ much as to the length of time the true Emerald has been known and valued; yet it is evident that it was known to the Ancients, for we ourselves have seen ornaments made of Emeralds, which have been excavated from Pompeii and Herculaneum. Similar ornaments have been found in the ruins of old Rome, and even on the Egyptian mummies. Pliny also alludes to some old Emerald mines on the Arabian Sea, which Caillaud discovered when sent by the Pasha of Egypt on an exploring mission. He found many of the caves or mines so large that 400 men could work together in them: and that they had been used long before was clear, as he there saw, ropes, levers, lamps, tools of various kinds, and many vessels. Pliny declares that the Emerald stood very high in the estimation of the Ancients.

We read also of Nero and Domitian using Emeralds as ornaments for their dress. Democritus of Thrace was famous for the art of imitating the Emerald. Seneca tells us that Democritus could put the fire and color of an Emerald into a common pebble.

Isidorus, Bishop of Seville (630 A.D.), says of the Emerald "that it surpasses in greenness all green stones, and even the leaves of plants, and that it imparts to the air around it a green shimmer; that its color is most soothing to the eyes of those engaged in cutting and polishing the stone."

Psellos, in the 11th century, says of the Emerald, "that it is leek-green, playing easily into gold and blue; and that it has power, when mixed with water, to heal leprosy and other diseases."

In the middle ages, it was much used to ornament church treasures; and in the tiara of the Popes there was an Emerald an inch long and one-and-a-quarter thick.

After the discovery of Peru, Emeralds became less rare, and jewellers and lapidaries much preferred those from Peru; hence the most beautiful of Emeralds are always called Peruvian Emeralds. Joseph D'Acosta, who himself visited the Emerald mines of New Granada and Peru, said that at first these stones came to Europe in such numbers, that on the ship in which he returned from America to Spain, in 1587, were two chests, each containing one cwt. of Emeralds. Most of the Emeralds now come from Santa-Fé and the valley of Tunka, between the mountains of New Granada and Popagan.

Europe.—Ural Mountains.

The Ural and Altai Mountains have of late years furnished true Emeralds of the finest quality. The first Emerald was found accidently by a charcoal burner in 1830, at the root of a tree on the east side of the Ural, in the district of Perni. This was at once followed up by a regular working of the bed, which yielded in the first year several good Emeralds, one of the extraordinary size of $101\frac{1}{4}$ carats; but unfortunately the yield gradually decreased.

Austria—Salzburg.

Those found here are dark-green, six-sided prisms, often covered with Glimmer, and not perfectly transparent.

Asia.

It is very doubtful whether any Emerald mines ever existed in India. Those that are imported from that country are never in the rough, but cut in an unfinished style by the Indian lapidaries. On arriving in Europe, it is always necessary to re-cut them, so as to develope their full beauty by perfect workmanship. It is very difficult to say whence they are obtained, as they are of quite a different quality from those found in South America.

In the kingdom of Burmah, near to Ava, they are found in the sands, or beds of small rivers, with pure gold and Spinel. The Sultan of Oude presented our Queen with a Burmese Emerald as large as a moderate-sized hen's egg.

There are some valuable beds of Emeralds and Topaz on the Chinese borders of Siberia.

Africa.—Egypt.

The Egyptian Emeralds have always held high rank in consequence of their richness of color. According to Pliny the celebrated mines in former times were in the rocks round about Coptos; and the stones were admired for their brilliant sheen. Mahommed Ben Mantur (13th century) describes the Emerald mines as being on the borders of the land of the negroes, and yet belonging to the kingdom of Egypt: the stones found here being dug out of Talc and also red earth. De Laet thinks that the same region supplied Emeralds as late as the 17th century.

The mines of which we know most are in the mountains of the Sahara (the beds being of mica-slate), and the bed of the River Harrach in Algiers, where it joins the River Qued Bouman. In the latter, Emerald-crystals have been found in white lamellated lime, which probably belonged to the chalk mountains. Large Emeralds have been found in the débris of Dolomite mountains.

America.—Columbia, Tunka Valley.

One of the most celebrated Emerald mines of the Tunka Valley, is that of Muzo, 5° 39' 50'' N. latitude, and 76° 45' W. longitude (from Paris), N.N.W. of Bogata. It was discovered by Lanchero in 1555, but the Spaniards did not commence working it until 1568. It is now worked by a company who pay an annual rent for it to the Government, and employ 120 workmen. It has the form of a tunnel of about 100 yards deep, with very inclined walls. On the summit of the mountains, and quite near to the mouth of the mine are large lakes, whose waters are shut off by means of water-gates, which can be easily shifted when the laborers require the water. When the waters are freed they rush with great rapidity down the the walls of the mine, and on reaching the bottom of it, they are conducted by means of an underground canal through the mountain into a basin. The matrix of the Emerald is a bituminous lime, rich in carbon, deposited on old red sandstone and clay slate. To obtain the Emeralds, the workmen begin by cutting steps on the inclined walls of the mine, in order to make firm resting places for their feet. The overseer places the men at certain distances from each other, to cut out a wide step with the help of pickaxes. The loosened stones fall by their own weight to the bottom of the mine. When this begins to fill, a sign is given to let the waters loose, which rush down with great vehemence, carrying the fragments of rock with them, through the mountain, into the basin. This operation is repeated until the horizontal beds are exposed, in which the Emeralds are found. The Emeralds are sometimes accompanied by beautiful crystals of iron-pyrites and now and then by parasite crystals. An Emerald is not unfrequently found in fragments which, when placed together, form one beautiful crystal. It has been supposed that in the moment of formation the stone became divided, and continued, when separated, its crystallization. Another remarkable circumstance is that the Emeralds break shortly after being separated from the matrix. This is sometimes prevented by a little foresight, viz., by placing the stones into a vessel for some days, and protecting them from the rays of the sun.

The Emerald is found cropping up out of the earth in low prisms or columns, without stripes and without any inclination to the cylindrical form. It is sometimes, though not often, found in pebbles or grains. The color varies from what is called Emerald-green, to grass-green, and greenish-white. Subjected to the Dichroscope, it shows clearly Emerald-green and sea-green. The variety of opinion as to the source of the beautiful color of the Emerald is very interesting. According to some authorities it is said to owe its beauty to the chrome which it contains. On the other hand Levy, who analysed with great care the Emeralds from the Muzo mines of New Granada, found that they contained an organic matter, a simple combination of carburet of hydrogen, and that the intensity of the color depended upon the amount of this organic matter contained in the Emerald. Of protoxide of chromium he found but .01 per cent. Blum, experimenting upon the color of the Emerald, exposed this stone for four minutes to an intense heat, and then threw it into the water, the consequence of which was that it fell into several pieces, some of which were of a black, and others of a greenish tint. The color of an Emerald loses somewhat of its intensity by long use, in consequence of the softness of the stone.

According to Mohs, its hardness varies from 7·3 to 8 ; the specific gravity 2·67 to 2·73.

The value of an Emerald depends greatly upon its color ; for example,—

A light color, almost white, is worth 5/- a carat.
Lightest green ... ... 20/- „
A fair body of color ... ... 100/- „
Good color, with flaws, from £10 to £15 „
Pure color and clear ... £20 to £30 „
Very fine dark color, velvety, and without flaws, as high as ... £50 to £60 „

This last, however, is very rare. Perhaps there is no stone which suffers more than the Emerald from inequality of structure, color and transparency, clouds and spots.

Fashion greatly influences the value of the Emerald. When retained to enhance the price, it yields to the potent attraction of other first-class gems and the demand subsides ; when freely admitted into the market the taste often revives, as fashion springs not infrequently from the exhibition of color under favorable circumstances. The Sapphire has now supplanted the Emerald in general estimation.

Pliny gives the following anecdote as an illustration of the fire and lustre of the Emerald. " In the Island of Cyprus stands the sepulchre of King Hermias, on which is a lion formed of marble, but with eyes of Emeralds, which shone so brightly on the surrounding sea that the tunny fish were frightened away ; the fishermen, having long observed this phenomenon, resolved to remove this disadvantage, and so have replaced the Emeralds by other stones which have not this property of sparkling brightness." What was due to the shadow of the figure was not considered.

In the Manta Valley, the natives are said to have worshipped an Emerald of the size of an ostrich's egg, under the title of goddess of Emeralds. The priests permitted her, to be seen by the worshippers only on high festivals, when the poor people were expected to bring Emeralds as offerings to their goddess; thus they became possessed of a large collection of these Precious Stones, which fell into the hands of the Spaniards after the discovery of Peru. Don Alvarado and his followers, who evidently knew nothing of the brittle character of the Emerald, had them broken to pieces, firmly believing that had they been genuine stones, they would have resisted the power of the hammer.

⁎ *For a representation of the Emerald in its native or rough state, see colored Illustrations.*

CHAPTER V.

SPINEL AND BALAS RUBIES.—VARIETIES.

a.—PRECIOUS SPINEL.

SMALL crystals are found loose, or embedded in granular limestone. Colors: carmine, carmoisine, cochineal, rose-red, to reddish-white, cherry-juice, hyacinth, and brownish-red, reddish-brown, yellowish-brown, and orange-yellow. It is transparent, translucent, and receives its red tinge from chromic acid.

It is found loose in the sand in the province of Mysore, in the Madras Presidency, and in Hindostan; but in Burmah, Pegu, Ceylon, Saffragan, and Matura, in well-formed, sharp-angled, and, for the most part, octahedral crystals. It is also found in the sands of rivers and in inundated lands, accompanied by Zircon, Garnet, and magnetic iron ore; and in granite, accompanied by Apatite.

North America.

In the region between Amity and Andover there is much granular limestone and serpentine in which Spinel abounds. Sometimes the crystals are as much as sixteen inches in diameter.

The Spinel-crystal belongs to the regular gem system, and its form has the octahedron for its base. Spinel is found in fragments or pebbles. Twin crystals frequently occur. It is distinguished from the Ruby by its peculiar formation and inferior hardness. Cleavage—very imperfect and parallel to the facets of the base; hardness—that of Topaz; specific gravity—3·5 to 3·8.

A peculiarity of Spinel is that the light which is reflected from the depth of the gem, no matter what the color of the stone, is always of a pale yellow. The lustre is vitreous, and displays every degree of transparency. The refraction is simple, and in no stone is this more real and abiding than in this species. It is rendered electric by friction, but not by heat.

Spinel is a combination of alumina and magnesia. The varieties of color are due to the magnesia being replaced partially by iron oxide (Fe.O), zinc oxide (Zn.O), or manganese oxide (Mg.O) and lime (Ca.O); and the alumina, by ferric oxide ($Fe^2.O^3$).

One of the finest specimens of Blue Spinel, a thickish oblong stone, was in the possession of Messrs. Pittar, Leverson & Co., a short time ago. It was an Indian-cut stone, weighing 31⅞ carats. They had it re-cut by Mr. J. N. Foster, of London, and it weighed after re-cutting 25 carats. There is a curious history attached to this stone; it was consigned from India as a Sapphire; subsequently it was found to be a Spinel, whereupon the purchaser returned it to the merchant, who at once wrote to the consignor in India, but the statement was not believed. The merchant determined to have it cut, and afterwards sold it for a much larger sum than it had obtained as a Sapphire.

In the Exhibition of 1862, we find there were two very fine Spinels; one exhibited by Messrs. Hunt & Roskell, which, when it arrived from India, was a cabochon-cut, octagon-shaped stone, of perfect color, and free from flaws.

It weighed 197 carats. This also was cut by Mr. J. N. Foster, to an 81-carat "perfection stone." The other Spinel was also an octagon-shaped stone, of perfect color, very "spread," and free from flaws. It weighed $102\frac{1}{4}$ carats, and was re-cut to $72\frac{1}{2}$ carats. It is strange that both these stones arrived from India in the same year, viz., 1861. One collected by Dr. Heron is said to weigh 49lbs.; it is in three pieces, and contains cavities studded with crystals of Corundum.

Europe.

In Meronitz, in Bohemia, little rose-red crystals are found, in company with Pyrites; also in the Liebenburgen, in gold sand. At Aker, in Sweden, pale-blue and pale-grey varieties are found in limestone.

Australia.

Crystals are found in the Ovens River, in Victoria, and also in the pearl rivers of New South Wales, and in other parts of Australasia.

b.—THE BLUE SPINEL.

In Sweden, Antwerp, and Ceylon, crystals are found, both loose and imbedded. They are easily distinguished by their foliated fracture; color generally of faint-blue, violet-indigo, and seladine-green. Translucent. Contain 3 to 4 per cent. of iron.

c.—PLEONASTE.

This mineral received the name of Ceylanite, from Romè d' l'Isle, who analyzed it with a number of others, brought from Ceylon. Haüy, seeing its crystal was like that of the Spinel, desired to give it a special position in the system of minerals, and named it *Pleonaste*, which signifies superfluity. Further investigation showed that it was in reality a black variety of the Spinel.

The specific gravity of this stone rises from 3·5 to 3·8. It consists principally of alumina, and about 10 per cent. of protoxide of iron. Its infusibility before the blow-pipe, and its formation with borax into an iron-colored glass, are the surest indications of Pleonaste. Acids have but little influence upon it. It is found in Russia and other cold climates, but it is also found in Ceylon, as well as in the Dolomite region in Ratan.

Spinel, in consequence of its lustre, color, and hardness, is used for personal ornament, and for objects of luxury; but it is only when the crystals are fine and large that they are considered gems. In cutting, it receives the same form as the Ruby.

Spinel Ruby or Balas Ruby varies in value according to its cut and color.

In the inventory of the French Crown Jewels, in the year 1791, we find the following:—

One Spinel Ruby of	56¼ carats	...	50,000	francs.
One ,,	4⅔ ,,	...	300	,,
One ,,	3¾ ,,	...	300	,,
One Balas Ruby	20⅜ ,,	...	10,000	,,
One ,,	12⅜ ,,	...	3,000	,,
At the present time, small stones range from		...	5/- to 10/- a carat.	
Medium stones, of fair color		20/- to 40/-		,,
Large stones ...	...	...	60/- to 100/-	,,

Specimen stones attain even a higher value.

BALAS OR BALAIS RUBY.

(*so called.*)

These gems are pale-red, or rose-red, with a tinge of blue appearing at the angles of the octahedron, which gives them a milky kind of shimmer and depreciates their value. The color is due to chromic acid.

The Balas Ruby varies much in price; for example, a dark rose-red of 10 millimetres, square-cut, and polished as a Brilliant, pure and lustrous, will sell for 300 francs; while a pale-rose of like size, will be worth 20 francs only; its value depends entirely on the demand and the character of the stone, occasionally a fine specimen of five carats will realize £50.

As long ago as the last half of the 13th century, Marco Polo collected them in Balascia or Ballahia, on the Upper Oxus, where they were found below the surface soil.

CHAPTER VI.

THE OPAL.

THE Opal is a non-crystalline, compact body, having a vitreous, which often inclines to resinous, or to pearly lustre. Its hardness is 5·5 to 6. The specific gravity is only 2 to 2·1, which is attributable, in some cases, to accidental cavities in the stone, which are sometimes filled with drops of water. Although possessing no color which can properly be called its own, it exhibits flashes of the most brilliant colors: this is the result of the number of fissures which traverse it, and which are filled with air and moisture. It is composed of 90 per cent. of silica and 10 per cent. water. When first taken out of the earth it is soft, but it hardens by exposure to the air. Before the blow-pipe the Opal is infusible, but the water driven out by heat renders it opaque. It has the curious property of improving by wear, as warmth brings out the brilliant tints for which the Opal is famed.

Nicols gives a quaint description of this stone. He says, "The Opal is a Precious Stone which hath in it the bright, fiery flame of the Carbuncle, the fine, refulgent purple of an Amethyst, and a whole sea of the Emerald's green glory; and every one of them shining with an incredible mixture and very much pleasure." Boetius says, "that it is the fairest and most pleasing of all other jewels, by reason of its various colors." Cardanus says, "I bought one for 15 crowns, which gave me as much pleasure as a Diamond of 500 aureos." Onomacritus, writing 500 years B.C., says, "The delicate color and tenderness of the Opal reminds me of a loving and beautiful child." Pliny says, "It is made up of the glories of the most precious gems, and to describe it is a matter of inexpressible difficulty."

The precious Opal, used in *bijouterie*, is found almost entirely in Hungary. It was called Oriental Opal by the Greek and Turkish merchants, who obtained it from the celebrated mines of Czerwenitz and carried it to the East for the purpose of giving the title Oriental to it, which always conveyed a sense of goodness and value to stones. If it were necessary to prove that Opal does not exist in India we could state that Dhuleep Singh, on revisiting that Empire, carried two Opals to his mother as a gift that should bear the charm of novelty.

The mountain range in Hungary, where the Opal is found, consists of a kind of porphyry, which likewise yields lead, silver, and gold; and near the celebrated Czerwenitz district traces of quicksilver also occur. The two highest mountains of this range are Simonka and Libanka, and it is from these that the precious Opal comes, and observation leaves no doubt that the Opal mass, originally in a liquid condition, filled up the cavities in the porphyry veins and gradually solidified. This stone is found in Honduras, Zimapan, Mexico, and Brazil. It also occurs in thin slabs in Queensland, and it has recently been discovered in other parts of Australia in large blocks. Opals are found at Sandy Brae, in Ireland, in porphyry, though not in specimens worthy of cutting; also in several parts of Denmark, and in Frankfort, embedded in dolerite. In South Australia the Opal in its play of color is similar to that of Hungary.

The Opal is cut and polished first upon a leaden plate covered with Emery, next on a wooden wheel with fine pumice powder, and lastly on a wheel covered with felt. Delicate handling is requisite to turn out an Opal to the best advantage.

The work of engraving the Opal requires great care on account of the numberless fissures, which it is dangerous to open to the air, yet there are several engraved Opals in existence. The oldest example is an Intaglio, on a moderately large Opal, of the portrait of Louis XIII. when he was a child; and the head of Juba is engraved upon an Opal in the collection of the Duke of Orleans.

The Hungarian Opals exhibit a uniform milkiness of surface, more or less iridescent. From their greater density, they resist the effects of wear longer than any other sort, hence their superior value. The Mexican stones are beautiful, but so porous, that if they are wetted they become colorless, or after some wear they turn opaque and brown; they are only worth a few pence a carat. A few years ago Hungarian Opals were sold by the piece, now they are sold by the carat: (1) the smaller stones, £1 to £1 10s. per carat; (2) medium ones, £2 to £3; (3) larger stones, £3 to £5; (4) specimens of great size and purity, on account of their extreme rarity, are well-nigh invaluable.

There is a peculiar history connected with an Opal about the size of a hazel-nut, which Pliny gives. This particular Opal was possessed by Nonius, and was valued at £20,000 of our money. Nonius, who was proscribed by Marc Antony for the sake of this gem, made his escape, carrying off the ring with him, as the sole relic of his fortune. He preferred exile with his Opal to living in Rome without it.

The two largest specimens of "Fire Opal" known in this country, were found in the Hungarian mines in 1866; and were exhibited by the late Madame Goldschmidt in the Paris International Exhibition of 1867. Both stones are of the "drop," or pear-shape form, one weighing 186 carats, the other 160 carats; this latter, a magnificent "Harlequin Opal," is reputed on good authority to be the finest gem of its class ever seen.

There is, in the Imperial Cabinet of Vienna, an Opal nearly as large as a man's fist, and weighing 17 ozs. Perhaps the finest Opal of modern times was that of the Empress Josephine, which was called the "Burning of Troy," from the numberless red flames blazing on its surface, the obverse being opaque, which is one of the forms of the Honduras Opal.

There are innumerable superstitions surrounding these gems. By the Ancients they were thought to bestow every possible good. In the middle ages the same belief was held; and in the early part of the seventeenth century the Opal was much more valued than in the present day. But by a strange freak of fashion, the Opal has lost its pristine glory, and is now falsely accused of bringing ill-luck. Sir Walter Scott is in a great measure answerable for this, as readers of *Anne of Geierstein* well know. It seems strange that in this enlightened nineteenth century, there should still be people believing in the bad fortune supposed attendant on the wearing of Opals. Yet withal it is a favorite stone with the Queen, and with the members of most of the European royal families; and without doubt the stone will, ere long, be as much appreciated as it was in earlier times. It is inevitable that the idea of ill-fortune attending the wearing of the Opal, should go the way of all superstitions.

BLACK OPAL.

This is a stone that has appeared lately in the market and, like anything new or uncommon, was immediately sought after. A heavy price is readily paid for it. The ordinary Opal is worth, say 60/- the carat if fine, but its black brother has a higher commercial value. Certainly the colors are very lovely in this Opal, yet how they acquire their blackness and deep tints is questionable. Some other hand than unassisted Nature may have been at work. Man is an adept at chemical operations. I may be wrong, and no doubt Baron Goldschmidt, the owner of the Hungarian mines, would say so; but still it is well to have an opinion based on experience. A specimen of the size of a hen's egg, was not long since sold in Paris for 25,000 francs. I have one in my possession of similar size, and the colors are certainly attractive. At present these stones are rare.

⁎ *For a representation of the Opal in its native or rough state, see colored Illustrations.*

CHAPTER VII.
THE CAT'S EYE.

MUCH confusion exists concerning this very curious and valuable gem, a confusion arising partly from the ignorance of many in the trade as to its true nature, but principally from the mistakes of those who have written about it. In mineralogical treatises it is usually confounded with, and described as, a particular variety of Quartz, which somewhat resembles it, but which is of little or no mercantile value, although it has occasionally been sent to Europe by unscrupulous merchants as the true Cat's Eye. This *chatoyant* Quartz is found in Ceylon (also the home of the *true* Cat's Eye) in large quantities, and occurs chiefly of various shades of yellow, or brown. It is semi-transparent, and when cut in a convex form (*en cabochon*) shews a more or less defined band of light, with a *silky* lustre, resulting from a reflection of the fibrous-like grain of the stone itself, or more probably from an intimate admixture of asbestos. This Quartz Cat's Eye, even when most perfect, cannot be compared for beauty with the real Cat's Eye, for which it would not be mistaken, even by the uninitiated. It is at once distinguished by its inferior hardness, and want of brilliancy.

Description of True (Chrysoberyl) Cat's Eye.	Description of Quartz Cat's Eye.
Color — Various shades of yellow, brown, and green, rarely black	Color — Various shades of yellow and brown only.
Ray—Iridescent.	Ray—Dull.
Polish—Brilliant.	Polish—Dull.
Hardness—8·5.	Hardness,—6 to 6·5.
Specific gravity—3·8.	Specific gravity—2·65.
Infusible and not affected by acids.	Melts with Soda to a clear glass. Soluble in Fluoric Acid.
Sometimes shewing a beautiful trichroism.	Never trichroic.
Chem. Com. { 80 alumina, 20 glucina, coloring matter — protoxide of iron.	Chem. Com. { 48 silicium, 51 oxygen, with a small amount of oxide of iron and lime.

The true Cat's Eye is a rare variety of the Chrysoberyl, of extreme hardness (in this respect being only inferior to the Diamond and the Sapphire), and is characterized by possessing a remarkable play of light in a certain direction, resulting it is supposed from a peculiarity in its crystalization. This ray of light, or "line," as it is improperly termed by jewellers, shines in fine and well-polished specimens with a phosphorescent lustre.

The Cat's Eye comes principally from Ceylon, where it is found with Sapphires, and is met with of various colors, ranging from pale straw-color through all shades of brown, and from very pale apple-green to the deepest olive. Some specimens, much sought for by Americans, are almost black. The line, however, no matter what ground-color the stone may possess, is always white, and more or less iridescent. This lustre is most beautiful when seen in full sun-light, or by gas-light, when the line becomes more defined and vivid.

This gem is valued principally according to the perfection and brilliancy of the line, which should be well-defined, not very broad, and should run evenly from end to end across the middle of the stone. The color does not influence the value much, some jewellers prefering one tint, some another. On the whole, perhaps, the most popular colors are the clear apple-green and dark olive : both of these form a splendid background, and contrast well with the line. It is quite impossible to give any satisfactory scale of values for this gem. Its estimation depends much on personal appreciation and taste : a ring-stone may be worth from £10 to £100., or even more ; and there are large specimens at present in the market which are worth upwards of £1000.

The Cat's Eye has become more and more fashionable of late years in Europe, and its value has greatly increased.

In India it has always been much prized, and is held in peculiar veneration as a charm against witchcraft, and is the last jewel a Cingalese will part with. The specimens most esteemed by the Indians, are those of a dark olive color, having the ray so bright on each edge as to appear double. It is indeed wonderfully beautiful with its soft, deep color, and mysterious gleaming streak ever shifting, like a restless spirit, from side to side as the stone is moved ; now glowing at one spot, now at another. No wonder that an imaginative and superstitious people regard it with awe and wonder, and, believing it the abode of some genii, dedicate it to their gods as a sacred stone.

CHAPTER VIII.

THE TURQUOISE.

THOMAS Nichols says, "The Turquoise is a hard gem, of no transparency, yet full of beauty: its color is sky-blue, out of a green, in which may be imagined a little milkish infusion. A clear sky, free from all clouds, will most excellently discover the beauty of a true Turquoise." This gem is throughout of the same beauty, as well internally as externally; it requires no help of tincture or foil to set it off in grace, the constancy of its own beauty being its support.

"It hath its name Turcicus," (or Turquoise) says Baccius, "either because of its excellent beauty, or because it is brought from the Turks."

Its exquisite color, which loses nothing by candle-light, is thought to be owing to a certain quantity of protoxide of copper. Those of the Oriental Turquoise, which retain their color perpetually, are said to belong to the "Old Rock;" while those that lose their color, or grow green, are ascribed to the "New Rock."

According to old writers, the Turquoise was found, in

their day, in the remote parts of India, and was conveyed to Turkey to be cut; whence, probably, it derived its name.

Most of the Oriental mineral Turquoise is obtained now from a mountainous district in the north-east of Persia, lying between Mushead and Neshapore, 35° N. Lat. and 58° E. Long.; or from the valley of the Galesteo River, south-east of Santa Fè.

The ore forms thin veins on flinty slate rock, and the people of Bucharest strike it off the matrix, with bullets covered with moss which are thrown from slings, the rocks being generally inaccessible. They then take the ore to the market of Moscow, where it is cut and polished. Boetius says he never saw a Turquoise larger than a filbert.

We only know of Turquoise as compact and uncrystallized, having no cleavage, and possessing a conchoidal fracture and a hardness which is represented by 6, together with a specific gravity of 2·6 to 2·8. Opinions vary as to its chemical nature. Looking at the results of the many analyses, they agree only in proving the presence of phosphate of alumina, oxide of copper, iron and water. It is infusible before the blow-pipe, and cannot be affected by acids. It is doubtful whether the Turquoise was known to the Ancients; but in the middle ages it was well-known and most highly valued, and few stones had such wonderful gifts and virtues attributed to them as this had. But to realise these advantages, it was a necessary condition that the stone should have been received as a gift. Even to this day, in the north-east, there is a proverb, "That a Turquoise given by a loving hand carries with it happiness and good fortune;" and another, "That the color of a Turquoise pales when the well-being of the giver is in danger." The Orientals cut or bored texts from the Koran on Turquoise, and filled up the interstices with gold. There are some very good specimens of engraved mineral Turquoise, but they are neither very ancient, nor many in number. Thomas Nicols speaks of one possessed by the Duke of Hetruria, which was the size of a hazelnut, and had the image of Julius Cæsar engraved on it. There are two in the collection of the Duke of Orleans: on one of which is engraved an image of Diana with her quiver, and on the other that of the Empress Faustina. A jeweller in Moscow has one two inches long, cut in the shape of a heart, and said to have belonged previously to Shah Nadir, who wore it as an amulet. It contains a verse from the Koran, in gold, and 5,000 roubles is the price asked for it.

In the year 1808, a magnificent necklace of Turquoise was sold for 9,000 francs. It consisted of twelve stones, of a beautiful pale blue, none of which were of any great size; but each of them was engraved in relief with a figure of one of the twelve Cæsars.

Major MacDonald lent a very fine Turquoise to the Exhibition of 1851, which had been found in a soft yellow sandstone quarry in the Desert of Arabia; but the so-called MacDonald, or Egyptian Turquoises are of hardly any value, as their color fades when exposed to the light. And so it happened with that exhibited in 1851: it was bought for a large sum of money, but within a year it had so faded as to be almost worthless.

The value of the Turquoise varies considerably: small stones from 1d. to 10/- each; small stones for rings from £1 to £10; large and fine stones for rings from £10 to £50; stones for lockets, bracelets, and other ornaments, increase in value according to their size and quality.

The Fossil Turquoise must not be confounded with the Mineral; as the former is really nothing more than the teeth of fossil mammalia, colored probably by contact with phosphate of iron and copper; it differs entirely from the mineral in composition and original structure, and rarely if ever loses its color. Abroad it is more valued than in England, in consequence of this freedom from outward change, but it is not so valuable as the pure rock Turquoise.

∗ *For a representation of the Turquoise in its rough or native state, see colored Illustrations.*

CHAPTER IX.

STAR-STONES, OR ASTERIA.

THE Orientals had, and still have, a deep veneration for Star Sapphires.

The localities of star-stones are the same as those of other Sapphire crystals.

When light shines upon these stones, stars of six rays are seen, an appearance which attracts much attention, and gives proportionate pleasure. This may be termed its speciality, and is more observable when the stone is convex. The color is a greyish-blue; occasionally blue and red specimens are met with.

These Star-stones, according to their color, are designated Star Ruby, Star Sapphire, or Star Topaz.

Only of late years have they been of any value in England. In Ceylon, but a few years back, they could have been purchased for a few shillings, as the natives had but little regard for them. The finest Star Ruby I have seen was valued at £200 and is in the possession of a private gentleman, who obtained it from a noted collection. If a pair of these stones could be obtained their value would undoubtedly be largely augmented. The price of these gems is mainly determined by their size and quality; small Star Sapphires range from £2 to £10;

large Sapphires, £10 to £100. Star Rubies obtain higher prices; but Star-stones, of a secondary rank, are of little or no value.

The River Sangaris (according to Plutarch) produces a gem called Aster, which is luminous in the dark, and called by the Phrygians "Ballen," "The King." A gem called "Asterites," found inside a huge fish called "Pan," from its resemblance to that god, is also described by Ptolemy Hephæstion. This stone was a potent love-charm, and when exposed to the sun shot forth flames. It was used by Helen of Troy for her own signet, and to it she owed all her conquests. Helen, however, was not of human origin simply, and her beauty was as great at seventy as at seventeen. The term Asteria has been used by different authors in various senses at various times; but Pliny understood by it the same gem that we do at present. The Star Sapphire, is also known under the title of Astrapia (lightning stone), from its supposed action in a colorless or an azure ground, sending out, as it were, rays of lightning diverging from the centre.

SECTION IV.

STONES OF INFERIOR VALUE.*

CHAPTER I.
AMBER.

AMBER is a fossil, and its exterior conditions, as well as its chemical composition, point to its resinous vegetable origin. This view is further strengthened by its occuring in connexion with brown coal and bituminous wood.

If further proof were wanting of the vegetable origin of Amber, it exists in the inclusion of insects, plants, pieces of wood, moss, seed, and little stones, all of which may be seen in that which is found on the coast of the Northern Seas. The condition of this inclusion shews the liquid nature of the resinous matter as it took up and involved the insects; and it shews, also, the subsequent slow process of their petrefaction.

When insects are caught and retained in the tenacious resin of our northern pines, we find as a rule that their

---

* I have thought it advisable to arrange these Stones in alphabetical order, without committing myself to any expression of opinion as to their relative values.

bodies are bent, their feet broken off, or their wings rolled together. It is not so, however, with the insects of the ancient world found buried in Amber, where the most delicate parts of the creature are preserved in the most natural position.

The innumerable organic remains, which this resin has preserved uninjured for thousands of years, give us a marvellous peep into the vegetable kingdom of the Tertiary period, to which Amber belongs. We here see plants quite unknown among the flora of the North sea-coast woods, but which have a relationship to the flora of the coasts of the Mediterranean. The insects embedded in Amber, on the contrary, are like those with which we are quite familiar.

Amber is somewhat brittle, and has a specific gravity of 1, as nearly as possible the same as that of sea-water. Its hardness is 2·4 to 2·5. Its fundamental or ground-color is yellow in all shades, running on one side into white and Hyacinth-red, and on the other into brown and black. The green and blue specimens are never pure.

From the following names given to Amber by various nations, we derive their idea and knowledge of it, viz.: "Yellow," "Gellatinous," "Sap of ligneous matter," "Extract of Straw."

Wherever Amber is found, whether in France, Holland, Greenland, Sweden, Italy, Sicily, Spain, Siberia, China, or India, it is in combination with the brown-coal formation of the Tertiary period. This combination is very instructive. The most prolific fields of Amber are the great plains of north Germany, and the North sea-coasts, between Lymfjord and the Elbe.

Commerce in Amber dates back to very early times, and as was the case thousands of years ago, large quantities are still sent to Breslau, Odessa, and Constantinople. Amber forms a very important industry not only in Dantzic, Königsberg, Stolpe, and Lubeck, but in Vienna, Constantinople, Calamia, and Sicily; indeed, in almost every town where "Galanterie" is acceptable. In Stolpe alone the Amber industry amounts yearly to about £10,000. In Paris the most exquisite wares are made of Amber, and command extraordinary high prices. Innumerable are the articles made of it, amongst others, microscopic lenses, aerometers, and busts. Necklaces, and bracelets of Amber are sent to Egypt and India, and the meanest Turk seeks a piece of it for his pipe, not only because it is pleasant to the lip, but because he has a belief that it will preserve him from inhaling pestilence.

Amber was much valued by the Ancients, particularly by the Romans. The Greeks very early received from the Phœnicians chains made of Amber, both for the neck and arms, and it is mentioned in connexion with heathen mythology from very ancient times. The sisters of Phaeton, mourning and weeping at his unhappy end, attracted the pity of the gods, who mercifully changed them into trees, so says the legend, and their tears still flowing on, became Amber. A still stranger origin is given to this fossil, in the well-known couplet of the fire-worshippers,—

"Around thee shall glisten the loveliest Amber,
That ever the sorrowing sea bird hath wept."

*** *For a representation of Amber in its native or rough state, see colored Illustrations.*

CHAPTER II.

THE AMETHYST.

HIS is a term now applied to all the violet, purple, blue, and other crystals of Quartz, which, when fractured, present the peculiar undulated structure described by Sir David Brewster. This is, however, an entirely distinct species from the true Oriental Amethyst, which is a variety of Sapphire, of a deep shade of violet, mentioned already under Corundum.

They are found in the galleries of old mountains, sometimes in iron, and sometimes in Agate beds. Those of the finest violet are found in Siberia, India, Ceylon, Persia, Carthagena, and Brazil. In cutting them, as many facets as possible are given, in order to intensify the color and lustre. This stone takes a beautiful polish, and as none harmonizes better with gold, it forms a gem of great beauty, but since the discovery of it in America, it seems to have lost caste. Brazil, of all the places above-mentioned, furnishes us with the best specimens of the dark-colored stones. In America it occurs of extraordinary size: a block sent thence to India is said to have weighed 98 lbs. A variety known as Spanish Amethyst is sometimes met with in very old-fashioned jewelery; it

GEMS (IN THE ROUGH.)

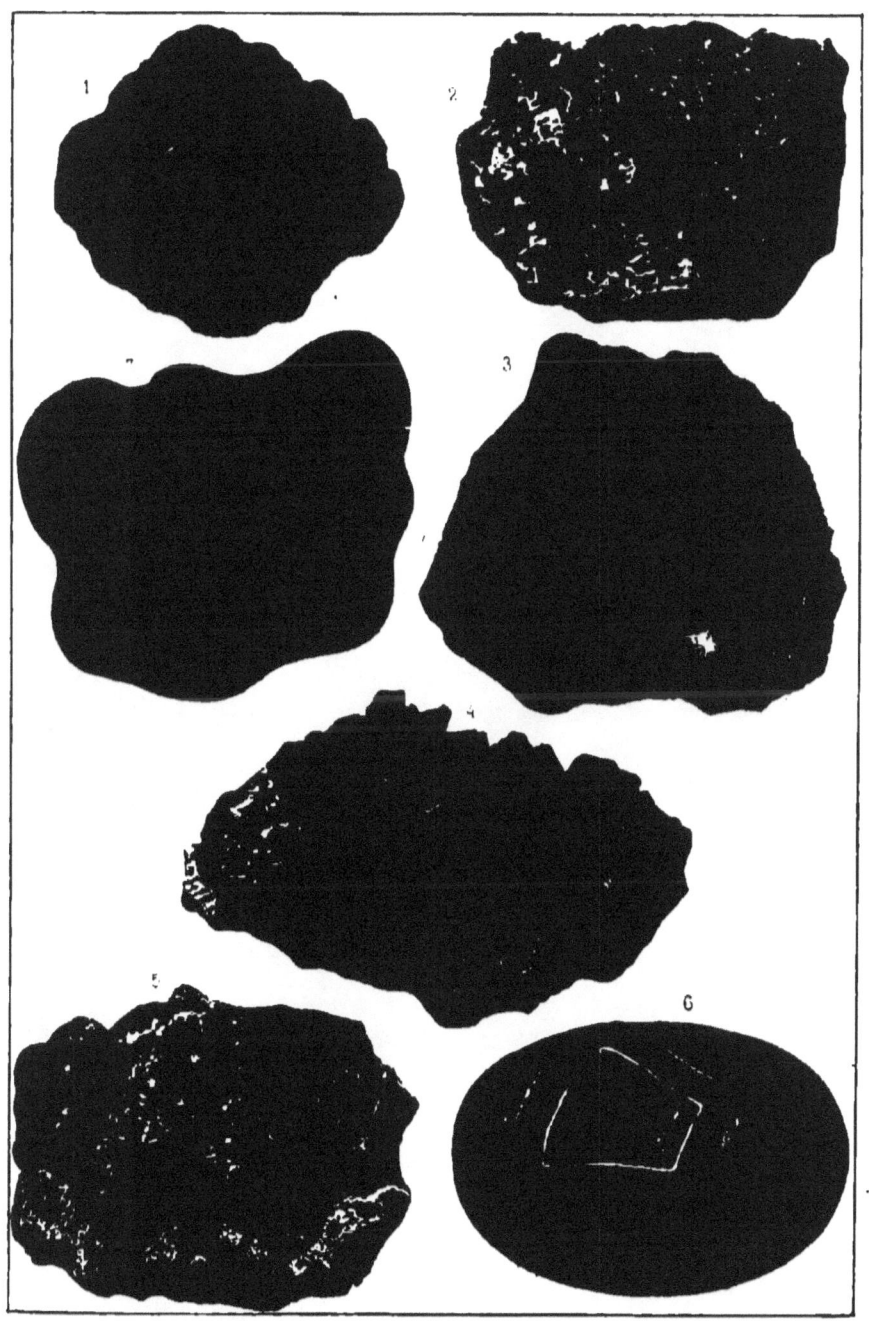

exhibits the true purple color at one time so much prized: whence they came is unknown. The common Amethyst is found in nearly all parts of the world. A block measuring a foot square, but with scarcely any color, was recently in my possession.

To show the fall in the value of this stone, we quote one instance, viz., the Amethyst necklace of Queen Charlotte. It consisted of well-matched and very perfect stones, although only of the common variety, and was valued at £2,000; it would now barely realize £100.

Intagli of very ancient date and in every style are met with in Amethysts. As a rule, stones of a pale color are used for engraving rather than the dark; as an exception to this rule, King says, he himself has seen, perhaps the grandest Greek portrait in existence, a head of Mithridates, cut in a large Amethyst of the deepest violet color, which was found a century ago in India. There is another very ancient intaglio of the head of Pan in the Uzielli collection.

In early times the Amethyst seems to have been a favorite stone for engraving. One of the largest of the kind was the gem, representing a bust of Trajan, of which the Prussian treasury was robbed during the Napoleonic wars.

∗ *For a representation of the Amethyst in its native or rough state, see colored Illustrations.*

CHAPTER III.

THE AGATE.

AGATE, strictly speaking, does not belong to mineralogy, which deals only with the characteristics of simple minerals, that is to say, those which, by their mechanical division, in all their fragments are essentially of the same quality and condition.

By the term Agate we understand a collective substance; it implies a conglomeration of certain silicates, or quartz minerals, which in texture, color, and transparency are diverse one from the other. These minerals are Chalcedony, Carnelian, Quartz, Jasper, and some others. Two or more of these in a conglomerate, forming a mixed cohesive mass and presenting spots and stripes, is denominated Agate. According to certain fancied similitudes, which this stone displays to things in common use, it receives a distinguishing name.

Riband Agate exhibits strata, or layers of different colors which play one into the other. Where the colors are beautiful and sharply defined, and the strata run parallel to the surface of the stone, it is called Onyx, or Agate Onyx ; and, in a narrower sense, that is called Band Agate, wherein there appear stripes of varied hues. If these stripes converge towards a centre, it receives the name of the Circular Agate ; and if in this centre there are other colored points, it is called the Eye Agate. In Rainbow Agate the stripes form a bow, presenting the colors of the Iris when the stone is held towards the sun or a strong light ; the thinner the stone the more this peculiarity is noticeable.

In speaking of Oriental and Western Agate, we understand that all the most beautiful and translucent sorts belong to the Oriental, and the less valuable to the Western variety.

The Agate, Onyx, and Chalcedony, are produced almost exclusively in a peculiar kind of stone, originating in Melaphyre, Black Porphyry and Trapp.

In a district of $8\frac{3}{4}$ square miles, stand the two little towns of Oberstein and Idar, the chief centres of the Agate industry. Not only is a great proportion of the inhabitants of these towns in some way occupied in cutting, polishing, and coloring these stones, but for miles round, every tributary of the Rhine is dotted with the homes of those who follow this business.

In 1770 there were only twenty-six cutting and polishing mills in Birkenfeld, whereas in 1870 there were 180, half of which were built within the twenty years preceding. In each mill there are four or five whetstones. These stones are firm quartzig sandstone, which is obtained from Zweibrücken ; two men ordinarily work together at the same stone. Much of the Agate is cleaved to the requisite form by means of the hammer, a work which exacts much skill from the artisan : He must be well acquainted with the natural planes and cleavage direction of the stone, and have dexterity enough to take advantage of them. The purchase of the stone in the rough is generally undertaken by professed dealers in Agate wares, who commit them to the cutters and polishers, to form them into articles in demand. The artificers are paid by the piece, or by the dozen.

₊ *For a representation of the Agate in its native or rough state, see colored Illustrations.*

CHAPTER IV.

ALEXANDRITE.

THIS is found in Takowaja, and as it contains the two chief military colors of the Russian Empire, red and green, it is called Alexandrite. It is transparent, but in consequence of its many crevices and rents, it cannot easily be cut and polished.

A small amount of chrome-oxide gives it its green color, which is much admired in day-light; and it contains just a trace of copper and oxide of lead, which makes it look dark-red by artificial light. By day-light these two colors intermingle, the green predominating. If the stone be turned towards the setting sun, or towards a flame, the red predominates. It is an extraordinarily good specimen of Trichroism.

CHAPTER V.
AQUAMARINE.

QUAMARINE partakes of the nature of the Emerald and the Beryl, both of which are varieties of the same species, but the Aquamarine contains oxide of iron in the place of the oxide of chromium. Its hardness, being less than that of first-class stones — 7·5 to 8, detracts from its value in the jeweller's estimation.

Most of the Aquamarine comes to us from Brazil, already cut; but the stones are found elsewhere, viz., in the granite regions in Siberia, in the Ural Mountains, and in the Altai Mountains. Formerly they were obtained from the frontiers of China.

This gem is a great favorite with the English, chiefly because it possesses the advantage of retaining its lustre in artificial light. Jewellers distinguish the varieties of this stone in a manner peculiar to themselves, viz.: the green and blue varieties they call Aquamarine, while the yellow variety receives the name of Beryl. But the former is again sub-divided: into (1) *Aquamarine*, pure, light sky-blue; (2) *Siberian Aquamarine*, light greenish-blue, bright lustre, and faintly colored; (3) *Aquamarine Chrysolite*, greenish-yellow, sometimes yellowish-green, with bright lustre.

Aquamarine is made into a variety of ornaments. It is said that the Emperor Commodus possessed an Hercules engraved on Aquamarine by Hyllus; and that in the treasures of Odescalchi, there was a stone engraved by Quintitius, representing Neptune, drawn by sea-horses. In the National Library in Paris, there is a beautiful engraving of the head of Julia, the daughter of Titus, by Evodus, on Aquamarine. An Aquamarine, $2\frac{1}{16}$ inches long and $2\frac{3}{8}$ in thickness adorned the tiara of Pope Julius II.

CHAPTER VI.

THE BLOODSTONE.

THE variety of Hematite used for ornament, is found generally in fibrous masses, having a curved, round, kidney-shaped, or clustered upper surface. It is opaque, and the cleavage is imperfect, fracture sub-conchoidal and uneven; its hardness 4·5. The color varies from dark steel-grey to blood-red and brownish-red, and possesses a slight and imperfect metallic lustre. It consists of Hematite in a pure condition, viz., oxide of iron; the chemical composition of which is, 69·34 of iron and 30·66 of oxygen ($Fe^2 O^3$). It is infusible by itself, but with Borax and subjected to a fierce heat, the part on which the outer circle of the flame impinges becomes a dark red, but turning to yellow when cool, whereas the centre remains a bottle-green.

Hematite is found in various formations, in Andreasburg in the Hartz; Saalfeld in Thuringia; Waldenburg in Silesia, Rothenfels and Hohenburg, in the Pfalz; and in Bohemia, France, and Spain.

The Hematite or Bloodstone is not much used for ornament, except for signet rings, but is most useful as a polish for other stones and for metals. We have noticed it here because of its value in ancient times. The art of engraving seems to have been first experimented on the Bloodstone. The largest number of the old Babylonish and Egyptian Intaglios, consists of the Hematite or Bloodstone.

CHAPTER VII.

THE CARNELIAN, OR RED CHALCEDONY.

SOME believe this stone to have derived its name from "Carien," the place where it was earliest found. Others, that it comes from "Caro" *flesh*. The Ancients called it "Sarda," either from the town of Sardis in Asia Minor, or from the Arabian word "Sard," (*yellow*). Luther translates the Hebrew word "Odem" or "Adam," (*red*) (Exodus, chap. xxvii. v. 17), by Sarda, so well-known was the stone at that early period.

Carnelian is chiefly found in dense, imperfect balls; often however, in obtuse-angled pieces. Its color varies from blood-red to wax-yellow, and reddish-brown; it is cloudy, seldom striated, semi-transparent and of waxy lustre. Its hardness is somewhat less than that of Chalcedony. By heat the color of Carnelian becomes intensified, probably because of its coloring matter, oxy-hydrate of iron being changed into oxide of iron. By an over application of heat it sometimes loses its color and becomes white, pale and friable. Carnelian is found mostly as rubble and as filling-up material in the air-bladder of Almandine. It is found with Amethyst and Chalcedony at Oberstein in the province of Birkenfeld, in sandstone at Waldshut in Baden, and of extraordinary beauty as rubble, at Barotsch in the province of Guzurale, in the East Indies. In the same manner it is found in the rivers of Uruguay. The jewelers and lapidaries distinguish the different kinds of Carnelian by the following names—1st, Masc. or Carnelian of old stone, dark red. 2nd, Fem. pale red passing into yellow. 3rd, Sarder, brown, passing into pomeranian and yellow. 4th, Sardonyx, where layers of the Sarder alternate with layers of white. 5th, Carnelian Onyx, blood-red stripes playing into white. 6th, Carnelian Beryl, a whitish yellow.

Carnelian is cut on a leaden plate with Emery, and polished on a wooden one with pumice-stone. It receives its last touch of polish, however, on a plate consisting of lead and tin, with water. It is generally cut into squares, hexagons, or octagons; sometimes round, or by giving to the upper part the *treppen* or graduated cut. To increase the lustre it often receives a silver or golden foil, or the under part is touched with color corresponding to that of the stone. The color is improved and intensified by means of heat, as has been above mentioned, which alters its yellowish hue into a pleasing red.

Carnelian is used for rings, seals, watch-keys, and other objects of adornment. It is very much employed for Cameos, and for engraving. In cutting a Cameo from Carnelian, the snow-white layer would be made use of for the figure; the red for a base or ground-work; and should it have a third layer of milk-white, it would serve for the hair in the figure of the Cameo. The Cameos which from time to time we receive from India are most *bizarre* in their appearance. The natives cover the whole stone with carbonate of soda, and subject it for a moment to intense heat, so that a hard molten mass is produced in which they cut the figure.

Carnelian of a beautiful color is of more value than the other varieties of Chalcedony. The blood-red stands first, and the pale-red next. Since the Oberstein industry of the artificial coloring of Precious Stones, the value has much diminished ; and probably the market has not been improved by the very large importation of Brazilian stones. Of course the price paid for this stone depends greatly upon the degree of transparency, purity, and beauty of color, and upon its freedom from flaws.

This stone was probably chosen by the Greeks and Romans for Cameos in consequence of its possessing a beautiful color and a certain hardness, affording a facility for manipulation. We shall mention only a few of the many famous specimens.

The oldest Greek gems known are in the collection of the Emperor of Germany. One of them is a Carnelian, on which is represented a winged Jupiter appearing to Semele, and the other an opaque Sardonyx, on which is engraved a draped figure of Venus. They are more modern, however, than the butterfly of the first epoch of the Etruscan art of engraving.

There is a Carnelian of the earliest period in the St. Petersburg collection, on which a man's head is engraved, with most artistically arranged beard.

The British Museum possesses an example of the second period, viz., a Carnelian butterfly, carrying a representation of Venus, of very fine workmanship. The dress of the goddess hangs in rich and graceful folds, and has a border round it, and she is furnished with large wings.

A Carnelian of the third period is in the Royal Collection of Vienna, and represents Helena, with wings on her shoulders.

On a small Carnelian, in the Collection at Florence, there is a head of Apollo, adorned with laurels and fillets.

The Carnelian, or Red Chalcedony.

In the Berlin Museum there is an unique Indian Carnelian, almost as transparent as the Hyacinth, engraved with the head of Sextus Pompeius.

One of the most famous of the ancient deep-cut stones represents the birthday festival of Dionysius, and was once in the possession of Michael Angelo.

₊ *For a representation of Chalcedony in its rough or native state, see colored Illustrations.*

CHAPTER VIII.

THE CHRYSOLITE OF LAPIDARIES
(CHRYSOBERYL).

THE crystalline form of the Chrysoberyl belongs to the rhombic system. It is usually found in the same sands as those which furnish crystals of Topaz and Corundum. Twins of two kinds and of great beauty are found in the Emerald mines of Takowaja, east of the Catharine mountains in the Ural. The cleavage is imperfect—parallel to the faces of the right-angled prisms: fracture conchoidal and uneven: hardness 8·5: specific gravity 3·6 to 3·8. It is brittle, transparent, translucent, and possesses in a high degree the power of double refraction, and a vitreous and oily lustre. The color varies from asparagus-green to grass-green, greenish-white, and yellowish-green. A peculiar bluish opalescence, in the inner part of the stone, is to be seen at times. The streak is white. Under friction it becomes electric, and remains in that condition for hours. Perhaps no mineral has had so many analyses with such a variety of results as the Chrysoberyl. Klaproth and Aredson considered it to be silicic acid and alumina. To Seybert we are indebted for the discovery of glucina in Chrysoberyl. He conceived it to be composed of silicic acid, alumina, and an aluminate of glucinum or Beryl earth. Thomson declared he could find no silicic acid in it, and was confirmed in this view by Mr. Rose. Chrysoberyl is therefore composed of a combination of alumina and glucina, a small portion of the latter being replaced by oxide of iron. It undergoes no change before the blow-pipe, but fuses with great difficulty into a clear glass by means of borax. Acids have no effect upon it, but with a solution of cobalt it becomes blue.

Asparagus or Yellow-green Chrysolite was known in very early times to the people of Ceylon and Brazil. In Ceylon it was found in the sand of the river in company with Tourmaline, Spinel, and Sapphire. On the east side of Borneo also, it is found in the river sand, and in flooded lands with crystals, gold dust, Diamond, Topaz and Emerald. In Pegu it is found amongst pebbles and loose river sand. In Brazil, pieces of this Chrysoberyl of the size of a hazel nut, and of yellowish-green color, are sometimes met with while washing for Diamonds. Of late years it has also been found in Connecticut, North America, in well-formed tables and prisms, with Tourmaline, Garnet and Beryl, in the granite strata; and at Saratoga and Greenfield in New York State, in regular twin crystals with Tourmaline, Garnet, and Apatite.

CHAPTER IX.
THE CHRYSOPRASE.

PLINY speaks of the Chrysoprase as a gem well-known to the Ancients, and tells us that they made vessels of it, and that the stone was obtained from India in great quantities. It has been said, however, that Chrysoprase was first discovered by a Prussian officer near a mill on the Kosemitz mountains in 1740. It is quite certain that the Chrysoprase has been known and used for centuries, although its true home has not been accurately ascertained until lately. The costly Mosaic walls of St. Wenzel's Chapel, in the Cathedral of St. Beit, at Prague, built in the 14th century, contain splendid specimens of Chrysoprase. Frederick the Great used this stone very largely in adorning Sans Souci. In the palace of Potsdam there are two tables formed of Chrysoprase, three feet long, two feet broad, and two inches thick.

Chrysoprase is found in Silesia, near Kosemitz, Glasendorf, and Baumgarten, not far from Frankenstein. It occurs in veins of serpentine, in company with other minerals, such as Quartz, Hornstone, Chalcedony, Opal, and Pimelite; the two last receiving their color in the same manner as the

Chrysoprase, viz., from oxide of nickel. The Chrysoprase as a rule, is laid bare by the heavy rains washing away the soil on the hills, and is occasionally also turned up by the ploughshare.

The Green Opal, which is found in company with the Chrysoprase, is called the Chrysopal. Among the less Precious Stones the Chrysoprase is perhaps the greatest favorite, possessing a beautiful apple-green color of many shades, and a transparency and capability of a high polish, together with the advantage of being found in large pieces. One of its peculiarities is, that by constant use (such as sealing), it partly loses its color and gradually becomes paler. Heat and sunshine even affect the color. This is caused by the fact of one of its constituent parts being nickel. It was the great chemist, Klaproth, discovered this fact, and also that it contained a small quantity of water. The nickel oxide is therefore probably united with water as a hydrate in the Chrysoprase, making the metallic oxide appear more varied and beautiful in color. If, by the influence of heat, a particle of water in the stone is lost, the beauty of the color vanishes more or less. The Chrysoprase is chiefly used for signet rings, buckles, and pins. The working of the stone must be done with great care, as if too great a heat be applied, it splinters and loses color. As a rule, it receives the table-cut or "*Cabochon*" form. The lapidaries of Warmbrun are the principal cutters and polishers of Chrysoprase.

The value of the Chrysoprase depends upon its color and freedom from flaws. It is not so much valued now as in former times, but it still obtains a higher price than any other variety of Chalcedony, good specimens realizing from £5 to £20.

CHAPTER X.

THE GARNET, CARBUNCLE, JACINTH, AND CINNAMON STONE.

THE Garnet or Carbuncle was a great favorite with the Ancients. Several antique Garnets have been found in Roman ruins, some being round, and some cut; the latter receiving the name of "Garnet Plates," the underside of which is ground convex, to give them a more perfect transparency. In former days it was very frequently engraved, and several beautiful specimens are now to be seen in Paris, Turin, Rome, and St. Petersburg; among which, is the grand masterpiece of art, the representation of "Sirius," engraved on the celebrated Marlborough Garnet. The small degree of hardness posssssed by this stone renders engraving on it comparatively easy.

The word Garnet, or, as the Germans call it, Granat, owes its origin to the similarity in color to the blossom and kernel of the pomegranate, a fruit of southern Europe; it is not a name of ancient date. Pliny calls it "Carbuncle" from "Carbo," a live coal; both names are derived from its bright red color. According to some authorities, however, it is thought that the origin of Garnet is "Graniun," a grain, because it is so often found in that condition. The Precious Garnet is sometimes called "Almandine," from the city of Alabanda, in Carien. Its color is blood-red, cherry, or brownish-red, which, unlike the Oriental Amethyst, gains nothing by candle-light. On the contrary, it assumes an orange-tint, which detracts from its beauty. The crystals are almost always embedded in the rock singly. Its specific gravity is from 4 to 4·2, and its hardness is 7·5. It possesses a bright lustre, and is transparent. It occurs very frequently mixed with a variety of other stones, and the places where it is found are so numerous, that only a few of the most important can be mentioned.

In the mountains below the River Enns, in Austria large transparent crystals of Almandine are found in serpentine. In the Zillerthal and Tyrol, crystals of an inch in size are found embedded in the stratum of chlorite slate, in granite. These are taken to Bohemia, and worked into ornaments. The crystals found in Bohemia are generally reduced to powder for polishing purposes.

In Norway it is found in granular masses, associated with Augit, Epidot, and Hornblende. Some specimens have been obtained of rare beauty. In Sweden, fine, large crystals are found embedded in schist.

Switzerland is rich in Garnet. On the St. Gothard, large and small crystals of blood-red color are found in mica-schist. In the Rheinwalde, extraordinarily large crystals of bright red color are found in rich Quartz-gneiss, and in the Simplon Pass they are found in the glacier streams, of small size but very beautiful.

They occur in great abundance near to Almeria, in Spain, with Cordierite, Diorite, and also in Gneiss.

In Hindostan, Garnet is abundant in the débris of mountains; and in Ceylon it occurs everywhere in Gneiss, particularly at Trincomalee and at Adam's Peak.

The crystals which come from Siria, in Pegu, and which are called Sirian Almandine, are more than ordinarily fine.

In Greenland they not unfrequently fall out of the matrix, which is a chlorite-slate, and leave a regular colored impression behind. In the United States they occur in Granite, Hornblende, and Gneiss. In Mexico, beautiful crystals occur in the fissures of Granite-rock, in Chalcedony, and in lime; and in Brazil in a variety of places; sometimes in chalk, or in Talc and slate, and not unfrequently in river-beds in company with Diamonds.

In Australia, very fine crystals are found near Oven and the Peel River.

There are several kinds of Garnet used for ornament, but the red varieties only have been used to any extent as jewels. They used formerly to command high prices, and retained their popularity to quite a recent date, and even lately a Carbuncle of the size of half-a-crown has been known to fetch as much as £50, but they may be said to have quite gone out of fashion. The several varieties employed by the jeweller are distinguished by their peculiarities of color or cutting, and are known by special names. The Almandine, a beautiful stone of a rich claret color is the most highly esteemed. The finest stones of this class come from Ceylon and Pegu.

The Pyrope, sometimes known as the Bohemian Garnet, is of a blood-red color, never purple. When cut like a Brilliant it is very bright, but owing to its occurring in small pieces, it is more usually Rose-cut and mounted as a *pavé*. Its chemical composition differs from the Almandine in having only 10 per cent. of protoxide of iron, 15 per cent. of magnesia, and 5 per cent. of lime. It is found principally in Saxony and Bohemia. Its specific gravity is slightly lower than that of the Almandine.

The Carbuncle is simply an Almandine cut "*en cabochon*," that is, with a convex surface, the back frequently being hollowed out so as to display the deep color of the stone, and enable the jeweller to "foil" it.

The Jacinth, sometimes called Hyacinth, is an orange-red variety, it differs in some respects in character from the deep red Garnets, and is considered by lapidaries as a distinct stone. This is a mistake, as its crystalline form and typical composition are identical with that of the other Garnets. Its chief difference, besides its peculiar color, is a lower specific gravity, and the presence of 30 per cent. of lime, in lieu of protoxide of iron. The specific gravity is 3·65. It is known to mineralogists as the Essonite or Cinnamon Stone.

Jacinth, or Cinnamon Stone, comes almost entirely from Ceylon, where it is found in large pieces in the strata of rocky mountains: these stones are generally finely colored and transparent. They are cut thin on account of the depth of color, with a pavilion-cut below and a broad table above, bordered with small facets.

At Dissentis, in Switzerland, beautiful crystals are found, of a reddish-yellow color, in a sort of Quartz, formerly called by the name of Hyacinth of Dissentis; and equally fine with Diopside in Piedmont and St. Gothard. From the Dolomite region of Mexico we obtain Cinnamon Stone of a beautiful red color, almost identical with Spinel.

A new variety of Garnet has recently come into the market from Siberia: in color it is a beautiful green, very brilliant, and unlike any other stone that we have.

*_** *For a representation of the Garnet, in its native or rough state, see colored Illustrations.*

CHAPTER XI.
THE JASPER.

THE different species of this stone, and the variety of opinions concerning it, render a description difficult. The Greek name, "Jaspis," according to Isidore, "signifieth green, and such a green as doth illustriously shine forth with a very supreme viridity, or greenness of glory." Pliny considers the "Jaspis," a gem of a dull-green color, like an Emerald, but not so transparent. In his 37th book, he reckons up no less than ten kinds of this gem. "The third of these," he says, "is like to air, and is called Ærizusa, because it resembles the morning of an autumnal heaven;" "and the tenth kind," he writes, "is like to crystal," which concurs with the description of it in Holy Writ; but he himself prefers the Purple Jasper to all other kinds, and next to this, that which resembles the rose. Baccius declares "that the pleasure which may be seen in a Jasper, the beauty of which ariseth from the mixture of many excellent greens and whites, cannot be expressed." The name itself is very ancient. This gem is the "Jaspeh," or eleventh stone, in the breastplate of the High Priest. The glory of the Jasper is often made use of in the Holy Scriptures to represent the New Jerusalem.

Pliny assures us that Eastern nations wore pieces of it as amulets ; and Nicols, who wrote in the middle of the 17th century, says in his quaint way, "Divers do very superstitiously attribute much power and virtue to the Cross-white Jaspers, if figures and characters be engraven upon them."

The Red Jasper was much valued in early times for engraving. In Florence the Yellow Jasper is largely employed for Mosaics, and the Riband Jasper for Cameos. "We have seen," says Pliny, "a large Jasper of 15 ounces in weight upon which was worked a likeness of Nero." For finer work, the piece of Jasper is divided by a copper-edged saw, used with fine sand ; or pieces of a more carefully selected size are cut and polished with Emery.

In the Vatican, there is a beautiful vase of Red Jasper, with white veins, and another of Black Jasper, with yellow veins. In China, the Emperor's seal is of Jasper ; and in that country the stone is valued highly.

It is found in compact masses of kidney shape, or in pebbles, very seldom in clusters. Its colors are green, yellow, and red of various shades, rarely blue. That known as the Egyptian Jasper is found in round or spheroid masses, and is of intense red, or ochre-yellow, deepening into chestnut-brown, according to the preponderance of one or other coloring matter. Very frequently the colors form stripes or zones in the stone, which are probably the result of decomposition of the upper surface. Genuine Jasper has a perfect conchoidal fracture, and a peculiarly dull lustre. The Brown Jasper, with its concentrated light or dark stripes, is found in abundance in the ridges and sands of the deserts. Near Cairo, it occurs in masses, which probably belonged to the chalk formation.

Its great capability of polish, and the abundance in which it is found in the birth-place of Moses, must have first drawn attention to it, and may account for the Jews examining into its character and properties, and making much use of it.

The Red Jasper is found in great plenty near Mühlheim, in Bresgau, in the granular iron of that district, which suggests a similar origin with that of flint.

Common Jasper, generally red and brown, but sometimes yellow and black, is found in iron and iron-stone, in a variety of places.

Riband or Striped Jasper occurs in compact masses with thin conchoidal fracture. It has stripes or zones of grey, green, yellow, red, and brown, and is mostly found in Siberia; but is also obtained in smaller quantities in Sicily, Corsica, the Hartz, and Tyrol.

The so-called Porcelain Jasper is only burnt clay. The many-colored Jasper has frequent rents, whereby the appearance and lustre suffer. In Sicily, they practice the art of filling up the fissures or rents with a cement made of nut-oil and tragacanth; but when this cement becomes quite dry the rents re-open.

Thomas Nichols writes: "This gem or stone of price, for its fulness of glory, and excellence of beauty, cannot admit of any foyl or tincture to commend its beauty withal;" and further, "It is ascribed, by way of glory, to the King of Egypt, that the first adulteration of the Jasper by tincture was from him; but the glory of this praise, if I be not mistaken, doth even become his shame."

CHAPTER XII.

THE LABRADOR.

THE Spaniards found amongst the ornaments of the Indians, dwelling upon the shores of the Amazon, grotesque figures formed of this mineral, supposed to have been exhumed from the tombs of the old Mexicans. It is now found principally on the coast of Labrador, and is sent home by the missionaries.

The crystals belong to the Triclinic system. The cleavage is perfect; the fracture uneven; and it possesses a pearly or vitreous lustre. The color is grey, brown, or greenish. Usually a play of various colors may be observed, in which blue and green are predominant. It is translucent. The stones which have the most beautiful colors come from the coast of Labrador and St. Paul's Island, where they are found in masses, and from Finland, where they are found in loose blocks.

Great care has to be taken in the manipulation of this stone to preserve the play of color; for if many facets are given to it, this wholly disappears. Large and beautiful specimens of this stone are highly valued. The first block of Labrador was brought to Europe in 1775; and it was discovered in Russia in 1781. Still later, two blocks were found on the shores of the Paulkovla, which exceeded all hitherto known specimens in size. One of these was a Russian ell in length, and the second weighed 1000 lbs. It is valued for jewelry and ornamental purposes on account of its beautiful colors. Value from £1 to £10, according to its lustre.

CHAPTER XIII.
THE LAPIS-LAZULI.

THIS stone is remarkable for its beautiful color. The Arabians call it "Azul" (blue). It is without doubt, the Sapphire of Pliny, who speaks of it as being "like to the serene blue heavens fretted with golden fire." The Lapis-Lazuli crystallizes in the Tesseral system. Its specific gravity is from 2·3 to 2·4, and its hardness 5·5. The color varies from pale azure to deep blue, with a tint of green; but is seldom quite pure, being subject to white and yellow spots, caused by the presence of iron pyrites, which considerably lessen its value. It is brittle, has but little lustre, and is transparent only at the corners. The chemical composition of this stone, according to Varrentrapp, is, silica 45·5, alumina 31·7, sulphuric acid 5·8, soda 9, and lime 3·5, added to which is a little iron, sulphur, and chlorine. The beautiful color is no doubt owing to the combination of a silicate with a sulphate, mixed with a little sulphuret of iron. It fuses with great difficulty, and expands before the blow-pipe, after which it becomes a porous, colorless glass; but if heated with saltpetre, it turns to a beautiful green. According to Field, the variety of this stone which comes from the Cordilleras, loses its blue color by heat, but regains it on cooling.

In the Cordilleras, near the sources of the Cazadero and Vias — little tributaries of the Rio Grande, not far from the high road leading to the Argentine Republic, and a short distance from the great watershed in the Chili dominions, the Lapis-Lazuli is found in a thick stratum of carbonate of lime, accompanied by small quantities of iron pyrites. This stratum rests upon slate, and is covered by another stratum consisting of rich iron-ore, which contains a large amount of Garnet. Over this last lies the granite formation constituting the summit of these mountains. This stone is also found in Siberia, on the shore of the Shudank, particularly on the lands near the Baikal lake, into which that river empties itself. Marco Polo in his travels to the princes of Tartary in 1271, found it in the upper district of the Oxus, mixed with iron, from whence the Armenian merchants bring it to the market of Orenburg, in eastern Russia. In many provinces of China, and in Bucharia, it is found in granular lime with iron pyrites, and on the banks of the Indus in a greyish limestone.

The Lapis-Lazuli was used in old classic times for Cameos and Intaglios, of which a number remain to this day. The Chinese have for a long period constructed out of it vases, caskets, buttons, cups, and the like, and have also used it for porcelain painting. There is a prejudice against Lapis-Lazuli, as it loses polish by constant wear and becomes dull. This stone is used for rings, pins, crosses, ear-rings, as well as for larger objects, such as caskets, vases, candlesticks, statuettes, watch cases, and handles for sticks and umbrellas. In Italy it is a favorite stone for ornamenting churches, and in the chapel of San Martini, at Naples, the Lapis-Lazuli is profusely employed for decorative and even as structural material. In the Zarskoe Palace, south-west of St. Petersburg, there is an apartment, called Catharine II's. chamber, formed entirely of Lapis-Lazuli and Amber. This stone was in early, times much valued by us, because it was the only material from which the true ultra-marine could be obtained. Thos. Nichols relates that in his day the fragments of it were worth ten crowns a pound to extract from it Azur (Aquamarine), for when very good this quantity would supply ten ounces of coloring matter, and every ounce of *pure* Azur was worth twenty crowns of the then currency.

⁂ *For a representation of Lapis-Lazuli in its native or rough state, see colored Illustrations.*

CHAPTER XIV.

THE MALACHITE.

HIS stone was known and valued by the Ancients. Pliny, who calls it "Molochitis," describes it as an opaque stone, of a rich Emerald-green, and says that its name was derived from the color of the "Malve;" and that it was much used for seals, and was worn by children as a certain protection against evil.

Malachite is not rare. It is found in Siberia, at Moldavia in the Bannal, at Saalfeld in Thuringia, in Prussia, at Chessy near Lyons, in Poland, Cornwall, and extensively in Queensland. It is generally the product of the decomposition of minerals containing copper. There is a beautiful variety composed of oxide of iron, which is found in great quantity in the Ural.

Malachite is found in crystals, but perfect specimens are very rare; its color is light-green, with a paler streak; and its lustre adamantine inclining to vitreous, but the fibrous incrustations are silky. It is translucent, nearly opaque, and brittle. Its hardness is 3·5 to 4, and its specific gravity 4. Its composition is generally, carbonic acid, oxide of copper, and water. When heated in a glass tube, it gives out the water, and becomes black; and it fuses with borax to a deep-green globule, and ultimately affords a head of copper. Owing to its magnificent color and capability of polish, Malachite is highly valued for ornamental purposes, and is frequently inlaid with, and often used to cover, inferior stones, for vases, tables, caskets, and the like. It is polished by means of Tripoli, on a tin plate. In the collection at St. Petersburg, there is a mass, 3½ feet square, of the most beautiful Emerald-green; it weighs 90 lbs., and is valued at 525,000 roubles.

From the mines at Nischne-Tagilsk, belonging to Mons. Demidoff, a block of beautiful green Malachite was taken out, 16 feet long, 7½ feet wide, and 8½ feet thick.

One of the most perfect specimens of Malachite work is the vase which stood for a long time in the great rotunda of the old Museum in Berlin. It is covered with tiny pieces, cut in little "tables," and so joined that it could not be perceived. It was made by order of the Emperor Nicholas in honor of King William III. of Prussia.

Of antique engraving on Malachite, Köhler speaks, in the highest praise, of a Cameo with the head of Isis. He says, "The head of the goddess is drawn with a definiteness, tenderness, and refinement that could not be surpassed."

Although the Ancients only knew of its existence in Arabia, the results of modern discovery shew a far more extended range of its habitat.

CHAPTER XV.

THE SELENITE, or MOONSTONE.

"THE Selenite," says Andreas Baccius, "is a kind of gem which doth contain in it the image of the moon, and it doth represent it increasing and decreasing according to the increase and decrease of the moon in its monthly changes." The Greeks, who call it "Aphroselenë" which signifies the splendour of the moon, or a beam of the moon, with their lively imagination, often discovered in natural objects resemblances to other organic forms, and ascribed to them virtues and properties according to their interpretation. The Moonstone is a good example of this. The Romans called it "Lunaris." Pliny mentions four varieties of it. The first or the female, was egg-shaped, white, and filled with a soft sweet clay. The second, or male, was externally reddish, and had within a stony substance. The third contained a sweetish sand. The fourth, or the Laonian variety, had a crystalline core. The best kind, he says, "were to be found in the eagle's nest only, whence the name Aëtites, Eagle's Stone." The substance itself, according to De Boot, is one of those calcareous hollow concretions, white, or sometimes tinged with iron, familiar to geologists. This gem is found in Macedonia, and in appearance is like frozen water. The stone now known as Moonstone, is found on the higher mountainous regions of India. Dioscorides says "it is found in Arabia, and is endued with virtues, as of making trees fruitful, and of curing epilepsy;" he adds "that in the night it will illuminate the place that is next to it, yet not by any transmission of light, but by the collection of light into itself." This stone is remarkable rather for the fables which cling to it, than for its substantial value or qualities.

CHAPTER XVI.

THE ORIENTAL ONYX.

ONYX is a very celebrated variety of tinted Agate, and is found almost exclusively in Melaphyre and Black Porphyry. The Oriental Onyx is obtained from India, Egypt, Arabia, Armenia, and Babylon. The inferior variety mostly comes from Bohemia.

Some stone, called by translators Onyx, ranked among the highest class of gems in the ante-christian world. It is often mentioned in the writings of Greek and old Hebrew authors. Pliny likens it in color to the human finger-nail; and it is upon this similarity that its Greek name Onyx is based. According to this author, the stone is marked with white, horn-colored, brown, and black bands or zones, which are arranged in flat, horizontal planes.

The Greeks attached the following mythological origin to this stone: "Cupid, with the sharp point of his arrow, cut the nails of the sleeping Venus, which fell into the Indus; but as they were of heavenly origin they sank, and became metamorphosed into Onyx."

The Onyx has been chiefly used for Cameos, and very costly vessels. In making the Cameo, the figure is carved out of the light color, and stands in relief on the dark ground. One of the most famous of the Antique Cameos is the Mantuan Vase; the base is brown, and on it, in relief, are groups of white and yellow figures, representing Ceres and Triptolemus in search of Proserpine. The vase is formed from a single stone, and is seven inches high and two-and-a-half broad. There is an Onyx Cameo in the Vatican library, representing Octavius Augustus; and, in the Emperor's Cabinet, at Vienna, there are some specimens of exquisitely cut Antique Onyx. In the Museo Nationale, at Naples, there are many specimens; among others, an Onyx Cameo (eleven inches by nine); representing the apotheosis of Augustus; and another with the head of Medusa carved on one side, and the apotheosis of Ptolemy on the other. Among the remarkable Cameos in the National Library of Paris, is one of Tiberius with an ox; a second, of Marcus Aurelius and Faustina; a third, of Aggripina with her two children; and a fourth, of Jupiter armed with lightning. An Antique Sard-Onyx Cameo, in the Mineralogical Museum of the Marquis Dree, representing the bust of Faustina, cut on a five-colored basis, was sold for 7,171 francs.

Onyx has been found in such large masses that small pillars have been made of it: there are six such in the Basilica of St. Peter, at Rome. At Cologne, in the Temple of the Three Magi, there is one broader than the palm of the hand. Appianus says that "Mithridates, King of Pontus, had 2,000 cups of this gem;" it is scarcely possible, however, to believe that they could have been the true Oriental Onyx.

Boetius mentions the Arabian Onyx, as "black, with white zones or circles, by reason of which many colors are caused in it. It is called an Onyx only when the black appeareth as it were under a white. It is a gem that hath many veins, compassed about with milky zones or girdles, and meeting in a pleasing concord and consent."

It is not at all probable that the Onyx which Professor Aaron Pick shews to be the *Shouham* of Holy Writ, was the same composite stone with that which modern writers designate by that name, for it is classed with the Ruby, Topaz, Diamond, Chrysolite, Jasper, Sapphire, and Chrysoprase. This great Hebrew scholar believes it to have been the Carbuncle.

The price of carefully selected stones, sufficient to form a necklace, may range from one hundred to five hundred guineas. No Precious Stone varies more in value than the Oriental Onyx. It is used chiefly for fine art jewelry, and is generally set with Diamonds, and it is also highly esteemed by the Indians, who wear it with Pearls. No stone is more difficult to determine than this, as the Common Onyx is now so skilfully dyed to represent the Oriental, as almost to escape detection, even by experienced judges.

CHAPTER XVII.
THE PERIDOT.

THIS is a very ancient stone, at one time considered of more value than the Diamond, and worn by ladies for many centuries as an ornament. It has a very pleasing yellowish-green color, and is susceptible of a fine polish, but it is so soft as to be easily scratched. The Oriental Peridot is a beautiful gem. Its crystallization, is rhomboidal; its lustre, vitreous; and it is translucent and transparent. As it is composed of silicate of magnesia, colored by peroxide of iron, it is less dense than stones of the first class. It is turned to jelly if macerated in sulphuric acid. Its specific gravity is 3·4; its hardness, 5·6; it possesses double refraction, and acquires electricity by friction. Formerly it was doubtful what its form of crystallization really was, as it was found in fragments much worn by the action of water, but well-defined crystals have been found in Vesuvius, which prove that they are rhomboidal prisms.

It is remarkable as having been discovered in masses of "aerolite" or meteoric stone (a union of iron, nickel, cobalt and other metals.) Although the Peridot has not retained its pristine repute, it is still occasionally in demand, and is much valued by some of the Society of Friends.

In the Wardrobe Book of Edward I., the Peridot is mentioned among the jewels of the deceased Bishop of Bath and Wells (escheated to the Crown). It is found in the Levant, in Brazil, Mexico, South Africa, Australia, and other countries, generally as small pebbles; the large pieces which have been preserved from the Middle Ages remain unrivalled by any modern discovery. The finest resemble in color the Emerald; the gem looks well if judiciously set in gold, and the deeper the green the more valuable the stone.

CHAPTER XVIII.

QUARTZ CAT'S EYE.

OR a description of Quartz Cat's Eye, and the True Cat's Eye, (Chrysoberyl), see pp. 166, 167, and 168.

CHAPTER XIX.

ROCK CRYSTAL.

ROCK Crystals are found in a variety of forms, sometimes of extraordinary size. Their color varies from pure white to greyish-white, yellow-white, yellowish-brown, clove-brown, and black. They possess double refraction and transparency. The electricity obtained by friction lasts about half-an-hour, rarely longer except under very favourable conditions. Before the blowpipe many colored crystals lose their tints. The frequent admixture of chlorite, asbestos, rutile, iron pyrites, gold, and radiolite in the crystals is very remarkable. The green color of the last is like a blade of grass inclosed in ice. The liquid or gaseous contents, which move as you turn the Crystal, are very interesting. There are pieces received from Madagascar, which have a thousand such bladders on a square inch, and when subjected to friction, give out a perfume like burnt oil.

The places from whence Rock Crystal is derived are so numerous, that we give but a few, chiefly those which yield it in large quantities for commerce.

In Europe, near St. Gothard it is found in company with Mica, Hornblende, Granite, and Felspar. A little distance from the "Grimsel" it is found as quartz-ore in the mines of Jochle Berg and Zinkenstock. In 1735 the yield from the mine of Zinkenstock alone was valued at £2,250. The most famous mine, perhaps, is that of Fischbach, in Visperthal, which supplied the crystal for the great Pyramid of Marsfeld, 1797. This block measured three feet in diameter, and weighed over 800 lbs. It is now in the Natural History Museum at Paris. The neighbourhood of Mont Blanc yields beautifully clear Crystal, which affords employment and wealth to the inhabitants of Chamounix. It is also found in Friedeberg, Salzberg and Gillerthal in Tyrol, and in Hungary, France, and Scotland. In the clear cells of the snow-white marble of Carrara it is found in great purity.

Ceylon affords it abundantly, and the natives use it for ornamenting their temples.

Madagascar supplies large blocks, and the common sand in this island is full of little crystals.

Rock Crystal was known to the Ancients. The Greeks valued it for its purity and its regular form. Theophrastus mentions that it was selected for seals. Pliny mentions several times in his Nat. Hist. 37. 9, that the Romans were well acquainted with its habitat in the Alps, and that they employed it largely for household luxury and adornment. They worked it into wine jugs, glasses, vases, and other vessels, such as moderns now obtain much cheaper from the glass factories. The Ancients believed it to be ice, and feared to expose it to great heat lest it should melt. Nero possessed two very beautiful drinking glasses and a ladle of Rock Crystal, for which he paid a large sum of money. When he heard of the loss of his kingdom, he is said to have broken the two glasses, in anger, to punish the age in which he lived, and jealous lest any one should thenceforward drink out of them.

The Empress Livia gave to the Capitol a piece of

Crystal weighing 50lbs.; and the Roman physicians used Crystal balls as lenses, in order to burn out sores. In the kingdom of Greece, the pure-water Crystal was rarer than the tinted; and, probably, was first made use of under the Roman Emperors. The Crystal was set for rings. un-cut much more frequently than cut.

We find an engraving on Rock Crystal mentioned, of the contest between Hercules and Antæus; and a representation of Arsinoe on a second.

As a rule Rock Crystal receives the form of the Brilliant, Rosette, or Table; the exception being the Rainbow Quartz, the Hair and Needle Stone, which are cut *en cabochon*. To cut or to engrave on Rock Crystal a Diamond point is used.

Rock Crystal is used for rings, pins, ear-rings, seals, caskets, gems, and other *Bijouterie*. It is also used for Cameos, Intaglios, lenses, and spectacles. For personal ornament, the clear, perfect, small Crystals are used, or the angles of the larger ones.

It is said that one of the finest works in Rock Crystal in existence, is an urn, 9½ inches in diameter, 9 inches high, and this, together with the foot or pedestal on which it stands, is formed of one piece. On the upper part is a representation of Noah asleep, his children holding a covering, and a woman with a basket of fruit in her hand. This urn belongs to the French Crown, and cost 100,000 francs.

The cups of Rock Crystal in the Vatican, and similar articles of domestic luxury in private hands, still retain a high value, although the large supply from Madagascar of the material itself, has greatly reduced its rarity, and therefore its price.

CHAPTER XX.

THE TOPAZ.

HIS interesting classic gem, called in Hebrew "Pittdoh," by Professor Aaron Pick, and "Pitdah" by Gesenius, (according as each reads the Massoreth), the latter of whom imagines that it is derived from Sanscrit "pita" (pale), and that the Greek "Topásion" is a transposition from "Pitdoh" to "Tipdoh," was certainly found in Ethiopia. Old mineralogists described it as a pale yellowish gem found in an island of the Red Sea. Boetius says it is of "diluted green color with yellowness added to it," and this is confirmed by the virtues then attributed to it "the Topaz calms anacreontic temperaments." The Topaz, although divided into Oriental and Occidental, should, strictly speaking, be divided into the variety composed of nearly pure alumina, (now designated Oriental), and the specimens which contain little more than 57 parts of alumina, the other parts, consisting of silica and fluorine, (called the Occidental). Its hardness is from 8 to 9; its specific gravity about 3·6; it possesses double refraction, and developes electricity by friction.

In Hindostan, in 1665, Tavernier saw a Topaz weighing 157¾ carats in the treasury of Aurengzebe which that monarch had purchased for a sum corresponding to £18,000 of our money.

The Topazes found in the beds at Capao, in Brazil, secured a net profit of £3,000 in twelve years. In the Ural, north of Katharinburg, it is found in Graphic, Granite, and Albite. In St. Petersburg is a heavy Crystal, 4¾ inches long and 4½ wide, weighing 31lbs. In the east of Siberia it is found in blue-crystals, in company with Beryl, Rock Crystal, and Felspar.

In Australia, the green and yellow crystals of Topaz are found, in Saxony, the pale violet, and in Bohemia, the sea-green variety. In Brazil, the red specimen, graduating from a pale to a deep carmine tint, has been discovered; here the prism is ordinarily rhomboidal, having at each end a four-faced pyramid, and its color is precisely that described as the Ethiopian Topaz. The varieties are described as the colorless, the Siberian, pale-blue, with a slight green cast, the red, the citron, and the Saxon straw-yellow.

Although the Topaz has a hardness little less than the Diamond, several have been found engraved: that in the Bibliotheque Royal, in Paris, is set in a signet-ring, having the portraits of Philip II. and Don Carlos deeply cut in it. There is also a Citron-yellow Topaz, representing an Indian Bacchus.

The antique Topaz in St. Petersburg, engraved with the constellation of Sirius, is of excellent workmanship. There was a celebrated Arabian Amulet composed of Topaz, having in Arabic, bored through it, "From God alone is success;" this now belongs to a Parisian jeweller.

The *Goutte d'Eau*, which is capable of exquisite polish, is a colorless Topaz. If cut as a Brilliant, with a small table, the pure gem forms a beautiful ornament; and some specimens found, both in New South Wales and also in Brazil, are worthy of careful cutting, polishing, and setting. It has been already stated that the so-called Diamond in the Portuguese Treasury is certainly a Topaz.

‗ *For a representation of the Topaz, in its native or rough state, see colored Illustrations.*

CHAPTER XXI.
THE TOURMALINE.

OURMALINE, known in Saxony as "Schorl," from '.the name of a village where it abounds, is mainly composed of alumina, silica, and boracic acid, although there are specimens which contain a small quantity of iron and manganese. The crystallization is rhomboidal; its cleavage is imperfect, and its fracture conchoidal. It is very brittle. Its hardness is 7 to 7·5, and its specific gravity 2·9 to 3·2. Tourmaline is rarely found of pure-water. Its colors are very varied, consisting of shades of greys, yellows, greens, blues, and browns; they all have a tendency towards the darker hues, even to black. A black or red kernel is not infrequently found in the midst of the stone.

Tourmaline possesses double refraction. Some specimens •polarize light perfectly, and by the aid of the polariscope it is easy to detect the pure gem from the yellow and green specimens.

Tourmaline, in common with other Precious Stones, developes electricity under friction, and is a mineral of the greatest interest from a thermo-electric point of view. Its dust is attracted by the magnet.

The Dutch introduced Tourmaline, somewhat more

than a century ago, into Europe from Ceylon. The first written history of it we find in a book published in Leipzig, 1707, called "*Curious Speculations of Sleepless Nights.*" It is mentioned also in the catalogue of a collection of stones sent over from Ceylon to Leyden in 1711. This stone was not sent in large quantities to Europe, and the German-Jews were almost the only purchasers of it.

Varieties of Tourmaline:—Siberian Tourmaline is of carmine, hyacinth, purple, or rose-red, running into violet-blue. When polished its lustre resembles that of the Oriental Ruby. We obtain it from Siberia, Ceylon, the Urals, Saxony, the Isle of Elba, and the United States, where it has been discovered in great perfection and abundance, which has caused a reduction in its value. That found in Peru is of a beautiful red, strongly resembling the Ruby. Indicolyte, or Brazilian Sapphire, is of a pleasing blue color. When very carefully polished it looks like the Sapphire. The Green Tourmaline, or Brazilian Emerald, is of an olive or darker green. It takes a perfect polish. Crystals of great beauty are found in Minas-Geräes, the Isle of Elba, the Urals, and St. Gothard. The Yellowish-Green Tourmaline (Ceylon Chrysolite) is very like Aquamarine, and is found in the river-beds of Ceylon and Brazil. Colorless Tourmaline occurs very seldom in pieces worth the cutting and polishing. The most beautiful specimens are found in Elba, and in Dolomite mountains. Brown Tourmaline is a variety not used for ornament. Ceylon and Switzerland yield a fair supply.

The value of the Tourmaline depends upon the color, quality, and size of the specimens; one of exceptional color and purity, of five carats weight, would be worth £20.

CHAPTER XXII.

THE ZIRCON, JARGOON, OR HYACINTH.

THE Zircon, Jargoon of Lapidaries, and Hyacinth, are all varieties of the same stone. Its name in Greek is " Uakinthis," in Latin " Hyacinthus," in German " Hyacinth," and " ein breuneder Jacinth," and in French "Jacinthe la belle." We apply the term Hyacinth to transparent and bright-colored varieties ; Jargoon to crystals devoid of color, and of a smoky tinge, which are occasionally sold as inferior Diamonds. Anselmus Boetius gives the following description of this gem. (1st) "There are some that flame like fire, or are similar in color to crimson or to natural vermilion, these the French jewellers call 'Jacinthe la belle,' and these they esteem the best. (2nd) Those with a yellow-red color. (3rd), Others which are like unto Amber, so that they can hardly be distinguished from it, but by their hardness. These are of no great value, by reason of the atoms they contain, and the multiplicity of small bodies which are in them, which do hinder their transparency and translucency."

"One of these," Cardanus says, "he was wont to wear about him, for the purpose of procuring sleep, to which purpose it did seem somewhat to confer, but not much."

(4th), "There is a fourth kind which have no redness at all in them, which are like to white pellucid Amber, and these are of least value."

We distinguish the Zircon by its quadrilateral crystals, terminating at both ends in a pyramid. It is of Adamantine lustre, transparent and sub-translucent. The fracture is conchoidal. This stone is most probably the Lincurium of Theophrastus. When looked at through a microscope, in front of a strong light, a watery texture is to be seen, which the French call "*Ratiné*," (nappy), and which has the appearance of water when spirit is poured into it. This cottony or "nappy," look is its special characteristic, and enables one to identify it among all other stones of a similar nature. When submitted to great heat, its lustre becomes stronger, but at the same time it loses color. In former times this gem was more highly valued than at present. In order to prepare the stone for ornaments, such as rings, pins, earrings, etc., it is ground on a leaden plate with Emery powder, and polished on a copper plate with powdered rotten-stone. The forms given to the Zircon are generally the Rose, the Table, and the Brilliant.

Inferior Zircons require peculiar setting to shew them to advantage; but a perfect one requires no aid, it is beautiful in itself, as well as valuable. There is a splendid specimen of a very ancient engraving on a Zircon in the Paris Museum, the workmanship of which is exquisite; it is 54 millimetres in length, and 34 in width, and represents Moses with the two tables of the law. Lord Duncannon has in his collection a Zircon with an engraving on it representing an athlete.

Nicols, writing 225 years ago of the Zircon, says, "They are found in Ethiopia, India, and Arabia. The Arabs distinguish three kinds: 1, Rubri Coloris; 2, Citrini Coloris; 3, Antimonii Coloris. Of these the worst is found in the River Isera, which is upon the confines of Silesia and Bohemia. The best and most excellent ones are brought from Cananor, Calicut, and Cambia." The number of places in which Zircon is now found has greatly increased, and it would not be too much to put them down at 120.

In the original beds nine-tenths belong to the volcanic or Plutonic stones. It is found in the refuse both of active and exhausted volcanoes, in porous and dense basalt, as well as in pitchstone, syenite, and granite. It is very remarkable that the Zircon has not hitherto been found in certain classes of volcanic stones, such as Melaphyre, Phonolite, and Trachyte. It occurs in very many localities which are not *volcanic:* for example, in the Island of Harris, in the Pfitsch Thal in Tyrol; in Gaston, Pennsylvania, and in Hammond, New York. It is found in small crystals in syenite, at Meissen, and in the Plauenschen-Gründ, both near Dresden.

In the Sieben-Gebirge, in Prussia, it is found in dense basalt; at Niede-Mindy, in porous millstone lava; in the Lacher Sea, in little white and red crystals, in volcanic bombshells. Little grains of Zircon are found in the valley of the Iser, in Bohemia; and small violet-blue crystals are obtained from the gold sands of the Ticino, and also from Vesuvius. It is obtained from Ceylon, which is one of the richest beds of natural wealth in the world, and also from Pegu, in the river sands.

SECTION V.

ANIMAL PRODUCTS USED AS GEMS.

CHAPTER I.

CORAL.

CORAL is the produce of gelatinous creatures which come under the class of Polypi: there are many varieties, but we have only to do with Precious Coral—"Isis Nobilis." This Polypus production is like a tree with leafless branches, the stem of which, in rare cases, is as thick as a man's body, but generally about a foot high, and an inch thick.

The calcareous axis of the "Isis Nobilis," is distinguished by its size, hardness, and capability of polish, as well as by its beautiful red color. It has a sort of leathery covering in the cells, to which the Polypi adhere. In the soft rind which surrounds the axis there are small lime-needles, and outside these the nets of the common canals which the little creatures weave.

The Polypi consist of a soft gelatinous substance. When they sit undisturbed in their cells, one can see distinctly, by means of a microscope, that each possesses eight soft, three-cornered, leafy feelers, which are notched on each side, and situated in a simple circle round the mouth, by means of which they catch their food, and convey it to this aperture. If one of these feelers is touched ever so slightly, this act is sympathetically conveyed to each creature in the Coral hive. There seems to be among naturalists, a conviction that the Coral insects, or Polypi, possess a common feeling, which by some wonderful organization vibrates through the whole root or axis of the Coral, so that both insect and web become as it were, one organized body. Although the Polypi shew such a remarkable sensitiveness, it has never been discovered that they possess nerves, or any of the five senses. Their digestive organs are developed only in the smallest degree. In the common living Polypi, as in the case of the Precious Coral, the food goes into a hole in the stomach, and is there well mixed with water, and circulated hither and thither in little vessels, and so conveyed to the whole mass of Polypi, which are in direct communication with each other. The nourishment of the Polypi is derived from tiny creatures, and particles of plants found in the water. They have a great dislike to the light, and to a disturbance of the water, either one or other of which will drive them suddenly back to their cells.

The home of the Precious Coral is the Mediterranean, more especially on the African coast. It is formed in clefts of the rocks by the creatures themselves—a very tedious operation, indeed, when we consider that it is found at a depth of 700 feet.

Obtaining the Coral is quite as fruitful a source of traditions and fairy tales among the fishermen of the Mediterranean, as the buried treasures in the hearts of the mountains to the Germans.

The Coral fishery is carried on with much zeal and

energy in many places, but especially on the coasts of Tunis, Algiers, Corsica, the Red Sea, Persian Gulf, and Sicily. On the African coast, which for centuries has been most celebrated for its Coral, is the sea-port of Calle, or Kalak, where the trade is most successfully carried on. Although the fishery has for years been worked by Corsicans, yet this particular industry has been taken up by French energy. In the year 1450, France had an establishment there whose occupation was, above all things, the Coral fishery. It was conducted by a company who received the privilege of working it provided they employed Provençals only.

In the year 1791 the fishery became free for all Frenchmen who traded with the Levant and states of Africa. Three years after a change in the arrangements took place. In 1802 England took possession of Calle, and restored it back in 1816. During this time the fishery was carried on vigorously, not less than 400 boats being devoted to this industry. In 1830, new arrangements were made, by which the Italians had to pay a duty for it, the French being exempted. Still, the Italian vessels predominated. Each Coral boat has twelve or thirteen sailors on board. The fishery begins in March and the fishers return home in October. Coral is obtained in the following manner: two iron rods about seven feet long, and having four prongs, are bound crosswise together, and wrapped up in hemp about half-an-inch thick, and bound to this is a net-work bag. In the middle of the rods a weight of lead is fastened. This machine is let down by means of a cable, and when drawn up again, it catches the projecting Coral in the hemp, which is gently brought to the surface. Very clever and experienced divers will themselves bring up a strong branch of it. The Coral is next cut in specified lengths, and separated according to thickness, size, and beauty, and then, with or without polishing, sold. Coral is bored by steel needles, and in Italy this is done by hand, but in Leipzig, Karl Hoffmann has invented a machine for boring, and has thereby rendered it much cheaper. The larger the Coral and the paler its color, the more valuable it is in our day. The most beautiful production is called "Flower of Blood." The working of Coral is principally carried on in Marseilles, Genoa, and Leghorn. In the last-named city, as many as 300 work-people are employed, and most of the Coral goes to India, China, and Japan. In India the dark-red variety has always been valued. Every Oriental strives to get a string of Corals for his turban, or at least sufficient to decorate the handle of his sword. They think that to leave their dead without ornaments of Coral, is to give them over to the hands of mighty enemies. There is scarcely an Indian to be found without at least one or two rows on one of his arms; those who can afford it have them on both arms, and the rich wear Red Coral on head, throat, and legs.

The Brahmins and Fakirs use Coral beads for rosaries to count their prayers. The Chinese mix the Red Coral with Jade beads, and wear them as ornaments for the neck and head.

The use of Coral in Europe, if we except England and Russia, is not large. At the commencement of this century, however, Coral of a beautiful blood-red, set in gold or silver, was fashionable for earrings, bracelets, necklaces, and baby rattles, in the nursery of the middle and upper classes.

The Pale Coral has been for the last twenty years rising in value: the rose tinted variety, when cut into a resemblance of the fanciful shapes assumed by Pink Pearls, obtains an enhanced value.

The price of the pale and sound Coral, is at present from £10 to £100 per ounce. The beautiful Rose-colored variety ranges from £100 to £200 per ounce; and the Red varies, according to color, from £2 to £20 per ounce.

It is often used for Cameos, being soft. At the sale of the Empress Eugènie's jewels, by Messrs. Christie and Manson, in 1872, a very fine suite of carved Coral and gold ornaments realized a high price: this probably may be explained by its having belonged to so distinguished a person. Fine specimens of carved Coral are not at all uncommon.

Coral was formerly in great repute as a talisman against enchantments, witchcraft, thunder, tempests, and other perils. It was consecrated to Jupiter and Phœbus.

It would not be wise to say that Coral either has lost, or will permanently lose, its share of popularity. It was only as the competitor of Wisdom that it was said, "No mention shall be made of Coral, or of Pearls, for the price of Wisdom is above Rubies."

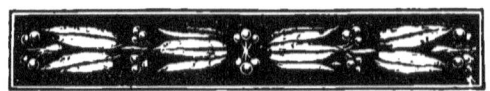

CHAPTER II.

PEARLS.

THERE is a large variety of Mollusca which exhibit certain deformities, known by the name of Pearls, and which, by their beauty and rarity, rank with the most costly of Precious Gems. The most highly valued are known by the name "Margarita" (the Sea Pearl Oyster), and "Unio Margarita" (or River Pearl Oyster). The first of these live on the coast of Ceylon, in the Persian Seas, on the Japanese coast, the coast of Mexico and California, and West Australia. The second is somewhat large, and drags itself along the sand and slime of the brooks and rivers of Europe and North America.

The Pearls in the inside of the hard oyster-shell, are generally bluish-white or yellow bodies of round or pear shape. They lie partly on the inner side of the shell, near the edge, and partly on or in the living creature. Pearls of the greatest value have a pure orient, white, black, or pink tint, that is to say, a fine color, with a lively lustre that sparkles in the light, or with the whiteness that reflects azure.

Tavernier says "that all Pearls are white, and that the yellow and other tints are induced by putrefied products, resulting from the treatment of the shells in the place of their production; the oyster shells being left in the air that they may open of themselves after the creature is dead. The work is thus accomplished without any expense, and without risk of breaking the Pearls, an accident that occurs very frequently if the shells are opened artificially;" and he further states "that Yellow Pearls are never found in shells that remain in the water."

The specific gravity of the Pearl is 2·684. According to their size they receive certain names; those of extraordinary size, are called Paragon Pearls; when the size of a cherry, Cherry Pearls; small, Piece Pearls; smaller, Seed Pearls; smallest, Dust Pearls. Then according to their form they receive names: oval and long, Pear Pearls; while the badly formed specimens are known as "*baroques*" Pearls.

Pearls frequently take grotesque shapes, and are used in works of art, and for caricatures. There is a very large collection of such in the Green Vaults at Dresden: one, a Spanish court dwarf of the time of Charles II., made out of a Pearl the size of a hen's egg.

There appear sometimes in the market, pieces of Pearl substances, which are taken out of the shells, consisting partly of Mother-of-Pearl and partly of a pearly substance. They are called Phantasy Pearls, and they are only valuable according to the purpose to which they are applied. Barbot mentions a strange circumstance about one of these Phantasy pieces. "A French Pearl merchant, in Mexico, bought one of these pieces of a fisherman, for a small sum of money, in order to learn something of them. He was not a little surprised, on cutting it in half, to find a perfect, round Pearl inside, of purest water and brilliant lustre, weighing 14½ carats, and which he sold some time after in Paris for 5,000 francs — about half of its value." Pearls are often peeled now, and a finer Pearl found underneath. In Ceylon, the Pearls are divided into classes according to their species and colors.

From time immemorial the real Pearl—that which is formed in the seas and rivers—has attracted the attention of mankind, by its pleasing and bright exterior, its regular form, and peculiarly soft union of prismatic cólors. It has been for ages past the emblem of purity, beauty, and nobility; and for an equally long period the mind of man has been occupied as to its origin. Most fantastic are many of the representations, viz.: that the Pearls are tears of fallen angels, or dew-drops from Heaven, which had fallen on a summer's night into the lap of the sea, and which had been taken prisoners by the oysters, who had opened their shells to receive them; or again (not so beautiful, but nearer the truth), that the Pearls were a diseased formation generated by the animal in the same manner as like diseases in man. A clearer insight into the being and reality of the Pearl, was obtained by Europeans after the perfection of the microscope. The first clear information which we owe to it, is that the Pearl is of the same formation as the oyster-shell. The shells of all the oysters which give Pearls have three layers; the outside is of a friable character, generally blackish-green in color, and of a horny nature; this is the outer skin, and consists of thin scales or leaves, which exhibit no regular form. Then follows a second, composed of innumerable diminutive, horny cells, filled with a calcareous mass: it is in these principally that the various pigments are deposited which give to so many shells their exquisite colors. The third and inner layer has a more foliated form, and an uniform foundation, which appears on the outside like fine folds, and when the light shines upon it produces a peculiar Mother-of-Pearl sheen which is so beautiful in many of the shells. The Mother-o'-Pearl owes its incomparable lustre, not to its material which is nothing but lime, but solely to the soft and tender unevennesses of its surface.

We owe a great deal of our knowledge of the Pearl oyster to Dr. von Heszling, who devoted much time and talent to the study of it. Almost every person who has written upon the origin of the Pearl, has an opinion of his own upon it, and we are not much wiser than the Ancients in this particular. One thing, however, is quite clear, viz., that the Pearl, whether it be free or attached, is not the healthful production of regular life, but, on the contrary, a disease, or produced by disease.

Here and there attempts have been made to form artificial Pearls, but it has not been very successful. The Chinese have done more in this trade than any other nation, but they can never produce them so perfectly as to deceive. They, however, have been able to produce grotesque figures, covered with a pearly substance, some curious specimens of which are now in the possession of W. J. Ingram, Esq., M.P. It is not an uncommon belief that the Pearl is the egg of the oyster.

With regard to River Pearl oysters it is well-known that some rivers are much richer in them than others; and the reason for this inequality has been sought, but not with satisfactory results.

The Pearl fisheries of the Ancients were in the Persian Gulf (which to this day produces the most beautiful Pearls in great abundance), in the Indian Ocean, the Red Sea, and the Coromandel coast. Those in the Red Sea are now partly exhausted. Ceylon was well-known to the Phœnicians, who went there for Pearls, and up to this time it has held its own as one of the most prolific of our Pearl fisheries; it is now closed for a year or two, in consequence of the diminution in its produce. The home of the Pearl-oyster is in sand-banks, lying off the west coast of the island, in the Bay of Manaar. The first Europeans who obtained firm footing in Ceylon were the Portuguese in 1506. They made a contract with the then ruler of the island, that he should pay them a yearly tribute of spices and Pearls, by which they made a great profit. At that time during the Pearl fishery, there were collected on the island from fifty to sixty thousand people of all kinds—divers, tailors, merchants, and tradesmen. The Pearls belonged generally to the people who sought them; but the Portuguese bought most of them at a very low price. In 1640, the Dutch obtained power, and seized upon the Pearl fishery in Ceylon. Under them the native Indians, who congregated there to the number of 200,000, were allowed for twenty alternate days to fish for themselves, and every other day for the Government; after which the produce was sold to the highest bidder. Such fishing took place every three years. In consequence of a dispute between the Dutch and the Rajah, fishing at the oyster bank at Manaar was forbidden, whereby for years it was left unworked, viz., from 1760 to 1796, until the English had rule there, who therefore had the benefit of the accumulation during those years. The gain in the one year of 1798, after deducting the cost, was £140,000. It is estimated that the same sum would be realized every seventh year, if the fishing of twenty days were restricted to the once in seven years. The fishing takes place in March and April, when the sea is calmest, and before the fishing commences the bank is tested by experienced divers.

Gathering or obtaining the Pearls is an occupation of

great difficulty and danger. It is performed by divers who are trained to their work from earliest childhood. Some time before the fishing commences, they take a particular diet, and all their limbs are daily rubbed with oil. At the appointed time they go to the Pearl bank, offer up their devotions, strip themselves of their dress, stop their ears with cotton-wool, compress their nostrils by means of an instrument made of horn, and bind over their mouths a sponge soaked in oil, which resists the water for a certain time. They then sling a rope round their body, and generally hang a heavy stone on their feet, and so throw themselves down to the Pearl bank. This stone they slip off as soon as they are on the right spot, and it is drawn up again. When the diver touches the bank, he takes a sharp knife and loosens the oysters from it, and collects as many as he can into a sort of net which he has upon his body. The time he is under the water is about a minute, his gain in that time from eight to ten oysters. With occasional breathing times, he descends forty or fifty times. If anything occurs while he is under the water, either that he is faint, or that sharks approach, he gives a sign with his rope, and is raised at once. Many at the end of the day bleed at the mouth and nose, and the strongest of them can only work at the fishery for a few years.

In modern times the diving is much less dangerous to life, owing to the diving-bell. It is only a pity that it is too dear to allow of its universal use. With this a single diver can gain from one to four thousand oysters in the fishing season. The divers either have a share in the gains, or are paid daily wages in money.

The oysters are deposited in a shut-up or enclosed space and left to get foul, whereby most of them open of themselves; but after three or four days the stench is intolerable. These foul creatures are then washed and rinsed in troughs with sea-water, until the Pearls are deposited on the earth. It is not every oyster that possesses Pearls. When the Pearls are dry, they are arranged according to size, and sold at once to agents for the market.

The first news of the presence of Pearls in the Persian Seas, which we of the West received, was from the Macedonian Greeks. Metasthenes, an officer of Seleucus, King of Syria, gives an account of them. In later times, from 1515 to the beginning of the 17th century, the Portuguese became masters of these fisheries; and during the subsequent period the native princes again became possessed of them. At the most favorable time for fishing, viz., from June to September, 30,000 men live there on the divers' boats. Except a small duty paid to the Sheikh of the harbour, the fishing is free. The method of diving and of obtaining the Pearl from the oyster is much the same as at Ceylon. The sword-fish is the great enemy here that the divers have to guard against; and every one has a dagger in his girdle to ward it off. The enormous sum realized here yearly is from £300,000 to £350,000, the purchasers being the Indian, Arabian, and Persian merchants. Most of the Pearls found here are sent by way of Mascate to Bombay, and on to China. The Chinese also receive many Pearls from the Sooloo Archipelago, lying between Borneo and Mindanao.

The Pearl fishery in the Red Sea was in early times very important. Under the Ptolemies, and later under the Egyptian Caliphs, merchants settled on the coasts, and by means of a successful trade in Pearls became extraordinarily rich. There are still Pearls to be found in the Red Sea, by the Island of Dhalak, opposite Massowa, on the Abyssinian coast. The negroes are generally the fishers here, and the fishing takes place in the winter months, from December to April, after the heavy rains; the average gain being one Pearl from five oysters. The other principal fisheries in the Eastern hemisphere, are Japan, Java, Sumatra, and the Bosphorus.

There are Pearl banks on all parts of the coasts of America, and since the beginning of the 17th century the Pearls of California have been rivals of the treasures of Panama. Hundreds of poor Indians are now employed in California as divers. On the coast of Columbia the Pearls are of a peculiar and beautiful lustre, and on the south coast of the island of Cuba the product is similar to that of the Persian Sea. On the coast of New Jersey Pearls were discovered by a farmer, who, when fishing for oysters, found in one of them a large Pearl: since then the product has been large, and of good quality.

Of late years Pearls have been discovered in Australia, from whence some of large size and good quality have been imported into England. The Fiji Islands also supply us with very fine specimens; the necklace presented to the Empress Eugènie being composed of Pearls found in those islands, and valued at several thousand pounds. It is computed that out of 20,000,000 oysters, 4,000,000, or one-fifth, only contain Pearls. The river Pearl-oyster is found largely in America, Asia, and Europe, particularly in the north. We obtain many also from France and Scotland, from the Ilz in Bavaria, the Vattava in Bohemia, and the Elster in Saxony, the last of which is famous for its Pearls. There are said to be 44 little rivers in the north of Russia and Finland in which Pearl-oysters are found. The most beautiful of the Elster Pearls are in the Green vaults at Dresden; they may not surpass the Oriental Pearl but can without depreciation take their place beside it.

The rivers in Scotland produce a great many Pearls,

which are mostly defective in form and small in size, but those of a pinkish hue however, are considered of great value, and necklaces made of them sometimes realize from £300 to £500, and are much prized by English ladies. A few Pearls are found in the Irish rivers, but they are of inferior value.

The price of Pearls depends upon their size, beauty, and rarity. In Europe perfectly white specimens and those slightly tinged with blue are most valued. The Indians, Arabians, and Chinese prefer those with a yellow tinge, which have this advantage over the former that they do not lose their lustre and tint from wear. All the sums mentioned by different authors as to the price of Pearls only mislead the buyer, for the value depends greatly upon their shape, and varies as much as that of a Diamond. For instance, a 1-carat Pearl may be worth from 24/- to 40/-; 2-carat Pearls, if fine, from £6 to £8; and large and fine Pearls range from £2 per grain, upwards. The variation being so great, I have gone from the beaten track, and have given no table of their value, which is only to be ascertained by a competent knowledge of the market.

Pearls were very highly valued in ancient times, especially in Asia and Egypt, for the inhabitants of those lands regarded them as the most beautiful gift of the elements in which they had their origin, and worthy of the honor of decorating their deities. They ranked next the most precious gems, and took their place with ivory and precious metals, and the sweet-smelling spices of Arabia, Sidon, and Tyrus. Pearls were an article of commerce among the earliest commercial people, viz., the Phœnicians. Theophrastus places them amongst the most loved and valued stones, and, speaking of their size, says, " They are like to the large eyes of fish."

In the Old Testament history they are mentioned with favor; and Job regarded them as a great and costly article. The Babylonians, Medes, Persians, and indeed all the then nations of the world, held the Pearl in the highest esteem. The Persian nobles used to wear in the right ear a golden earring containing Pearls; and in Athens the same kind of earring was worn in the right ear by youths of noble birth. These golden earrings generally contained two or three Bell Pearls, which made a sound every time the head moved. In Pompeii, on a skeleton of a lady, were found two golden earrings, each containing two beautiful Pearls. The Ethiopian, and Egyptian princes and nobles, used this gem more than any other in the adornment of their persons. The Pearl is intimately bound up with the history and traditions of India, one of which says that their god *Vishnu* discovered Pearls and employed them for the adornment of his daughter. Indian women from the earliest times have worn gold and ivory richly set with them. There was a remarkable law in India that anyone who bored Pearls and Precious Stones unskilfully, should not only make good the mischief, but pay a fine of 250 Panas. Among the ancient Chinese, the Pearl was highly valued as an amulet, the possession of which was supposed to increase the beauty of the body. Pearls are said to have been paid as "tribute" 2,300 years B.C., and it is stated that 100 years B.C., the exorbitant and wilful luxury in Pearls was written against by the authors of that day.

The Romans called the large ball-shaped Pearls, "Uniones;" the pear-shaped Pearls, "Elenchi;" and the half-ball shape, "Tympania;" and those which possessed the most beautiful white color received the name, "Exaluminatœ Margaritæ." Pompey, the victorious Roman general, the conqueror of Pontus and Syria, found in the palace of Mithridates a wonderful collection of Precious Pearls, which laid the foundation, in later years, of a most valuable museum in Rome. In his third great triumph against the Asiatic Princes, 61 years B.C., he took thirty-three crowns of Pearls. After this period the Pearl luxury became quite a disease in Rome. The philosopher Seneca spoke very sharply against the Roman women for wearing so many Pearls. He declares that they would not bend nor give obedience to their husbands, until double or treble the value of their own settlements was dangling from their ears. Roman ladies wore necklaces of Pearls which cost 200,000 francs, also ornaments for the breast, consisting of thirty-four half-ball Pearls, and thirty-four cylinder-form cut Precious Stones, dresses, shoes, and bracelets richly covered with costly Pearls. Julius Cæsar presented to Servilia, mother of Marcus Brutus, a magnificent Pearl which he obtained as booty in Egypt, the value of which was estimated at 990,000 francs. Another famous Pearl, in possession of the Egyptian Queen Cleopatra, was, after her death, presented by a Roman Ambassador to the then Imperator, Septimus Severus, for his wife; but he, to set an example against the ever-increasing tendency to this luxury, ordered it to be sold for the good of the State. No purchaser, however, could be found to pay for it according to its value, whereupon the Emperor had it cut into two pieces, and made into two earrings for the image of the goddess Venus, which was in the Pantheon, saying, that the Empress would be setting a very bad example to his subjects if she wore in her ears things too valuable to be paid for. The Romans used also to decorate their temples and dwelling-houses with Pearls, and ladies used to hire them for their own personal adornment at great festivals; the Pearl merchants, called " Margaritarii," thus drove a flourishing trade by letting them for the occasion. The wife of Caligula wore in her parure Pearls to the value of 7,000,000 francs: Nero distributed them lavishly on his favorites: and it is stated that Claudius dissolved Pearls of great value in a strong acid and gave it to his guests. In ancient times, pulverized Pearls were used as medicines, but they acted simply in the same manner as chalk.

The story of the extravagant and luxury-loving Cleopatra, Queen of Egypt, is well known. She is said to have once made a bet with Marc Antony that in a single meal she would swallow the value of two millions of francs. Antony, of course, deemed this impossible, but he was soon convinced to the contrary, when Cleopatra took the Pearl from one of her ear-rings, dissolved it in vinegar, and drank it. She was about to take the Pearl from the other ear, when Lucius Plautus staid her hand, declaring she had won the wager without further loss. This Pearl, which was saved, afterwards came as we have said into the hands of the Romans.

Later on, Pearls still retained their great value. Pliny places them next in value to the Diamond; and Isidore ranks them as first among the pale-colored Precious Gems. Not only among the Eastern nations, but also among the aborigines of America, the Pearl held a high place; this was seen by the Spaniards, who disturbed them in their possessions. In old Peru, none but those of princely blood were allowed to wear them; and the temple of Montezuma, in Mexico, was lined with gold and silver, adorned with Pearls of the highest value. In Florida, also, the Spaniards found a perfect treasure of Pearls.

One of the largest known in Europe, was called La Perigrina, the Incomparable. It weighed 126 carats, and was pear-shaped. Gongibus of Calais brought it from India in 1620. When laid before Philip IV., King of Spain, he said, "How could you concentrate your whole fortune upon so small a thing?" to which the merchant replied, "Because I knew that the world held a King of Spain who would buy it of me." This gem is now in the possession of Princess Youssopoff. (Value, 80,000 ducats.)

Another large Pearl, of the form and size of a pigeon's egg, weighing 134 grains, came from Panama: it belonged to Philip II. of Spain, and was valued at 50,000 ducats. The Emperor Rudolph II. possessed one of 180 grains; and Napoleon I. had one nearly as large. The Pearl which the King of France gave to Madame de Maintenon, and which was offered for sale in 1819, weighed 27⅞ carats. The Pearl belonging to the Shah of Persia is above an inch in diameter, and in 1633 was valued at 1,600,000 francs; and that in the possession of the Arabian Mascate at 800,000 francs. The Crown Prince of Prussia gave a necklace of thirty-two Pearls, valued at 500,000 francs, to his bride, the Princess Royal of England.

CHAPTER III.

COLORED PEARLS.

IT is very difficult to determine whether colored Pearls were known to the Old World, our own Saxon word *pærl* signifying "a gem or white speck;" the name, by which the black, azure, bronze, green, or pink Pearl was designated, has not been satisfactorily ascertained. The value set therefore by the Ancients on this beautiful animal product, which is found of every tint and shade, is not to be easily assigned. In modern times the value of tinted Pearls is better gauged.

Pink Pearls are found in the rivers of South America and in the Bahama Islands, and vary in value according to their quality, shape, and size, the price ranging from 5/- to £6 per grain. Black Pearls are found in the Gulf of Panama, in the Pacific, and in Western Australia, and rise in value from £1 to £10 a grain. Pearls of rare color, or of any fanciful tint or shade, obtain prices commensurate with their demand and scarcity.

The specimen known as *La Perle rosée* ranks with the clear white Pearl, but it has this drawback, that its irregularity of form sometimes presents so inelegant a shape, as to prevent its being used for a personal ornament.

It is not unusual to find specimens of pale pink Coral cut and shaped like a *perle rosée* offered for sale as such; but an experienced eye will not fail to detect the special sheen of the concentric layers of which the Pearl is composed, and distinguish it from the glistening of the cellular structure of the Coral.

Inferior colored Pearls are sometimes dyed black or russet brown, and sent into the market; but the absence of the true Oriental tint and lustre is so marked, that only a very inexperienced eye can be deceived by them.

The famous necklace of the Empress Eugènie, consisting of a row of matchless black Pearls, realized the large sum of £4,000, after the removal of the Pearl forming the snap, which was subsequently sold for 1,000 guineas, to form the centre of a bracelet.

Hematite, an important iron-ore, is frequently used in the manufacture of imitation Black Pearls.

General Remarks upon the Term "Carat."

THE word Carat is probably derived from the name of a bean, the fruit of a species of *Erythina*, which grows in Africa. The tree which yields this fruit is called by the natives "Kuara" (Sun), and both blossom and fruit are of a golden color. The bean or fruit, when dried, is nearly always of the same weight, and thus in very remote times it was used in Schangallas, the chief market of Africa, as a standard of weight for gold. The beans were afterwards imported into India, and were there used for weighing the Diamond.

The Carat is not of the same weight in all countries, for instance :—

One Carat in	England is equal to ...	205,4090 milligrams.
,,	France ,, ...	205,5000 ,,
,,	Vienna ,,	206,1300 ,,
,,	Berlin ,,	205,4400 ,,
,,	Frankfurt-on-Maine ...	205,7700 ,,
,,	Leipzig ,,	205,0000 ,,
,,	Amsterdam ,,	205,7000 ,,
,,	Lisbon ,,	205,7500 ,,
,,	Leghorn	215,9900 ,,
,,	Florence ,,	195,2000 ,,
,,	Spain ,,	205,3930 ,,
,,	Borneo ,,	105,0000 ,,
,,	Madras ,, ...	207,3533 ,,

72 carats make... One Cologne oz.
151½ carats make ... . One English oz.

The ounce weight is used for weighing small, and Baroques Pearls, Coral, Peridots, and rough Garnets.

INDEX.

	PAGE
Acids do not affect Corundum	133
Adamant, known to Plato	17
Adamantine, lustre of the Diamond	50
Aerolite, containing Peridot	215
Agate, attempts made to dye it	39
———— full account of	180—2
———— Onyx	181
———— Circular, Eye, and Rainbow	181
———— where and how found	181
Agate-almond in Arabia, curious treatment of	38
Agnes Sorrel sets the fashion in the use of Diamonds	127
Alexandrite, where found	182
———— its color, components, &c.	182
Algeria, Emeralds found in	152
Alkalis, powerless to affect Corundum	133
Almandine Garnet	34, 196
———— where found	197
Alphabet of Precious Stones	20
Amber, known to Plato	17
———— full account of	177—7
———— origin of	175
———— organic remains preserved in	176
———— specific gravity, hardness of	176
———— various names of, where found	176
———— trade in	177
———— valued by the Ancients	177
America, North, said to yield Sapphires	135
Amethysts, how burnt	37
———— full account of	178—9
———— where found	178
———— fall in the value of	179

	PAGE
Amethysts, Intagli of	179
Amsterdam, its trade in Diamond-cutting	26
———— Diamond, its history	117
Ancients, Art of cutting gems, imperfectly known to	22
———— Stones preferred by them for engraving	35
———— skilled in stone engraving	36—7
Animal products used as gems	229—248
Antique gems used as signet rings	35
———— where preserved	37
Antwerp Diamond workers	26
Apostles, The twelve, gems emblematic of each	19
Aquamarine, its nature, hardness, &c.	184
———— where found	184
———— its varieties	184—5
———— rare specimens of	185
Arabian Onyx, described by Bœtius	213
Aristotle's extensive knowledge of Precious Stones	18
Asteria, or Star Sapphire, under the microscope	134
Asteria, or Star Stones	173—4
———— colour, varieties of	173
———— value and prices of	173—4
Astrapia, see Asteria	
Australian Diamonds	75—80
———— when and where first discovered	75—6
———— the first brought to England	79
———— probable future Diamond yielding districts in this colony	80
Babinet's test of the reflecting power of the diamond	49

Index.

	PAGE
Baroche in India, home of the Oriental Carnelian	37
Badakshan, Ruby mines of	135
"Bahias" or Bahia Diamond...	83
Bahia Diamond-fields, how first discovered	87—8
Balas, a variety of the Ruby	156—160
—— colours, forms, where found	156—159
—— fluctuating prices of	160
Balascia, or Ballahia, Balas Rubies found in ...	160
Barbot, his pretended power of removing the colouring matter from the Diamond	50—1
—— his experiment with Diamond phosphorescence	51
Barberini Palace, its collection of antiques ...	32
Baroques Pearls	235
Beau Sancy, a Diamond cut by Berquem	24
—— its history ...	119—20
Bedford, Duke of, his engraved Diamond ...	128
Berlin, its collection of antiques	37
Bernardi, Gio., Carnelian engraver	36
Berquem, the Diamond cutter	24
Beryl, of Siberia and Brazil	13
Bingera Diamond field, N. S. Wales	77
Birkenfeld, its Agate industry	181
Blacas collection of antiques, in British Museum	37
Black Diamonds, extraordinary hardness ...	51
—— of Borneo ...	51

	PAGE
Black Opal	165
Bloodstone, full account of .	186—7
Blue Diamonds	101—9
—— where found ...	102
—— first specimen brought to Europe ...	102—3
—— its history... ...	104
—— other specimens in Europe	105
Blue Sapphire, hardness of.	133
—— the Sapphire in its limited sense... ...	134
Blue Felspar in Badakshan	135
Blue Spinel, rare specimens, its history	157
—— where found, form, etc.	158
Bœtius, his description of the Arabian Onyx ...	213
Boetius, Anselmus, his description of the Zircon	226
Bohemia, Sapphires found in	136
Borgio, Hortensio, cutter of the Koh-i-noor ...	26
Borneo, Black Diamonds of	51
—— Diamond fields ...	99, 100
Boron, its relation to carbon	109
Boron Diamonds	109—10
—— graphite	110
—— its crystalline form	110
Bort, technical meaning of .	73
—— use of	73
—— how obtained ...	107
Boyle, Robert, fails to burn the Diamond ...	52
Brabant Rose, the ...	33
Braganza Diamond, its size, value, and history ...	111
Brahma Diamonds ...	94
Brazil, massive Diamonds in black pebbles found in	46
Brazilian Ruby, a Pink Topaz	138
Brazilian Topaz	37
Brazilian Diamond fields ...	81—90

	PAGE
Brazilian Diamond Fields primary deposits	81—2
—— secondary deposits	82
—— when first discovered	83
—— process of obtaining the stones	85
—— large stones rarely found	85
—— total yield	88
—— consequences of the discovery of the Cape Diamond fields	89
—— future prospects	90
Brewster on the refraction of the Diamond	49
—— on the origin of the Diamond	57
Brilliant, its nature and invention	31
——treatment of	32
Brillonètes, definition of	32
British Museum, Blacas collection in	37
Brittleness of the Diamond	46
Bruges, its guild of Diamond workers	24
Brunswick, Duke of, his "Blue" drop Diamond	104—5
Bruzzi, Vincenzio, his discovery	25
Bultfontein dry diggings	68
Bunsput Diamonds	99
Burmah, Emeralds found in	151
—— home of the finest Rubies and Sapphires	134
Burning of Precious Stones	37—8
—— various methods of	37
Cabochon, style of cutting	34
—— Rubies so cut	140
Caire, M. inventor of the "star."	32
Caltura, its Ruby and Sapphire cutters	41
Cameo, technical definition of	34

	PAGE
Cameo, the best stones for	35
Capelan Mountain in Pegu, yields Sapphires	135
Capas, its Topaz beds	222
Cape Diamonds	60—74
—— when and how first discovered	61—2
—— Diamond fields, their total area	63
—— the dry diggings	68—9
—— their probable origin	71
—— large size of the Diamonds here found	71
—— their unique character	74
—— see also under S. African Diamond fields	
Caradossa, Ambrosius, said to be the first Diamond engraver	36'
Carat, general remarks upon this term	249
—— table of weights in various countries	249
Carbon-dioxide gas	53
Carbon, Carbonate or Carbonado	107—8
—— its chemical component	107
—— its use in drilling rocks	108
—— its affinities with boron	109
—— graphite	110
Carbonado, not occurring in S. Africa	74
—— found in the Bahia Diamond sand	83
—— see also Carbon	
Carbuncle, full account of	196—7
—— engraved specimens of	196
—— where found	197
—— varieties of	198
Cardanus, his use of Zircon	226
Carnelian, Oriental, cause of its beautiful color	37

	PAGE
Carnelian, Oriental, where found	37
——— attempts made to dye it	39
——— of Brazil	40
——— full account of	188—91
——— where found, varieties of	189
——— how treated, uses of	189
——— rare specimens of	190—1
Cativos, meaning of the term	84
Cat's Eye	166—7
——— where found	166—7
——— compared with Quartz	167
——— the test of its value	167
——— prices of	167
——— superstitious regard for	167
Ceylon, abundance of Precious Stones in	41
——— value of its export trade in gems	42
——— its Rose-red Sapphires	134
Ceylanite, Pleonaste so called	158
Chalcedony, attempts made to dye it	39
——— dyed blue	40
Chapada Diamond field in Bahia	88
Charlemagne, clasp of his mantle set with Diamonds	23
——— his signet ring	35
Charcoal, a good conductor	51
Charles the Bold, his Diamond cut by Berquem	24
Chedra Diamonds	94
Cherry Pearls	235
Chrysoberyl, see Cat's Eye and Chrysolite	
Chrysolite, form, hardness, where found	192
——— its color, components, varieties	193

	PAGE
Chrysoprase, general account of	194—5
——— where found, varities of	194—5
——— value of	195
Cimento, Academy of, its experiment with the Diamond	52
Cinnamon Stone in Ceylon	42
——— or Essonite	199
Cincor Diamonds	89
Clark, his experiment with Diamond burning	55
Claude Briaque, see Clemens Birago	
Claudius de la Croix, a gem cutter	23
Cleaver, the, his art	28
Clemens Birago, inventor of Diamond engraving	36
Cleopatra, famous Pearl belonging to	244
Cleopatra, anecdote concerning	245
Clouds in faulty gems	44
Cohesion of the Diamond	46
Colesberg Kopje on the Vaal river	68
Colombo, its Ruby and Sapphire cutters	41
Colored Pearls, see under Pearls	
Columbia, Emeralds found in	152—3
Connecticut, a greyish Corundum and other crystals found in	135
Convex cut, how employed	34
Copenhagen, its collection of antique gems	37
Coral, full account of	229—233
——— its formation	229—230
——— fisheries	231
——— trade, uses of	232
——— varieties, current prices of	233
——— used as a talisman	233
Corundum, its technical meaning	132

	PAGE
Corundum, Diamonds	93
—— various species of	132
—— various forms of ...	132
—— physical properties of	132—3
—— its general tints and reflective index	133
—— chemical properties of	133
—— where found	134
—— a boulder of, found in North America	136
—— spar, its forms, colors, and localities...	137
Coster, G., cutter of the Koh-i-noor	27, 116
Coster, Messrs., their polishing rooms	29
Crown Jewels of England, Professor Tennant's account of	123, 124
—— of France, list and value of the Diamonds in Napoleon's inventory of Gems in	125
—— Napoleon's inventory of Gems in	126
Crystal, how rendered perfectly clear	38
Crystals, groups of	45, 46
—— their primitive form	132
—— most prominent forms	134
—— masses of, found in North America	136
Crystallisation of the Diamond, its peculiar character...	45
Cuddapah Diamond field ...	92—94
—— various kinds of stones in	93
Culasse, the	34
Culet, or Culette, meaning of the term	32
Current prices of cut Diamonds	128—9
—— of Gems, see under their respective names	
Cut Brilliants, prices of ...	128
Cutter, the, his art	29

	PAGE
Cutting of Precious Stones.	30
Daria-i-noor Diamond ...	27
Davy proves that Diamonds contain no hydrogen...	53
Deville discovers how to crystallize boron and silicon	·109
Diagonal facets of the rose	33
Diamantina Diamonds ...	88
Diamond, surface of ...	46
—— massive, in black pebbles	46
—— primary form of ...	46
—— described by Pliny	47
—— its best test	47—8
—— optical properties of	48—9
—— lustre of ...	50
—— color of ...	50
—— phosphorescence of	51
—— a non-conductor ...	51
—— chemical properties of	52—8
—— component of	52
—— combustion of, experiments on...	52—3
—— combustion of, results obtained...	56
—— resists all dissolvents	56
—— origin of, various opinions on the	56—9
—— localities where found	.59
—— colored	101
—— Rock Boring Company	108
—— celebrated specimens	111—22
—— largest known ...	112
—— in the French crown list of...	125
—— when first used as ornaments	127
—— spar, a Corundum so named	137
Diamonds cut as pyramids	23
—— belonging to Louis, Duke of Anjou	23

Index.

	PAGE
Diamond dust, or bort	27, 107
—— cleaving or splitting	27
—— cutting	28
—— polishing	29
—— sculpturing, invention of	36
—— fluctuating prices of	43—4
—— crystalline forms of East Indian and Brazilian	45
Diodorus acquainted with the Topaz or Chrysolite	18
Dionysius Periegetes, his knowledge of various Precious Stones	18
Dominico dei Camei, intaglio and cameo cutter	36
Double cut Brilliants	32
—— refraction wrongly attributed to the Diamond	49
Doublet, or counterfeit Sapphires	148
Drayson, Ch. his green Diamond	106
Dry diggings, South African	68—9
Drytzehen, Andreas, a gem cutter	23
"Dudley" Diamond	73
Dunn, on the origin of the "pipes"	69
Dust in faulty gems	44
—— Pearls	235
Dutch style of Brilliant cutting	32
—— Rose, the	33
—— East India Company, its trade in Gems	43
Du Toit's Pan, its origin	68
Dyeing of Precious Stones	38—9
—— known to the Ancients	38
—— at Oberstein and Idar	39—40
Echuca Diamond field	79
Egypt, art of dyeing Chalcedony successfully practised in	40
—— Emeralds found in	151
Egyptian Turquoise	171
Electricity of the Diamond	51
Elenchi "Pearls"	243
Eliason, D., his "Blue" Diamond	103
Ellore Diamond fields	94—6
—— geological conformation of	96
Emerald column at Tyre	17
—— known to Plato	17
—— full account of	149—155
—— antique specimens of	149
—— Mediæval uses of	150
—— Peruvian	150
—— where found	150—55
—— its matrix	152
—— how obtained	152—3
—— its various tints	153
—— its value, current prices	154
—— anecdote concerning the	154—5
Emery, where found, components, use of	137—8
England, stone engraving in	36
—— Crown Jewels of, Professor Tennant's account	123—4
English treatment of the girdle in Brilliant cutting	32
Engraved stones, how copied	37
—— Diamonds, rarity of	128
Engraver, his art	22
Engraving	34
—— in Mediæval and Modern times	35—7
—— revival of, in Italy	36
—— of Diamonds	36
—— of stones in Germany	36
—— in France, England, and Rome	36

	PAGE
Engraving, excellence of modern artists	36—7
Essonite, or Cinnamon stone	199
Eugénie, the Empress, black Pearl necklaces belonging to	241, 248
Facets of the Brilliant	32
——— of the Rose	33
Feathers in faulty Gems	44
Feijao or Lydian stone	82
"Fire Opals"	164
Fisheries, Coral	231
——— Pearl	237—240
Fischbach, its rock crystal mine	219
Florence, its collection of antique gems	37
Florentine Diamond, its history	119
Form, graduated, meaning of	34
Forms of Precious Stones	30
Fourcroy, his experiment with Diamond burning	55
Forster, J. N., famous Rubies cut by him	141
——— Blue Spinel, cut by him	157
——— Spinels cut by him	158
Fossil Turquoise	171
France, stone engraving in	36
Francis de Sales, his beautiful allusion to the purifying effects of honey	39
Francis I., first collection of engraved stones	37
French crown the, list and value of the Diamonds in	125
——— Napoleon's inventory of	126
Friction, effects of on the Diamond	51
Gajja Diamonds	93
Galle, its trade in gem cutting	41

	PAGE
Gani Diamond mine	95
Garnets cut and polished in Ceylon	42
——— a variety of the Sapphires	136
——— origin of the word	196
——— See also under Carbuncle	
Gems used as amulets	19
——— proper for each month of the year	19
——— emblematic of the Twelve Apostles	19
——— See also under "Precious Stones"	
Germany, stone engraving in	36
Girdle, technical meaning of	32
Göbel on the origin of the Diamond	57
Golconda Diamond district	95
Goutte d'Eau, the, a species of Topaz	222
Graduated form, meaning of	34
Grammagoa Mountain in Brazil, Diamond bearing	81
Graphite, a good conductor	51
Great Mogul Diamond	92
——— where found	95
——— its history	112—17
——— See also under Koh-i-noor	
Greek artists, stone engraving in Italy revived by	36
Green Diamonds	106
——— Vaults of Dresden, remarkable Brilliants in	122
——— its Elster Pearls	241
Green Pearl, collection in	235
Griqualand West, its Diamond fields	62—63
——— its geological features	63—65
Guttenberg learns Gem cutting	23
Guyton de Morveau, his experiment with Diamond burning	54

Index. 257

	PAGE
Half Precious Stones, price of, how determined	43
———— definition of	11
Halphen, J., his Red Diamond	105
Hardness of the Diamond	46—7
Hausmann on the origin of the Diamond	57
Helmreicher, V. von, collector of colored Diamonds	101
Hematite, used for imitating Black Pearls	248
Hermann, a famous Diamond cutter	24
Herodotus, his acquaintance with Precious Stones	17
Hindu, classification of, Diamonds	94
Holland, its thriving trade in Diamond cutting	26
Homer, his references to the Precious Stones	16
Honey, used in preparing the Agate almond	38
———— beautiful allusion to its purifying properties	39
Hope Diamond, the	103
Hornblende, blocks found at Cuddapah	93
Hungary, home of the Opal	162—3
Hyacinths, how burnt	37
———— full account of	199
———— where found	199
———— See also under Zircon	
Idar, its method of dyeing stones	39—40
Ilmenite	70
India, Diamond cutting in	26
Indian cut of the Brilliant	33
———— Diamond fields	91—100
———— five groups or districts	91
———— geological features of	91—2
Intaglio, technical definition of	34
Inventory, Napoleon's, of Gems in the French Crown	126
Isidorus of Seville, his treatise on Precious Stones	19
———— his account of the Emerald	149—50
Isis head in Malachite, in the Russian collection of jewels	35
Isis Nobilis, the precious Coral	229
Iser Mountains, Bohemia, Sapphire crystals found in	136
Itacolumite, the matrix of the Diamond	81
———— character of the stones extracted from	82
Jacinth, see under Hyacinth	
Jameson, on the origin of the Diamond	57
Jargoon, see under Zircon	
Jasper known to Plato	17
———— full account of	200—2
———— great variety of	200
———— used as amulets	201
———— where and how found	201
———— described by Nicols	202
Jet-stone in the Bingera Diamond field	78
Jewels, see under "Gems" and "Precious Stones"	
Jewels in the Imperial Crown of England, summary of	124
Jews of Alexandria, introduce engraving into the west	35
Jochle Berg, its Rock Crystal mine	219
Job, book of, references to the Precious Stones	16

2 K

	PAGE
Kandy, rulers of, their former monopoly of Precious Stones	41
———— its trade in cutting Gems	41
Kanna Diamonds	93
Karla Diamonds	93
Kentmann acquainted with point cut	33
Kiat-pyan, in Burmah, home of the Sapphire and Ruby	134
Kimberley mine in S. Africa	68
Koh-i-noor Diamond	26, 112
———— its history	112—17
———— identical with the Great Mogul	113
———— cut by Borgio and Coster	26—27, 116
———— the Persian	27
Labrador, full account of...	203—4
———— where and how found	203
———— rare specimens of	203—4
Labora, meaning of the term	27
Lapidary, his art	22
Lapis-Lazuli, full account of	205—7
———— color, specific gravity	205
———— where found	204
———— various uses of	204—5
Lavoisier proves that Diamonds are combustible	53
Lazulite in the Brazilian Diamond fields	83
Leipzig market, fall in price of Diamonds at	43
Leonard on the origin of the Diamond	56
Liebig on the origin of the Diamond	57
Light not polarized by the Diamond	49
Lisbon, its former trade in Gems	43

	PAGE
Loadstone known to Plato	17
Lorenzo de Medici encourages engraving	36
Louis, Duke of Angou, inventory of his Diamonds	23
Louis de Berquem, his discovery	24
Lustre of the Diamond	50
Lydian Stone, or Feijao	82
Macdonald Turquoise	171
Macquer, his experiment with Diamond burning	52
Maillard, his attempt to burn Diamonds	53
Malachite Cameo, in the St. Petersburgh collection	35
———— full account of	208—9
———— where found	208
Malay dealers in Precious Stones	41
Manik Diamonds	99
Mann, his anecdote about a Brazilian Diamond	101
Manta Valley, Emerald worshipped in	155
Marco Polo, Balas Rubies collected by	160
———— Lapis-Lazuli found by	206
Margarita, see under Pearls	
Margaritarii	244
Matan, Rajah of, his Diamond	111
Matrix of the Diamond	81
———— of the Emerald	152
———— of the Turquoise	170
Matura, its Gem-cutting trade	41
Mazarin, Cardinal, first to have the Diamond polished	128
Mazarins, the twelve	25
Meronitz, Bohemia, Spinel found in	158

	PAGE
Meteoric stones containing Peridot	215
Minas-Geraës Diamond fields	82—6
—— their great productiveness	84
—— value of the stones hitherto found	84
—— character of the stones	84
Minas-Novas, its richness in Precious Stones	43
Mo-gast in Burmah, home of the Ruby and Sapphire	134
Months of the year, Gems proper for each	19
Moon stone, full account of	210—11
Mother-of-Pearl	235
Motichul Diamonds	99
Mudgee Diamond drift	76
Muzo, Emerald mine in Columbia	152—3
Nassac Diamond, the	122
Naples, its collection of antique Gems	37
Naxos, Emery found in	138
New Mine Stones	13
New S. Wales Diamond fields, their yield to the present time	78
—— various localities where Diamonds have been found	78
Newton on the combustion of the Diamond	48
—— on the origin of the Diamond	57
Nicols, his description of the Opal	161—2
—— his description of the Turquoise	169
—— his description of Jaspar	202
—— his description of the Zircon	227

	PAGE
Nürnberg, Diamond polishing and table cutting, when first introduced	23
—— Stone engraving in	36
Oberstein, its method of dyeing stones	39—40
Odescalchi Museum, its antiques	37
Old English cutting	26
—— cut Brilliants	32
Old Mine Stones	13
Onomacritus, his knowledge of Precious Stones	17
Onyx, the best kind for Cameos	35
—— Oriental, fully described	212—14
—— where found	212
—— Greek legend concerning	212
—— antique cameos of	213
—— pillars made of	213
—— prices of, uses of	214
Opal, superstition regarding	17, 164
—— full account of	161,—5
—— its hardness, specific gravity, components, colors	161
—— described by Nicols	161—2
—— where found	162
—— treatment of	163
—— prices of	163
—— antique, history of	163
—— "Fire," specimens of	164
—— black	165
Orange River, its Agates and other pebbles	65
Oriental Ruby, description of	139
—— celebrated specimens	140—1
—— popular superstitions regarding	142
—— laws regulating the finding of	142

	PAGE
Oriental Ruby, prices of ...	143
—— the Siamese species	144
——Onyx, see under Onyx	
Orloff Diamond, its history	117
Ounce weight, Precious Stones weighed by this measure	249
Panna Diamond district ...	98—99
—— configuration of the land	99
Pans, S. African, nature of	68
Paragon Pearls	235
Paris, Gem and Diamond polishing, when first introduced	23
—— Diamond workers in	24
—— its trade in Diamond cutting	25—26
Parrot, on the origin of the Diamond	57
Partala, see Gani	
Pasha of Egypt Diamond...	122
Pavilion, technical meaning of	32
Payen, on the countries where the Diamond is found	59
Pearl River, N. S. Wales, said to yield prisms of beautiful Rubies and Sapphires	136
Pearls, full account of ...	234—248
—— most valued species	234
—— specific gravity, various names of ...	234
——extraordinary specimen of	235
—— formation of ...	236
—— artificial	237
—— fisheries, Ancient and Modern	237—40
—— banks in America, Australia, &c. ...	241
—— necklace of the Empress Eugénie ...	241

	PAGE
Pearls, value and current prices of	242
—— Biblical references to	243
—— Indian legends and laws regarding ...	243
—— mania for, in Rome	244
—— pulverised, used medicinally	245
—— rare specimens of...	245—46
—— necklace of the Princess Royal ...	246
—— Colored, full account of	246—47
—— where found, prices	246
—— dyed black ...	248
—— famous necklace of	248
Pegu, its trade in Gems ...	41
—— its brilliant Sapphires	135
Pennsylvania, a greyish Corundum found in ...	135
Pepin, King, his signet ring	35
Peridot, the, fully described	215—16
—— its form, components specific gravity ...	215
—— where found ...	216
Perigrina, the incomparable	245
Perle rosée, the ... * ...	247—48
Peru, Emeralds found in ...	150
Peruzzi, Vincenzio, his invention	31
Petzholdt, his experiment with Diamond burning	54
—— on the origin of the Diamond	* 57
Phantasy Pearls	235
Phœnicians, their trade in Gems...	16
Phosphorescence of Diamonds	51
Piece Pearls	235
Pigott Diamond	122
Pistazite Diamonds ..	93
Pitt Diamond, its history...	118
Plato acquainted with various Precious Stones	17

	PAGE
Pleonaste, in the Australian Diamond drift	...76, 158—9
Pliny, on lavish use of Gems	18
——— on the art of dyeing stones...	38
— — — his account of the Diamond	47
——— of a famous Opal.	163
Plutarch, his account of the Aster...	174
Point cut, nature of	33
Polycrates, his famous ring	16, 17
Porcelain, Jasper...	202
Portrait stones, description of	33, 34
Precious Stones, definition of the term...	11
——— science of...	12
——— where found	13, 14
——— distribution of	14, 41
——— Biblical references to	15
———lavish use of, in time of the Roman Empire.	18
——— proper for each month of the year	19
Precious Stones, alphabet of	20
——— working of	22—40
——— burning of...	37, 38
——— dyeing of ...	38, 39
——— required for dyeing, how tested	39, 40
——— trade in	42, 43
——— prices of, how determined	43
———'faults in ...	44
Price current of cut Brilliants	128—9
Pyrope, the, account of	198
Quartz, Cat's Eye...	166
——— references to	217
Randial Diamond fields	94
——— character of the stones...	94
Ratnapura, its jewel market	42
Ratoos Diamond fields, Borneo	99, 100

	PAGE
Recoupé Brilliant ...	25
Red Diamonds	105, 6
——— the only known specimens	105
——— Sapphire same as the Ruby ...	134
——— Chalcedony, see Carnelian...	
——— Jasper	201
Reflection of the Diamond	48
Refraction of the Diamond	48
Regent Diamond, its history	118
Riband Agate	180, 81
Ritter, Karl, his treatise on the Indian Diamond fields ...	91
River Pearl oysters	237
——— where found	241
Rock Crystal, fully described	218—19
——— varieties of, where found...	218
——— known to the Ancients...	219
——— uses of, rare specimens ...	220
——— art of dyeing	38
Rose, when first introduced	27
——— account of this form of Diamond cutting ...	32, 33
——— how determined ...	33
——— Recoupé ...	33
——— character of its reflection	49
Rough Diamonds ...	130, 31
——— points to be considered in valuing them	130
——— best forms of	130
——— from the Cape	131
Ruby, white spots how removed from ...	38
——— is the Red Sapphire	134
——— rare in Ceylon, common in Pegu...	135

	PAGE
Ruby mines in Badakshan	135
——— large, supposed to occur in couples	135
——— the Oriental, see under Oriental	
——— Spinel and Balas, varieties of	156, 60
Saffragam, its trade in Gems	41—2
Sahara, the, Emeralds found in	152
Salzberg, Emeralds found in	151
Sancy Diamond, see Beau Sancy	
Sand in faulty Gems	44
Sandy Brae, Ireland, Opals found in	162
Sapphire, how burnt	37
——— Blue, hardness of	133
——— specific gravity of	133, 145
——— various tints of	134
——— red, the Ruby	134
——— where found	134—5, 146
——— a fine Red, said to have been found in S. America	136
——— Blue and White in S. Australia	136
——— origin of the term	144
——— its form, color, hardness	145—6
——— celebrated specimens of	147
——— value and prices of	148
——— counterfeit, how detected	148
Sard, known to Plato	17
Sardonyx, the best kind for engraving	35
Saxon, Switzerland, yields Sapphire Crystals	136
Schorl, see under Tourmaline	
Schrabracq in Paris	26
Scotland, Pearls found in	241—2
Seed Pearls	235

	PAGE
Selecting Precious Stones, art of	30—31
Selenite, full account of	210—11
Shah Diamond, its history	118
Shouham, the, of Scripture	214
Siberia, Emeralds found in	151
Siberian Aquamarine	184
Signet rings of Charlemagne and Pepin	35
——— engraved with the king's signature	36
——— used by betrothed lovers	36
——— worn by the Greek rulers	16
Silicon crystallized by Wöhler and Deville	109
Simler on the origin of the Diamond	58
Single cut Brilliants	32
South African Diamonds	60—74
——— their quality	73
——— see also under Cape Diamonds	
Specific gravity of Corundum, Emery, Rubies, and Sapphires	133
Spinel, fine specimens of	157—8
——— where found	158—9
——— in the Australian Diamond fields	76
——— often found with the Sapphire	135
——— in the Brazilian Diamond fields	83
——— a variety of the Sapphire	134
——— see also under Ruby	
——— Crystal, form, components, &c.	157
——— Rubies in the French Crown	159
——— current prices of	159
Splitter, the, his art	28
St. Petersburg, its collection of Antiques	37

	PAGE
Star-stones, see under Asteria	
—— Sapphire, or Asteria	134
—— facets of the Rose	33
—— facets of the Brilliant	32
—— cut Brilliants, invention of	32
—— of S. Africa Diamond	71
—— of the South Diamond (Brazilian)	85
—— its history	120—21
Step-cut, definition of	34
"Stewart" Diamond, history of its discovery	72
Stow, his view of the glacial origin of the Diamond-bearing drift	67
Strasburg, stone engraving in	36
Sudra Diamonds	94
Sukariuh Diamond mine in Panna	99
—— four kinds of stones here found	99
Sumatra Diamond district	100
Sumbulpoor Diamond districts	96
—— the Diamond seekers of	97
—— methods of obtaining the stones	97—8
Sweden, Spinel found in	158
Table, technical meaning of	32
—— the original cut of the Diamond	127
Tavernier, his Blue Diamond	102—3
Telloe Bendu Diamonds	93
Temperature required for the combustion of Diamonds	53—4
Tennant, Professor, his communication on the Crown Jewels of England	123—4

	PAGE
Tenth Mazarine, the Brilliant known as such	128
Test of the Diamond in Brazil	48
Theodorus of Samos, first engraver of Gems	16
Theophrastus, his treaty on Precious Stones	18
Tobin, his Diamond expedition	66
Topaz, the, fully described	221—3
—— origin of the name, components, hardness of	221
—— where found, antique specimens	222
Tourmaline, cut and polished in Ceylon	42
—— Black, in the Bingera Diamond field	78
—— full account of	224—5
—— its form and various properties	224
—— first written account of	225
Tourmaline, varieties and value of	225
Tunka Valley, Columbia, its Emerald mines	152—3
Turquoise Cameos, in the Vienna collection	35
—— described by Nicols	169
—— where found	170
—— form, hardness, components	170
—— proverbs regarding	170
—— engraved specimens	171
—— current prices of	171
—— fossil	171—2
Tympania Pearls	243
"Uniones" Pearls	243
Ural Mountains, Emeralds found in	150
Vaalite	70

	PAGE
Vaal River, its Agates and other Chalcedonic pebbles	65
Venice, its Diamond trade in the time of Peruzzi	31
Vermiculite	70
Victoria, Diamonds found in	79
———— Queen, her state crown, description of	123
Vienna, its collection of antique Gems ...	37
———— curious double Diamond in	46
———— its collection of colored Diamonds ...	101
Vysea Diamonds	94
Wilson, G., on the origin of the Diamond ...	58
Wöhler, on the origin of the Diamond ...	58

	PAGE
Wöhler his method of crystallising Silicon and Boron...	109
Zinkenstock, its Rock Crystal mine	219
Zircon, found in the Australian Diamond drift	76
———— a variety of the Sapphire	134
———— full account of ...	226—28
———— various names of, varieties	226
———— described by Anselm Boetius	226
———— form, appearance, properties of	227
———— rare specimens of ...	227
———— varieties described by Nicols	227
———— where found ...	228

www.ingramcontent.com/pod-product-compliance
Lightning Source LLC
Chambersburg PA
CBHW032101230426
43672CB00009B/1604